The Gospel According to
Flannery O'Connor

The Gospel According to Flannery O'Connor

Examining the Role of the Bible in Flannery O'Connor's Fiction

Jordan Cofer

Bloomsbury Academic
An imprint of Bloomsbury Publishing Inc

B L O O M S B U R Y
NEW YORK · LONDON · OXFORD · NEW DELHI · SYDNEY

Bloomsbury Academic

An imprint of Bloomsbury Publishing Inc

1385 Broadway	50 Bedford Square
New York	London
NY 10018	WC1B 3DP
USA	UK

www.bloomsbury.com

Bloomsbury is a registered trade mark of Bloomsbury Publishing Plc

First published 2014

Paperback edition first published 2015

Library of Congress Cataloging-in-Publication Data
Cofer, Jordan.
The Gospel According to Flannery O'Connor : Examining the Role of the Bible in
Flannery O'Connor's Fiction / Jordan Cofer.
pages cm
Summary: "Illustrates how Flannery O'Connor's stories dramatize elements of
the Bible coming alive, anachronistically, in different times and social settings"–
Provided by publisher.
Includes bibliographical references and index.
ISBN 978-1-62356-088-1 (hardback)
1. O'Connor, Flannery–Criticism and interpretation. 2. Bible–In literature. I. Title.
PS3565.C57Z6247 2014
813'.54–dc23
2013049295

ISBN: HB: 978-1-6235-6088-1
PB: 978-1-5013-1427-8
ePub: 978-1-6235-6804-7
ePDF: 978-1-6235-6227-4

Typeset by Integra Software Services Pvt. Ltd.

*Dedicated to my lovely wife, Rebecca, my family
who encouraged me at every step of the way,
and to my mentor, Thomas Gardner*

Contents

Acknowledgments

My lifelong fascination with Flannery O'Connor began when I first picked up a copy of her *Collected Works* in the public library, after reading *The Violent Bear It Away* in an American Novels seminar, under the direction of fellow O'Connor enthusiast Susan Guymon. O'Connor believed that good writing "hangs on and expands in the mind," and, for me, this certainly was the case as unpacking the novel soon became an obsession. In my first clumsy attempts at literary research, I read journal articles, notes, and different translations of Matthew 11:12, all in an attempt to understand exactly what it meant for the violent to "bear it away." It was this obsession with the novel that continued long after the seminar was finished that led me to devour her work. Yet, as I began to read *Collected Works* cover-to-cover, it was not her fiction, but her letters that fascinated me. Her writing intrigued me in a way in which no other writer had ever captured my interest. I found myself reading her letters, highlighting advice that she gave, and feeling as if I had a deep personal connection with this writer. It was not just that her stories were funny or entertaining, but there was a level of depth—a vision—that I'd never encountered before (or since). After I finished my bachelor's degree and headed out into the strange and exotic land of graduate school, I went armed with my well-worn copy of *Collected Works* and the steadfast intention of studying Flannery O'Connor.

The germ of this book, the idea that O'Connor was rewriting Bible stories, came from an afternoon preparing to teach "A Good Man Is Hard to Find" to a classroom full of very talented freshman at Virginia Tech. From there, Thomas Gardner not only helped me to develop and expand the idea, but he helped me at every stage of the publishing process from beginning to end. Through countless hours in his office, on the phone, and frequent email exchanges, he not only helped me to develop a small idea into a thesis, and later a book, but he taught me almost everything I know about academic writing—lessons I have since tried to pass on to my own students.

During my doctoral studies, I also received amazing advice and direction from Dr. James Whitlark, who was supportive and integral in assisting with this study, while receive great insights from the other members of my dissertation committee, John Samson and Bryce Conrad. From there, editor Matt McCullough offered me some extensive feedback that helped this book to take shape.

Along the way, I also received much more help and encouragement than I deserved from a large number of Flannery O'Connor scholars, the most kindhearted and encouraging academic community out there; fellow Flannery O'Connor scholars did more than offer me direction—they took me seriously, took my ideas seriously, and treated me like a professional as they encouragingly fanned the flame of my enthusiasm for Flannery O'Connor. These generous scholars, from Jean Cash, who read early drafts of my thesis, to Bruce Gentry and Robert Donahoo, both of whom put up with my frequent questions, requests, and so on, all helped me immensely. I also received financial support from *The Flannery O'Connor Review*, which awarded me the Flannery O'Connor research fellowship (2007), and the Sarah Gordon award (2008), which I received for my essay on "Parker's Back." Both awards helped to fund the project. Furthermore, I received some great advice from many O'Connor scholars such as Jon Han, who published my first scholarly essay, Ralph Wood, John Sykes, Farrell O'Gorman, Jay Watson, Doug Davis, Craig Amason, Steve Watkins, and many more—all of whom gave me some amazing feedback and encouragement. Truly, the Flannery O'Connor community is one of the most gracious and supportive interpretative communities around. Parts of Chapter Three and Chapter Five, drastically altered, previously appeared as "The All-Demanding Eyes: Following the Old Testament and New Testament Allusions in Flannery O'Connor's 'Parker's Back.'" *The Flannery O'Connor* Review 6 (2008): 30-39 and "From Dishonor to Glory: Flannery O'Connor's Pauline Allusions in 'Judgment Day'" *Intégrité: A Journal of Faith and Learning* 5.2 (2006): 45-53.

I would like to further acknowledge the amazing editors, staff, and crew at Bloomsbury. They were so supportive and were great to work with, and without them, this project would not be possible.

Finally, I would like to thank my wife for her support and encouragement, for allowing Flannery O'Connor to remain as the "other woman" in our marriage. She read multiple drafts, printed off many, many copies of the book, helped in the editing process, and listened to me talk incessantly about O'Connor. Thank you so much for your support.

List of Abbreviations

CW   *The Collected Works of Flannery O'Connor*

CS   *The Complete Stories of Flannery O'Connor*

HB   *The Habit of Being*

MM   *Mystery and Manners*

Towards a New Approach to Flannery O'Connor's Fiction

An individual story's full significance may depend upon the reader's recognition of an allusion.

Driskell & Brittain 11

Regarding Fyodor Dostoevsky's *The Brothers Karamazov*, a novel which admittedly influenced Flannery O'Connor, Vladimir Nabokov once commented, "I do not like this trick his characters have of 'sinning their way to Jesus.'"[1] However, Nabokov could have very well been speaking about Flannery O'Connor's fiction since her work is littered with characters like Hazel Motes, who starts a heretical church and commits murder before his conversion, or O. E. Parker, who goes from a life of tattoos and debauchery into prophecy, all of whom sin their way to Jesus. This technique, of which Nabokov complains, however, predates Dostoevsky and can be found in several biblical narratives, the same place where O'Connor herself learned the trick. Throughout the Bible, readers encounter figures such as Paul, who began sinning his way to Jesus as a persecutor of the early Christian church before his conversion at Damascus, or Moses, who murders an Egyptian and flees to Midian before being called by God to free the Israelites. Although Nabokov chides Dostoevsky's use of this biblical trope, ironically Nabokov's critique is the hallmark of Flannery O'Connor's fiction.

As most readers know, O'Connor's Catholicism was absolutely essential, shaping the development of her writing, yet at the same time, the more apt concern should be avoiding a monologic reading of O'Connor's work. It is important to avoid assigning O'Connor to a strict master narrative of a Southern writer or a Catholic writer, while also recognizing O'Connor's own artistic intent. As with any artist, the ultimate fear is that the art, stripped of complexity, becomes reductive—interpretation becomes an epistemological act based on our own interest; however, considering the motive behind her methods adds new dimensions to her work. Readers and critics must always be aware that "interpretation is not isolated act, but takes place within a Homeric battlefield, on which a host of interpretive options are either openly or implicitly in conflict."[2] For any artist the issue of interpretation is fundamental, but it is especially relevant to the work

---

[1] Vladimir Nabokov, *Lectures on Russian Literature*, ed. Fredson Bowers (New York: Harcourt Brace, 1981), 104.

[2] Fredric Jameson, *The Political Unconscious: Narrative as a Socially Symbolic Act* (New York: Routledge, 1983), 13.

of Flannery O'Connor—an artist whose authorial intentions and techniques have not always been satisfactorily understood. Herein lies the central conflict in reading and interpreting O'Connor's fiction. Knowing how adamant she was in her own statements on her work, it becomes necessary to keep her theological perspective in mind. In other words, as much as some would like to ignore the religious underpinnings of her work, such a position would miss out on the complexities of her fiction.

This has, of course, happened repeatedly within O'Connor criticism. Early analysis of O'Connor's work completely misconstrued her aim, believing she was embracing the very same nihilist doctrine she parodied. Yet, some more recent readings have reduced O'Connor to a Christian apologist without understanding the method or approach that she uses. As Hawkins notes, "with both O'Connor's work and her views quite readily available, it is unusual to find readers so far afield from her intentions."[3] Hawkins, among others, have highlighted the importance of approaching O'Connor's work on an anagogical level, an approach which O'Connor herself advocated:

> The action or gesture I'm talking about would to be on the anagogical level, that is the level which has to do with the Divine life and our participation in it. It would be a gesture that transcended any neat allegory that might have been intended or any pat moral categories a reader could make. (*MM* 111)

O'Connor understood the complexity of a text as well as the need to consider context as a part of the act of interpretation. In fact, she recommends reading in the spirit of "medieval scriptural exegesis, in which three kinds of meaning were found in the literal level of the sacred text: the moral, the allegorical, and the anagogical."[4]

Perhaps this theological approach is what is missing from O'Connor criticism, as readers often misunderstood the grotesqueness and complained of gimmicky repetition throughout her corpus. In fact, Sarah Gordon's excellent study *Flannery O'Connor: The Obedient Imagination* includes a flowchart produced by Man Martin, which outlines how to write your own O'Connor story. Martin insinuates that O'Connor's fiction is so formulaic that it can be predicted or easily replicated. Although I disagree with this assumption, it is by examining her theological and artistic vision that the repeated patterns emerging out of O'Connor's fiction, beginning with her debut novel, *Wise Blood*, become clear. These patterns maintain some predictability, yet her approach is not formulaic as much as it is liturgical—that is, in some ways these repetitions match the traditional liturgical layout. The fact that her fiction follows preset patterns should serve as another indicator of the impact her religious inclinations had upon her fiction.[5]

---

[3] Peter Hawkins, *The Language of Grace: Flannery O'Connor, Walker Percy, and Iris Murdoch* (New York: Seabury Classics, 2004), 43.

[4] Flannery O'Connor, *The Presence of Grace*, ed. Leo Zuber (Compiler) and Carter Martin (Athens: University of Georgia Press, 2008), 94.

[5] Although O'Connor was influenced by a variety of biblical texts, arguably, the most influential are the Pauline epistles. It has been frequently cited that the Pauline epistles all follow the same model "from which Paul could have developed his own epistolary style" (Goulder 479). Thus, much like the comparison to liturgy, O'Connor's trademark approach—which others critique as formulaic—is actually a sign of the influence these texts had on her rhetorical approach to fiction.

While there has been much valuable critical scholarship that has helped us to understand her work, those familiar with O'Connor will know that she believed her art and faith were invariably intertwined and hoped that "the resonances of the anagogical will be available to the good reader."[6] This intent explains why her fiction "seizes again and again on biblical metaphors or familiar pious texts and fixes them in her fictional landscape."[7] Although there are many studies of how her beliefs and theology affect her fiction, I argue that O'Connor is heavily influenced by the text itself, noting her intentions and examining her reimagining of biblical narratives. Throughout O'Connor's work, there are significant biblical allusions which have been overlooked; more importantly, the methodology behind these allusions as a whole has been neglected. While it is necessary to acknowledge her biblical source material, it is critical to understand the impact it has had on her fiction. O'Connor's stories engage their biblical analogues in unusual, unexpected, and sometimes violent and grotesque manipulations, while conveying essentially the same message as their biblical counterparts. Theologically, her modus operandi was to argue many of the same points about grace that her biblical sources did, but to a modern-day audience.

O'Connor's unique approach, that is, her attempt to engage her biblical source material in a unique way in order to reach a mass audience, grows out of her frustration over her parish's "tendency to avoid the intellectual and spiritual problems confronting Catholicism in the twentieth century" since she was opposed to "practiced forms of worship that enabled people to recite 'readymade' prayers instead of searching their own souls"; instead O'Connor "frequently encouraged growing interest in Biblical studies."[8] Needless to say, this synthesis of her artistic and religious vision manifested itself within her writing. Instead of attempting to fit into the paradigmatic mainstream Catholic fiction, her subject matter focused on freaks, blind prophets, nymphomaniacs, gorings, homicidal criminals, and all types of grotesque images not often associated with "Christian" fiction. In fact, O'Connor consistently takes both the contemporary Catholic writer and reader to task for this limited vision:

> Ever since there have been such things as novels, the world has been flooded with bad fiction for which the religious impulse has been responsible. The sorry religious novel comes about when the writer supposes that because of his belief, he is somehow dispensed from the obligation to penetrate concrete reality. He will think that the eyes of the Church or of the Bible or of his particular theology have already done the seeing for him, and that his business is to rearrange this essential vision into satisfying patterns, getting himself as little dirty in the process as possible. (*MM* 163)

---

6   Marion Montgomery, "Flannery O'Connor: Realist of Distances," in *Realist of Distances: Flannery O'Connor Revisited*, ed. Karl-Heinz Westarp and Jan Norby Gretlund (Aarhus: Aarhus University Press, 1987), 229–230.

7   Frederick Asals, *Flannery O'Connor: The Imagination of Extremity* (Athens: University of Georgia Press, 1982), 77.

8   Jane Hannon, "The Wide World Here Parish: O'Connor's All-Embracing Vision of the Church," *Flannery O'Connor Bulletin* 24 (1995): 5,7.

As Brinkmeyer observes, it comes as no surprise that "O'Connor frequently railed about those she called vapid Catholics, believers who never allowed their faith and its tenets to be challenged or examined in any critical way."[9]

Of course, like her literary forbearers, her methods were not divorced from controversy. As Friedman noticed, O'Connor "failed to please only the most rigidly party-line Catholics who find her brand of Catholicism not orthodox enough and the most 'textual literary critics' who find her language too bare and experiments with structure not eccentric enough."[10] Meanwhile, several others believed her experiments with the Bible to be sacrilegious. Ironically, like Milton, O'Connor "has been accused of belonging to the devil's party unawares."[11] Of course, this was to be expected, as O'Connor complained of frequent misinterpretations of her work: "I've really been battling this problem all my writing days" (*HB* 554). Yet, this is telling when considering her approach follows in the tradition of writers from Dante to Donne, who integrate biblical texts into their work and were no strangers to controversy. Her approach completely shocked contemporary audiences who expected her to write simple and positive fiction. Kinney contends that "O'Connor's monstrous readers did not always get the point—and *precisely because* they did not always *want* the point, because too they *were* the point. But she kept on warning them even when paralysis spread upward and outward through her body."[12] Responding to criticism for her seemingly grotesque fiction, she argued, "My own feeling is that writers who see by the light of their Christian faith will have, in these times, the sharpest eye for the grotesque" (*MM* 33). In her essays, letters, and lectures, O'Connor consistently reiterated the fact that she never intended to write romantic or sentimental fiction, lamenting, "We have become so flooded with sorry fiction" (*MM* 39). She was also very clear about the problem with many religious readers and writers, claiming that the Catholic reader "has reduced his conception of the supernatural to pious cliché … … able to recognize nature in literature in only two forms, the sentimental and the obscene" and that a religious reader is often "so busy looking for something that fits his needs, and shows him in the best possible light, that he will find suspect anything that doesn't serve such purposes" since "Poorly written novels—no matter how pious and edifying the behavior of the characters—are not good in themselves" (*MM* 147, 182, 174). O'Connor argued that instead, "The Church should make the novelist a better novelist" (*MM* 170). The central irony lies in the backlash she received from her own Catholic community and the praise she received from secular artists, in many ways exemplifying "the dilemma of a writer who wants to communicate a mystery clearly, to write Christian fiction for a non-Christian audience."[13] Seemingly

[9] Robert Brinkmeyer, *The Art and Vision of Flannery O'Connor* (Baton Rouge: Louisiana State University Press, 1989), 159.

[10] Melvin J. Friedman, "Flannery O'Connor: Another Legend in Southern Fiction," *The English Journal* 51, no. 4 (1962): 233.

[11] Ralph Wood, *The Comedy of Redemption: Christian Faith and Comic Vision in Four American Novelist* (Notre Dame: University of Notre Dame Press, 1988), 97.

[12] Arthur F. Kinney, "Flannery O'Connor and the Fiction of Grace," *Massachusetts Review* 27, no. 1 (1986): 95.

[13] Hawkins, *The Language of Grace*, 39.

describing her own vision, she believed that "most of the best religious fiction of our time is most shocking precisely to those readers who claim to have an intense interest in finding more 'spiritual purpose'—as they like to put it—in modern novels" (*MM* 165).

It only seems appropriate then to look toward O'Connor's often-quoted personal mantra as the clearest explanation of her own authorial intentions:

> When you can assume that your audience holds the same beliefs you do, you can relax a little and use more normal means of talking to it; when you have to assume that it does not, you have to make your vision apparent by shock—to the hard of hearing you shout, and for the almost-blind you draw large and startling figures. (*MM* 34)

This book argues that these biblical patterns emerging throughout O'Connor's fiction are no coincidence; rather I intend to show how O'Connor's fiction was influenced by the Bible itself. In essence, I aim to show how O'Connor was *shouting* to have her message heard, as her religious and artistic ambitions intersected within these *startling figures* found in her fiction. I will also analyze the techniques and biblical underpinnings she used to communicate this vision. The overall point that I will make is that O'Connor sees herself as a type of prophet, to these very readers she considered deaf and blind and, therefore, turns to the Bible in three general ways to get their attention. The readers do not need to know this—in fact, at points she seems to presuppose that they will not fully recognize her source material—but a scholarly examination of these techniques can be helpful in understanding how her fiction works as well as in gaining a fuller understanding of her texts, in general. These three methods, which will be explicated further in this chapter (and dealt in depth in subsequent chapters), are: her recapitulation or retelling of biblical stories, so their power can once again be felt; demonstrating the redemptive power of violence through her prophetic figures (grounded in the Bible); and, finally, allowing the reader to feel the full power of the Bible's reversing vision. The stories that I take up in this study are all part of a larger effort to understand O'Connor's own vision; however, all of these stories use one of, or often several, applications of these three techniques.

In Chapter 2, I will trace the development of these three biblical-based approaches as she hones her craft within her debut novel *Wise Blood*. By highlighting and elaborating on each of these three methods, I will show how the novel recapitulates the story of Paul. Furthermore, the novel gives birth to O'Connor's bizarre, backwoods prophet figure and her method of redemption through violence. Finally, the chapter traces the ironic reversals throughout *Wise Blood*, such as her method of reconciliation of opposites.

Chapter 3 will expound on her method of biblical rewriting, pairing one of her early short stories, "A Good Man Is Hard to Find," alongside one of the final pieces she completed in her lifetime, "Judgment Day." The stories seem to share little commonality; "A Good Man Is Hard to Find" reworks the story of the rich young ruler (Mt. 19:16–30, Mark 10:17–30, Luke 18:18–23), while "Judgment Day" is a literalization of 1 Corinthians 15. However, these two examples present O'Connor's cogent awareness of the Bible, yet underscore her methodology and anagogical vision throughout her career since this method is present with her earliest and latest fiction. Certainly, this process of understanding and acknowledging her distorted source material surely opens up a fresh new approach to reading O'Connor's fiction, both for scholars and general readers alike.

Chapter 4 highlights three common traits of her prophetic archetype and argues that these unconventional figures follow a very distinct pattern based on their biblical predecessors. While tracing the biblical origins and explicating her prophetic archetype, this chapter focuses on "A Circle in the Fire," "The Lame Shall Enter First," and *The Violent Bear It Away* and examines various prophetic figures throughout her corpus.

Chapter 5 focuses on the reversals found in "Parker's Back," "Revelation," and "A Temple of the Holy Ghost." By examining these three stories, I will show how O'Connor often shifts the polarity of the biblical stories she recapitulates, providing the antithesis of readers' expectations. Through her techniques of reconciling opposites and polarity reversals, she shifts these stories in order to get them back to where they were originally supposed to be: reversing the typical archetype, writing about God extending grace to the faith-poor, often times by means of violence. In doing so, her use of biblical retelling, prophetic archetypes, and reversals, synthesize and serve as "devices that guide the reader."[14]

Exploring O'Connor's method of biblical recapitulation

While the biblical influence on O'Connor's fiction cannot be overstated, Shinn asserts that "it is immediately apparent that her writing is based upon at least two traditions—the Roman Catholic and the Southern Gothic."[15] Though the area may have been burdensome—many were suspicious of Catholicism—she greatly respected the gravity of their beliefs. For those around her, Christianity was to be understood literally and seriously, the same way in which she understood the Eucharist, as she famously scolded Mary McCarthy for implying that the host was just a symbol by saying, "If it's a symbol, to hell with it" (*HB* 125). O'Connor took her faith very literally, and she found that among the Protestant South, this was something they shared. In fact, O'Connor once quipped that "if she were not a Catholic, she would not be Episcopal but Pentecostal Holiness."[16] Characteristic of her devotion, she argued, "I have heard it said that belief in Christian dogma is a hindrance to the writer, but I myself have found nothing further from the truth. Actually, it frees the storyteller to observe." She further commented, "I see from the standpoint of Christian orthodoxy. This means

---

[14] Brian Ragen, *A Wreck on the Road to Damascus: Innocence, Guilt & Conversion in Flannery O'Connor* (Chicago: Loyola University Press, 1989), xviii.

[15] Thelma J. Shinn, "Flannery O'Connor and the Violence of Grace," *Contemporary Literature* 9, no. 1 (1968): 59.

[16] Quoted in Farrell O'Gorman, *Peculiar Crossroads: Flannery O'Connor, Walker Percy, and Catholic Vision in Postwar Southern Fiction* (Baton Rouge: Louisiana State University Press, 2004), 164.

that for me the meaning of life is centered in our Redemption by Christ and what I see in the world I see in its relation to that" (*MM* 31–32). Alice Walker, fellow Southern writer and middle Georgia native, has recounted a famous anecdote of the young man who studied under Eudora Welty, O'Connor's contemporary, who told Walker, "wherever we reached a particularly dense and symbolic section of one of O'Connor's stories she would sigh and ask, 'Is there a Catholic in the class?'"[17] Though this story may be apocryphal, it certainly demonstrates what most O'Connor scholars have long suspected: that O'Connor's Catholic upbringing has had a major impact on her fiction and how it is interpreted. In her essay, Walker reminds readers, "It mattered to her [O'Connor] that she was a Catholic,"[18] a fact which O'Connor would gladly confirm: "Why people have told me that because I am a Catholic, I cannot be an artist, I have had to reply, ruefully, that because I am a Catholic, I cannot afford to be less than an artist" (*MM* 146).

By retelling these narratives and setting them in the poor South, as Whitt acknowledges, O'Connor knew that "most readers will be repulsed by these people," yet after examining the theological dilemmas these characters face, readers realize they are no more repulsive than we are.[19] In this sense, O'Connor targets her message to the complacency of middle-class Christians of the 1950s and 1960s who practiced their religion with a similar approach. Within American Christianity, the focus shifts from the humble origins of a religion for the masses to a middle-class religion, which ignored its roots. O'Connor challenges complacency by upending it, since in her "fictional world God seems to us to spend his grace on the unlikeliest of people. Often they do not appear to deserve His blessing," yet this is the paradox of her artistic vision.[20] Although it may not be warranted, they are, ultimately, offered grace through violent or untraditional means.

The marked impact of O'Connor's religion and region manifests itself throughout her fiction, which explains why she was attracted to using biblical narratives. O'Connor believed:

> The Catholic writer may be immersed in the Bible himself, but if his readers and his characters are not, he does not have the instrument to plumb meaning—and specifically Christian meaning—that he would have if the biblical background were known to all. (*MM* 204)

Her personal opinion sheds light upon her theological vision in her stories, especially considering O'Connor's method of biblical recapitulation, since she often used these biblical allusions to add meaning, specifically Christian meaning, into her fiction. O'Connor personally "addresses the importance of writing stories with a Biblical

---

[17] Alice Walker, "Beyond the Peacock; The Reconstruction of Flannery O'Connor," *Ms* December (1975): 56.

[18] Ibid., 55.

[19] Margaret Whitt, *Understanding Flannery O'Connor* (Columbia: University of South Carolina Press, 1995), 11.

[20] Kinney, "Fiction of Grace," 71.

context," as she argues that "To be great storytellers, we need something to measure ourselves against … It takes a story of mythic dimensions, one which belongs to everyone, one in which everybody is able to recognize the hand of God and its descent"; and for her, "the Scriptures fill this role" (*MM* 202). Although O'Connor is remarkably explicit in her dependence upon the Bible, the importance of biblical influences upon her fiction has been overlooked. She often complained of modern readers' lack of biblical literacy, as she believed that for most of her audience, the "Biblical mythos of the Western Judeo-Christian tradition of which she strongly declared herself to be a part, once familiar to all … were no longer accepted, or in many cases even recognized in reference."[21] This explains why she often set her stories in the South: "Unfortunately, where you find Catholics reading the Bible, you find that it is usually a pursuit of the educated, but in the South the Bible is known by the ignorant as well," adding that the Southern writer is fortunate "because here belief can still be made believable" (*MM* 204).

In Frank Kermode's exploration of the Gospel of Matthew, he notes that though the Gospels have quite a few similarities, these texts—which are supposed to tell the same story—actually "differ to a remarkable extent. The differences no doubt arise in part from … the needs of the communities for which each of the evangelists was writing."[22] In a sense, Kermode's description explains not only the reason for O'Connor's approach but why it has been overlooked. As Kermode asserts, the authors all "saw the basic material differently, worked it differently, and impressed upon it a distinctive literary method and talent."[23] In a very real sense, as Harold Bloom writes, "Christian, Jewish, or secular, the contemporary reader has been nurtured by literary suppositions that frequently are alien to the nature of the ancient Hebrew text," yet O'Connor's method of biblical recapitulation is an attempt to bridge this gap.[24] By reworking the source material from several different biblical sources, O'Connor transposes these stories, radically altering their setting and characters, yet the point is still the same. Through Hazel Motes, in *Wise Blood*, O'Connor offers a comic retelling of the story of Paul as a Christian *malgré lui*, a prophet undergoing a miraculous transformation, and her intentions are the same as the author in The Acts of the Apostles. By modernizing it, she makes it fresh, palpable even, for her audience.

While it is not a straight rewriting or an extrapolation of the text, it is a type of retelling; however, O'Connor's success is due to her innovative approach. In an almost entirely unique way, O'Connor transforms these biblical narratives. She takes the essential elements and ideas, but places them in the contemporary South. In "Judgment Day," through T. C. Tanner's literal understanding of the Pauline theology, O'Connor

---

[21] Karl-Heinz Westarp, "Flannery O'Connor's Development: An Analysis of the Judgment-Day Material," *Realist of Distances: Flannery O'Connor Revisited*, ed. Karl-Heinz Westarp and Jan Nordby Gretlund (Aarhus: Aarhus University Press, 1987), 12.

[22] Frank Kermode, "Matthew," *The Literary Guide to the Bible*, ed. Robert Alter and Frank Kermode (Cambridge: Harvard University Press, 1987), 387.

[23] Ibid.

[24] Harold Bloom, Introduction to *On the Bible: Eighteen Studies* by Martin Buber, ed. Nahum N. Glatzer (New York: Schocken Books, 1982), xviii.

transfigures Paul's descriptions of the resurrection of the dead in 1 Corinthians 15. She is able to bring Paul's conception of resurrection to life through T. C. Tanner's own misconception of Judgment day, setting portions of the story in Corinth, GA.

However, her success ultimately masked this technique since she is not as explicit in her vision as authors such as Milton, whose epic *Paradise Lost* "was an exercise in intertextuality" based on his "'unfolding' the vast design of the biblical story."[25] Yet, works of more contemporary works such as Faulkner's *A Fable* (1954), Emil Ludwig's *The Son of Man* (1945), and Nikos Kazantzakis' *The Last Temptation of Christ* (1953) have all relied heavily on biblical texts. Kreyling notes that "Faulkner's attraction to the story of the life of Jesus Christ... sparked reams of Christian explication," but O'Connor conscientiously avoids rewriting the life of Christ.[26] In fact, O'Connor's approach is completely different. While Milton, Ludgwig, and Kazantzkis do not contemporize their works and Faulkner relies heavily on allegory of the life of Christ, O'Connor's success derives from the uniqueness of her approach, an "unfolding" of various biblical narratives. She is drawn to specific biblical texts and subtly integrates the ideas into her fiction.

The ending of *The Violent Bear It Away* offers an interesting example of O'Connor's method of biblical recapitulation. The novel centers around her prophetic archetypes, Mason and young Tarwater, who exemplify the Elijah–Elisha relationship. O'Connor has the young prophet re-enact the story of Gideon in the novel's end. As young Tarwater accepts his prophetic calling and plans to return to the city to bring the message of God, he finds a well, ignores the dipper, and "put[s] his face to the water and drank" (*CW* 466). By sticking his head in the water, he mimics Gideon, who was told by God to take his 10,000 men to the spring and "separate everyone who laps the water with his tongue as a dog laps, as well as everyone who kneels to drink" (Judges 7:5). From those 10,000 men, Gideon separates the 300 to accompany him. When young Tarwater comes to a well, he laps the water in the same manner as Gideon, which, for those who recognize the allusion, only strengthens the readers' belief that Tarwater is on his way to following in Mason's footsteps and becoming the prophet he was raised to be.

Yet, this scene also has a resonance in the New Testament. When Tarwater reaches the well, he approaches the little boy, "I want me some water," to which the boy replies, "Yonder hit" (*CW* 466). However, after drinking, Tarwater notices that the "water had strangely not assuaged his thirst" (*CW* 466). Tarwater's encounter is almost an inverted retelling of Jesus' encounter with the Samarian woman at the well. When Jesus was in Samaria, "There came a woman of Samaria to draw water. Jesus said to her, 'Give Me a drink'" (John 4:7). The Samaritan woman responds, "How is it that You, being a Jew, ask me for a drink since I am a Samaritan woman?" (John 4:9). Yet Jesus responds, "If you knew the gift of God, and who it is who says to you, 'Give Me a drink,' you would

[25] David Jasper, *The Study of Religion and Literature: An Introduction* (Minneapolis: Fortress Press, 1989), 83–84.

[26] Michael Kreyling, *Inventing Southern Literature* (Jackson: University Press of Mississippi, 1998), 137.

have asked Him, and He would have given you living water," adding, "Everyone who drinks of this water will thirst again; but whoever drinks of the water that I will give him shall never thirst; but the water that I will give him will become in him a well of water springing up to eternal life" (John 4:10, 4:13–14).

The similarity lies in the fact that in both encounters two opposites meet at a well. In the biblical account it is a Jew and a Samarian, and in O'Connor's story it is a Caucasian and African-American. Jesus brings a message of living water quenching a spiritual thirst; meanwhile, Tarwater's own thirst after drinking from the well is indicative of the void in him that must be filled. The fact that drinking in the well doesn't quench Tarwater's thirst indicates to readers that Tarwater still harbors an internal emptiness.

Although this scene in *The Violent Bear It Away* is one of many examples of O'Connor's method of biblical recapitulation, by explicating O'Connor's methods of retelling these biblical stories, I hope that discriminating readers can fully realize the intricacy of Flannery O'Connor's artistic and religious vision. When we recognize the parallels and allusions to her stories' biblical origins, we are able to understand the theological implications of O'Connor's work in a richer and more nuanced way. What I'm contending is that we can appreciate her incarnational writing—her theological explorations that are grounded in specific, complex, tormented people in unusual situations—by looking at the ways in which these explorations are predicated on specific biblical texts, which she subverts, in order to shock and teach readers. In essence, O'Connor does not merely reference these stories; she rewrites them. Of course, when one searches the Bible for the faithless Misfit who kills a family alongside the highway or a despondent ex-sailor who finds comforts in body art, one finds no such tale. Rather, with shocking freedom, O'Connor twists open the original references, redistributing their basic elements; thus, her works "never show the least tendency to become tracts or essays instead of stories."[27]

By highlighting her technique of biblical recapitulation, illustrating the way in which she rewrites, reimagines, and contemporizes these biblical stories, I hope to underscore her methodology and anagogical vision. Chapter 3 will expound on this method by partnering her early short story, "A Good Man Is Hard to Find," with one of her latest works, "Judgment Day." This chapter will explicate O'Connor's method of biblical recapitulation by examining her rewriting of "A Good Man Is Hard to Find" (Mt. 19:16-30, Mark 10:17-30, Luke 18:18-23) and "Judgment Day" (1 Corinthians 15). Both "A Good Man Is Hard to Find" and "Judgment Day" offer typical prototypes of her method of biblical recapitulation and, furthermore, serve as a testament to her career arc since they represent the book ends of her early and late mature works. However, more than anything, by demonstrating how O'Connor retells these stories, this study seeks to illustrate the significance and structuralist influence of the Bible within O'Connor's fiction.

---

[27] Ragen, *Wreck*, 197.

Backwoods prophets

The Gospel of Mark begins with the emergence of one of the Bible's prominent prophets, John the Baptist, who is described as appearing "from the wilderness," living on a diet of locusts and honey (Mk 1:4). By the time we are introduced to him, he has already acquired a large and faithful following. Some view him as a messianic figure and others believe him to be the resurrected Elijah, as prophesized by Malachi.[28] However, upon encountering this quixotic figure, New Testament readers may be a little confused. John the Baptist seems like an Old Testament carryover, yet his prophetic status is never in doubt. Instead, John the Baptist brings a message saying, "I am not the Christ ... I am a voice of one crying in the wilderness, 'Make straight the way of the Lord'" (John 1:20,23). Like many of the prophets found throughout O'Connor's corpus, John comes bringing the message of grace: "For of His fullness we have all received, and grace upon grace" (John 1:17). As Northrop Frye noted, "The prophets bring a message that often causes their contemporaries to regard them as traitors, fools, or madmen"; it is a concept embodied by figures such as John the Baptist and internalized by O'Connor.[29]

If prophecy involves the "human transmission of allegedly divine messages," there is unequivocally nothing that stipulates that the prophet must be respectable.[30] Perhaps the most "dominant conservative misconception, evident in manifold bumper stickers, is that the prophet is [solely] a future-teller, a predictor of things to come." Rather this reductive reading overlooks that fact that the prophet embodies much more.[31] However, this idea is indicative of a long-running conversation that emerges in the Old Testament: the divide between the temple prophets and the country prophets, especially during the years of the divided kingdom. Although the biblical authority figures, such as Jeroboam, were often more comfortable with temple prophets, readers are far more interested in the bizarre country prophets, such as Amos, who lives in the wilderness, or Levi, who marries strange wives, or Hosea, the prophet of doom. Perhaps, this is why O'Connor's fiction is so fascinating, as she was admittedly enamored with these anomalous prophet figures, comparing them to the grotesque characters of Southern literature:

> They seem to carry an invisible burden; their fanaticism is a reproach, not merely an eccentricity. I believe they come about from the prophetic vision peculiar to any novelist whose concerns I have been describing. In the novelist's case, prophecy is a matter of seeing near things with their extensions of meaning and thus of seeing far things close up. The prophet is a realist of distances and it is this kind of realism that you find in the best modern instances of grotesque. (*MM* 44)

---

[28] Malachi 4:5–6 "Behold, I am going to send you Elijah the prophet before the coming of the great and terrible day of the Lord. He will restore the hearts of the fathers to *their* children and the hearts of the children to their fathers, so that I will not come and smite the land with a curse."

[29] Northrope Frye, *The Great Code: The Bible and Literature* (New York: Harcourt Brace, 1982), 218.

[30] Martti Nissinen and Peter Machinist, *Prophets and Prophecy in the Ancient Near East* (Atlanta: Society of Biblical Literature, 2003), 1.

[31] Walter Brueggemann, *The Prophetic Imagination* (Minneapolis: Fortress Press, 2001), 12.

For O'Connor, the prophet is the imperfect messenger who brings a divine message. Since these prophets can see the distant up-close, they are able to make the word of God clear, visible, and striking. Sometimes they dress strangely or marry prostitutes; other times, they just speak forcefully. Yet, in order to re-create the "prophetic experience" in her works, she "had to go direct to the Bible for precedents."[32] Hence, O'Connor's prophets often mix the comedic with the deadly, often bringing a terrifying, yet cleansing, message of grace.

Although several of O'Connor's characters are often deeply grounded in her biblical source material, none were more so than her prophet figures. O'Connor's corpus is populated with wild-eyed fundamentalist Protestant mystics who inhabit the woods and hills of her fiction, making a living operating stills and performing healings. Her prophets destroy property, court violence, and live on the fringes of society. While her prophet archetypes are often peculiar, strange, and always out of the ordinary, they are never fantastic: nor do they challenge the willful suspension of disbelief. Her grotesque prophets—perhaps more than any other aspect of her fiction—have gained her much notoriety, whether wanted or unwanted, yet their message cannot be ignored. These figures take their job and their message seriously, warning "the mercy of the Lord burns" (*CW* 342). Thus, they are more than just backwoods fundamentalists or a satirical portrait of Southern grotesqueries: they are a reimagining of her biblical source material, firmly rooted in the prophetic tradition found in both the Old and New Testaments.

O'Connor acknowledged, "[M]y Protestant prophets are fanatics"; however, these characters who carry the message of God cannot be written off as crazy or a parody of Evangelical fundamentalism of the South (*HB* 517). Much like O. E. Parker, standing barefoot in front of a burning tree, or young Tarwater, who, feeling like Habakkuk, realizes "that he was called to be a prophet and that the ways of his prophecy would not be remarkable," her characters re-create the prophetic experience (*CW* 388–389). O'Connor considered her depictions of backwoods prophets a tribute to the tangible belief she experienced living in the Protestant South.

Furthermore, O'Connor found a companion in St. Thomas Aquinas[33] noting, "The ordinary person does not have prophetic vision but he can accept it on faith. St. Thomas also says that prophetic vision is a quality of the imagination, that it does not have anything to do with the moral life of the prophet" (*HB* 365). In St. Thomas Aquinas, O'Connor found a kindred spirit who believed in the power of prophecy as he wrote, "prophecy, properly and simply, is conveyed by Divine revelations alone."[34] O'Connor, like Aquinas, believed in a prophetic view of history—viewing the relationship between humankind and God as being directed and influenced by prophets carrying the message of God. For both O'Connor and St. Thomas, prophets serve as social critics, bringing the message of God to the people.

[32] Asals, *The Imagination of Extremity*, 216.
[33] See Marion Montgomery's *Hillbilly Thomist: Flannery O'Connor, St. Thomas and the Limits of Art* (Jefferson, NC: McFarland, 2006).
[34] St. Thomas Aquinas, *Summa Theologica* Vol. 4 (Part 3) (New York: Cosimo Classics, 2007), 29.

Through her focus on the biblical archetype of the marginalized prophets and by bringing these quixotic figures into the contemporary South to convey the message of God to a fallen world, O'Connor herself functions as a prophet, a role she embraces. Re-creating the prophetic experience in her fiction was her way to make the Bible clear and forceful as well as visible to her audience. She believed that a writer's vision should be a "prophetic vision" since "the prophet is a realist of distances, and it is this kind of realism that goes into great novels. It is the realism which does not hesitate to distort appearances to show a hidden truth" (*MM* 179). O'Connor's intention as a writer was to serve as a prophet, showing a hidden truth, an objective she achieves by reimagining the prophets of the Bible. Through her integration of these archetypes into the twentieth century, she re-creates their fundamental message of a mercy and grace, which burns. For O'Connor, "the prophetic vision is not simply a matter of his personal imaginative gift; it is also a matter of the Church's gift," hence, O'Connor's use of this archetype (*MM* 179). It is more than a way of writing interesting characters: it is a way of integrating her anagogical—a vision she believed belonged to the Church—into her fiction to reach a large audience.

Ironic reversals

As readers progress through the Gospels, several patterns emerge; however, what becomes most apparent are the teachings of Christ, specifically, his frequent use of reversals. What seems to perplex all of those around him—followers and Pharisees alike—is Christ's tendency to flip the script on his audience. Throughout his ministry, Jesus makes proclamations such as "I came into this world, so that those who do not see may see, and that those who see may become blind" (John 9:39); "the last shall be first, and the first last" (Mt 20:16); "whoever wishes to become great among you shall be your servant, and whoever wishes to be first among you shall be your slave" (Mt 20:26–27). It seems like every time Jesus begins to teach, he offers another *peripetia*. So many of his lessons lead to a complete polarity shift in messianic prophecy: "In the Sermon on the Mount the Beatitudes are nearly all paradoxes: blessed are the poor, mourners, the meek the persecuted, the reviled."[35] Noticing this pattern of reversal found in the New Testament, Ralph Sockman makes a similar observation: "A thoughtful person, reading the story of Jesus for the first time, might think of it as a book of riddles."[36] Through these teachings, Jesus continuously (and conscientiously) upends the traditional views in much the same way that O'Connor intends to upend contemporary views of religious fiction.

In fact, in several ways, the reception of Jesus' message serves as a perfect ancillary for O'Connor's fiction. When Jesus makes his proclamations of deity, many, understandably, had difficulty believing the claim that the son of an obscure carpenter was the fulfillment of an age-old prophecy. Recalling the messianic prophecies of

---

[35] Kermode, "Matthew," 391.
[36] Ralph Sockman, *The Paradoxes of Jesus* (Nashville: Abingdon Press, 1964), 14.

Jeremiah, most were waiting for a great king.[37] However, Jesus repeatedly claims, "I did not come to abolish, but fulfill," he repeatedly "replaces what has been 'said by them of old time' with commands of his own so radically different that the defenders of tradition rightly looked upon him as revolutionary"[38] (Mt 5:17). By returning as a humble laborer, Jesus makes a claim as a realization of Messianic prophecy which completely reverses these previous prophecies. In an ironic twist of fate, many who knew O'Connor expected her to write romantic Southern fiction in the style of Margaret Mitchell, yet many early reviewers viewed O'Connor's works as nihilistic.

The teachings of Jesus rely on a reconciliation of opposites, or paradoxes. This use of chiasmus, which pairs opposites, is a rhetorical device meant to lead readers to a higher truth. In Jesus' case, it was a way to confound listeners into understanding a broader point. When he tells his followers "Truly, truly I say to you, unless a grain of wheat falls into the earth and dies, it remains by itself alone; but if it dies, it bears much fruit," they do not understand the implication of his statement until after his death (John 12:23–24). Yet, as Jesus tells the crowd, "He who loves his life loses it, and he who hates his life in this world will keep it to life eternal," his message essentially embodies this same method of reversals toward which O'Connor gravitates (John 12:25). This message, which emphasizes the need to die in order to gain life, is obviously paradoxical to his audience since death is the cessation of life; thus, it seems incomprehensible that one could die in order to live. Frequently throughout the Gospels, people approach Jesus with their own agendas, yet he only highlights their folly since Jesus turns upside down what they believed to be true.[39] Perhaps this is why many did not initially believe Jesus' message—a message not of "a poor carpenter who triumphs over difficulties and becomes rich, but of a Carpenter who dies 'poor, yet making many rich.'"[40] O'Connor's attraction to both paradoxes and reversals are deeply grounded in the biblical texts, which were so influential to her development as a writer. O'Connor herself noted, "Much of my fiction takes its character from a reasonable use of the unreasonable…The assumptions that underlie this use of it, however, are those of the central Christian mysteries" (*MM* 109). While this method is not exclusive to the Bible, it is a method employed by a great many prophets and biblical figures, most notably by Christ.[41] While, this study focuses on O'Connor's use of biblical sources, arguing that she was drawn not only to stories from the Bible but also to the structural and rhetorical techniques she found there, of all these techniques, the most prevalent is her use of ironic reversals, which she uses as a means to revive these biblical texts in the modern era.

O'Connor's reversals often interject humor into a story—we can't help but laugh when Manley Pointer opens his suitcase to reveal whiskey, condoms, and risqué playing cards—but there is something more serious at stake. Her method of shifting

---

[37] See Jeremiah 23:5–6.

[38] Sockman, *The Paradoxes of Jesus*, 14.

[39] See Jesus' encounter with Nicodemus; John 3: 1–21.

[40] Sockman, *The Paradoxes of Jesus*, 18.

[41] In some ways, O'Connor's technique mirrors Jung's principle of *enantiodromia* (the tendency of extreme psychological effects to turn into their opposites).

our expectations is both compelling and appalling. Yet, when measured against the biblical source material, which is what O'Connor often wanted readers to notice, what emerges is the parallel between O'Connor's message and the Christian message. For her, these stories, often memorized and repeated, have become blunted, commonplace, and ordinary, and the message—now socially mainstreamed—is foolish to those who do not believe it. Peter Gomes elaborates by arguing that to make the Gospel appealing to a large audience, "its rough edges have been shorn off and the radical edge of Jesus' preaching has been replaced by a respectable middle, of which 'niceness' is now God."[42] Essentially, O'Connor is following the model of Paul, who argues that his mission is to preach the message of Jesus "so that the cross of Christ would not be made void. For the word of the cross is foolishness to those who are perishing" (1 Cor 1:16–17). O'Connor notices what Paul notices, that these stories have been emptied of all their meaning. However, by reversing the stories, by siding with the foolish, readers see the message in a whole new light. By bringing Christ, literally on his back, Parker reminds us of both the message of Moses and of Paul, since what Parker really offers Sarah Ruth is grace—freedom from her legalistic system. This same freedom is extended to Mrs. Turpin after Mary Grace accosts her with a condemning prophecy, "Go back to hell where you came from, you old wart hog" (*CW* 646). When examined closely, the pattern that emerges from all of these stories is based on the same biblical pattern. It is a pattern that O'Connor uses to revive the same old message for a new generation, to add a freshness, to add the edge to a message whose point has long been shorn off. In a sense, she came not to bring laughter, but a sword.

Frequently, she retells biblical stories in a reverse fashion, using very different characters to achieve the same results as their biblical counterparts. As Asals notes, within O'Connor's fiction, "the incarnation of biblical language in fictional action reverses the relation between literal and metaphorical: as the Bible's metaphors become her literal actions, so their underlying actuality is made part of her metaphorical implications."[43]

***

One of the best examples of these three techniques working together can be found examining "Good Country People," a story which features Manley Pointer as a backwoods prophet who, posing as a naïve Bible salesman, makes a living as a nomadic conman, resembling Tom T. Shiftlet in "The Life You Save May Be Your Own." His target is Joy-Hulga, an unemployed PhD in philosophy with a wooden leg who lives with her mother, Mrs. Hopewell, a woman who "had no bad qualities of her own but she was able to use other people's in such a constructive way that she never felt the lack" (*CW* 264). Besides legally changing her name to Hulga, Joy-Hulga believes herself to be intellectually superior to everyone around her. Thus, the story thrives on subverting the readers' expectations beginning with O'Connor's tongue-in-cheek title.

---

[42] Peter Gomes, *The Scandalous Gospel of Jesus: What's So Good About the Good News?* (New York: Harper, 2007), 31.

[43] Asals, *The Imagination of Extremity*, 78.

Providing an example of her use of biblical rewriting, Mrs. Hopewell's reference to "Good Country People," much like the grandmother's reference to the "good man" in "A Good Man Is Hard to Find," echoes Jesus' response to the rich young ruler in the Gospel of Luke. As the ruler approaches Jesus he says, "Good Teacher, what shall I do to inherit eternal life?" (Luke 18:18). Instead of answering his query, Jesus deconstructs his salutation by asking, "Why do you call Me good?" (Luke 18:19). This is the question O'Connor poses within the story; why do both Hopewells call Manley good, especially since Jesus instructs that "No one is good except God alone" (Luke 18:19). Much like in "A Good Man Is Hard to Find," O'Connor is able to shock both readers and Joy-Hulga when Manley is revealed to be a Charlatan rather than an upstanding young man devoting his life to Jesus—reminding readers that no one is good, including the Hopewells.

Mrs. Hopewell's disappointment in her daughter is clear. At the age of 32, Joy-Hulga is unemployed and still lives at home.[44] As Mrs. Hopewell critiques her daughter, Joy-Hulga responds, "If you want me, here I am—LIKE I AM," strangely echoing Hazel Motes' declaration "I AM clean" (*CW* 266, 54). The biblical allusion is important here, not only to highlight O'Connor's reference to her biblical source text, but due to the irony as these two supposed nihilists both play on Yahweh's proclamation to Moses, "I AM," since both, through nihilism, claim to be their own gods (Ex. 3:14).

Of course, there is another important biblical allusion as well serving as an undiscovered source for Joy-Hulga's character. There is an interesting link between O'Connor's scholarly protagonist, Hulga, and the Old Testament prophetess Huldah, since the name is altered in the same way she altered Elihu (Job 32–35) into Elihue in her story "Parker's Back" (*CW* 267). The biblical Huldah, who appears in both II Kings and II Chronicles, is a scholar, prophetess, and "the certifier of the first Bible."[45] Upon discovering an ancient scroll in the renovated temple, King Josiah ordered, "Go, inquire of the Lord for me and the people and all Judah concerning the words of this book," hoping Huldah can validate the scroll (II Kings 22:8, 22:13). The cabinet officials go to Huldah and accept her authority since "she verifies that the scroll contains God's message."[46] Of course, Huldah is "not only a prophetess, but taught publicly in the school," conducting an academy.[47] Herein lies the connection: Joy-Hulga, with a PhD in Philosophy and who dreams of nothing more than taking a university job, "lecturing to people who knew what she was talking about," seems to be a rewriting of Huldah, the biblical scholar (*CW* 283). In doing so, O'Connor combines the method of biblical recapitulation and biblical archetypes with her method of reversals. Huldah is an oracle, a prophetess, the bringer of divine revelation, who authenticates and preaches the Bible. When King Josiah brings Huldah the Bible, she confirms it, but while young Manley Pointer brings revelation—and literally a bible—to Hulga, she rejects it. This, in and of itself, serves as a microcosm for O'Connor's method of reversals.

---

[44] Those familiar with O'Connor have noticed that the "autobiographical references are unmistakable," as one O'Connor biographer notes, "there is a good deal of O'Connor herself in Joy-Hulga Hopewell" (*South* 201, Cash 30).

[45] Samuel Terrien, *Till the Heart Sings* (Philadelphia: Fortress Press, 1985), 81–82.

[46] William E. Phipps, *Assertive Biblical Women* (Westport: Greenwood Press, 1992), 85.

[47] Isidore Singer, ed., *The Jewish Encyclopedia* Vol. 6 (New York: Funk and Wagnalls Co., 1912), 488.

Yet, Joy-Hulga isn't the only one who is fleeced by this swindler; Mrs. Hopewell is quite intrigued by both Manley's simplicity and his earnestness as he flatters her, "I know you're a Chrustian [sic] because I can see it in every line of your face" (*CW* 270). Mrs. Hopewell is attracted to Pointer for—what she perceives as—his genuineness, something entirely different from her cynical daughter. However, Mrs. Hopewell's empathy for Manley peaks when she realizes the parallel between Pointer and her own daughter, Joy-Hulga, when he tells her, "I got this heart condition. I may not live long" (*CW* 271). To Mrs. Hopewell, Manley represents everything that Joy-Hulga is not, yet what she naively hopes that Joy-Hulga will become. Both Mrs. Hopewell and Joy-Hulga are drawn to Pointer by pure ego. Mrs. Hopewell enjoys Manley's flattery, as she tells Mrs. Freeman, "He was so sincere and genuine. I couldn't be rude to him. He was just good country people, you know" (*CW* 274).

Joy-Hulga is fascinated by Pointer's simplicity and intends to corrupt him. She fantasizes seducing Manley, initiating him "into a deeper understanding of life" (*CW* 276). Like her mother, Joy-Hulga believes Manley Pointer to be an uneducated country bumpkin and tries to shock him with proclamations such as "I don't even believe in God," "In my economy ... I'm saved and you are damned," as well as patronizingly telling Manley, "I don't have illusions. I'm one of those people who see *through* to nothing" (*CW* 277, 278, 280). In their own ways, both mother and daughter are condescending to Manley as he embraces the guise of the inexperienced, yet honest clod. This allows readers to believe that as Joy-Hulga and Manley enter the isolated barn, she will seduce him as planned.

However, O'Connor subverts readers' expectations as Manley opens his suitcase filled not with Bibles, but with vice—prophylactics, an adult-themed deck of playing cards, and a flask of whiskey. Joy-Hulga realizes that Manley has been seducing her as she asks "aren't you just good country people" (*CW* 282). Manley's reply is certainly ironic and unexpected as he tells her, "Yeah ... but it ain't held me back none. I'm as good as you any day in the week" (*CW* 282). Joy-Hulga realizes that she does not have as accurate a perception of the world as she originally believed, since O'Connor describes Hulga's stare as "the look of someone who has achieved blindness by an act of will and means to keep it," perhaps because amidst all the commotion, Joy-Hulga "didn't realize he had taken her glasses" (*CW* 265). As with her debut novel, *Wise Blood*, O'Connor has accurately foreshadowed the protagonist's own blindness, preparing readers for the shocking ending.

At this point, Joy-Hulga's leg quickly becomes the objective correlative of the story, indicative of her incompleteness, as she treats her leg "as someone else would his soul" (*CW* 281). With this, readers realize that Manley is not the good person that everyone, including Joy-Hulga Hopewell, thought he was. In fact, it is Joy-Hulga who is haunted by her own naivety due to her own poor judgment of character. Yet, Pointer, like the prophets of the Old Testament who bring devastation and destruction, disabuses her of her illusions: "you ain't so smart. I been believing in nothing ever since I was born!" (*CW* 283). Joy-Hulga finally encounters a genuine nihilist in Manley Pointer. As Wood highlights, her final interaction with Pointer "reveals that the core of nihilism is no mere mental worldview but a calloused way of life, a cold and heartless bent toward annihilation."[48] While Hulga may have believed herself a nihilist, she encounters in Pointer one who can act, like young Tarwater. Her encounter with this country prophet leads Edmondson to comment that "the message of 'Good Country People' seems clear: roll in the hay with a nihilist and you'll be left without a leg to stand on."[49]

This story provides a synthesis of O'Connor's techniques, incorporating both biblical recapitulation and prophetic archetypes, yet "Good Country People" hinges on the ironic reversal of Manley Pointer, whom O'Connor transforms from a guileless salesman into a jaded scam artist. This exchange is foreshadowed by Manley's own admission: "He who losest his life shall find it" (*CW* 272). It is no accident that he cites this specific verse (Mt. 10:39).[50] It is, after all, one of the most famous reversals in Jesus' ministry. Joy-Hulga's surrendering her leg, after being seduced by Manley, and, by association, herself to the Bible salesman, an act that "was like losing her own life and finding it again, miraculously, in his" is a literalization of Christ's own reversal (*CW* 281). Joy-Hulga loses her life to Pointer and gets nothing in return except for humiliation, blindness, and a reminder of her own helplessness. Yet, through Pointer, O'Connor reminds her readers just how risky the Christian message is. It is potentially dangerous, as she warns readers against investing wholly in a false sense of security and ending up like Joy-Hulga, completely stranded. Yet, Wood insists that this isn't a bad thing: "Pointer is, in fact, Hopewell's unintentional savior, having stolen not so much her wooden leg as her false faith."[51] Similar to the ending of *Wise Blood*, O'Connor's ending is an optimistic one. Joy-Hulga is offered grace through the theft of her leg, as Manley Pointer places it in his suitcase. Thus, O'Connor has put "the gospel, the Word, which exists right next to the sins of the world—in the same briefcase."[52] This juxtaposition, the Bible and vice living side by side becomes a mainstay of O'Connor's fiction, the indiscriminate offer of grace to everyone. O'Connor's message, ultimately, reflects that of Christ, since Joy-Hulga has physically lost her leg and, by association, her life through her interaction with Manley Pointer. Yet, if Christ is to be believed, she will find it again, as Manley aptly quotes, "He who has lost his life for my sake shall find it" (Mt. 10:39).

Of course, not every one of O'Connor's stories falls into this framework; however, much of O'Connor's fiction incorporates specific theological dilemmas grounded in often extreme situations which seek to wake the theologically uninformed reader. By noticing how O'Connor rewrites biblical narratives, reuses prophetic archetypes, and is drawn to the rhetorical techniques of the Bible, readers get a richer understanding of these stories. Through this approach, I hope to open up a new way of responding to O'Connor's biblical echoes.

---

[48] Ralph Wood, *Flannery O'Connor and the Christ-Haunted South* (Grand Rapids: Eerdmans Publishing Company, 2004), 208.

[49] Henry T. Edmondson III, *Return to Good and Evil: Flannery O'Connor's Response to Nihilism* (Lanham: Lexington Books, 2002), 90.

[50] This specific verse is quoted in different variations throughout the four Gospels (Mt. 16:25, Luke 9:24, Luke 17:33, John 12:25).

[51] Wood, *South*, 208–209.

[52] Jill P. Baumgaertner, *Flannery O'Connor: A Proper Scaring* (Wheaton: Harold Shaw Publishers, 1988), 38.

2

Wise Blood as a Primer for
O'Connor's Religious Vision

The publication of Flannery O'Connor's debut novel, *Wise Blood*, in 1952 garnered the little-known author national attention. Unfortunately, it was not always the type of attention she hoped to receive. The novel earned national acclaim, such as Caroline Gordon's generous blurb for the dust jacket which read, "I was more impressed by *Wise Blood* than any novel I have read for a long time," and influential critic R. W. B. Lewis' ringing endorsement claiming "that Nathaniel West and Kafka have contributed generously to *Wise Blood*"; however, the reviews, on the whole, were mixed, at best.[1] More often than not, early readers of *Wise Blood* either misread her intentions or were shocked by her reliance on the Southern grotesque tradition since the novel "gives the Devil his due."[2] Although *Wise Blood* did not initially receive the reaction that she had expected, years later, it serves as an early exemplar of the many themes and practices common among her fiction. Thus, having outlined the ways in which she turns to the Bible in her fiction, I hope to highlight how *Wise Blood* contains all three approaches in embryonic form: the story of Paul's conversion recapitulated in Motes' experiences; O'Connor's first attempts at developing her backwoods prophet figures, associated with strange and violent acts; and O'Connor's early uses of ironic reversals.

Of course, early critics could not have predicted *Wise Blood*'s impact on O'Connor's later work, yet among the novel's early reviews two clear patterns emerged: critics either fixated on her violence or misconstrued her religious vision, widely viewing the novel as a scathing critique of American Christianity. The *Savannah Morning News*, where O'Connor spent her formative years as a child, included a negative and error-ridden review of the novel about "a young boy reared by an evangelistic father who sets out at first to preach the gospel of salvation," but "is moved to preach in the name of the Church without Jesus."[3] The review concludes that *Wise Blood* "represents the loss of hope in today's world and the substitution of lust, violence, self persecution and fanatical passion" before dismissing it since "It is not a book which will find a wide reading audience."[4] Meanwhile, Martha Smith of *The Atlanta Constitution* believed

---

[1] R. W. B. Lewis, "Eccentrics Pilgrimage," review of *Wise Blood*, by Flannery O'Connor, *The Hudson Review* 6, no. 1 (1953): 144.
[2] Shinn, "Violence of Grace," 68.
[3] "Damnation of Man." *Savannah Morning News* May 25, 1952.
[4] Ibid.

that the novel was a dark "allegory of modern life" adding, "I can hardly wait to read what Miss O'Connor may write about some happy people."[5] Besides perplexing critics, there were many, such as Martin Greenburg, who believed that the "rather labored" point of the novel was "This is a horrid and hollow and unbelieving world we live in. Haze's crazy faith in nothingness is a true religiosity that shows up the emptiness of our own 'normal' canting."[6] A prophet without honor in her hometown of Milledgeville, many of the local readers complained, "What is this thing that Mary Flannery has written here!" and a "distant cousin recalls that family members were aghast at the book, wondering where she 'had ever learned anything like that—that they had never known people like that.'"[7] Before reading the book, people at Georgia State College for Women hosted an autograph party in the Ina Dillard Russell Library. Several years later, O'Connor's mother, Regina, noted, "They never had another one."[8]

Her novel was shocking to many, especially those who knew her best, yet it marked the beginning of the Southern gothic style, for which she was known. In many facets, *Wise Blood* is heavily indebted to both her own reading habits and the New Critical approach she learned as a graduate student at the University of Iowa. O'Connor later acknowledged, "I didn't really start to read until I went to Graduate School and then I began to read and write at the same time. When I went to Iowa I had never heard of Faulkner, Kafka, Joyce, much less read them" (*HB* 98). During this time O'Connor began to read works by "the best Southern writers like Faulkner and the Tates, K. A. Porter, Eudora Welty and Peter Taylor" (*HB* 98).

Although Faulkner is lauded as one of the greatest Southern authors, O'Connor publicly resisted his influence on her writing, stating, "The presence alone of Faulkner in our midst makes a great difference in what the writer can and cannot permit himself to do. Nobody wants his mule and wagon stalled on the same track the Dixie Limited is roaring down" (*MM* 45). Later, she privately wrote to Betty Hester: "I keep clear of Faulkner so my own little boat won't get swamped" (*HB* 273). Yet, of all the Faulkner she read, O'Connor was most impressed by *As I Lay Dying*, a novel she often recommended to her friends. The early drafts of *Wise Blood* demonstrate Faulkner's influence. Asals points out that her short story "The Train," which became the novel's opening chapter, "is unquestionably in debt to Faulkner, particularly *As I Lay Dying*, both in conception and stylistically. The train journey, the loss of the mother, the central coffin image, the use of the name Cash" are all echoes of the Bundren family.[9]

It was more than just the violence that disturbed readers; rather it was the grotesqueness of her characters and Taulkinham in general, which seems more akin to West than Faulkner. In fact, *Miss Lonelyhearts*' influence on *Wise Blood* is clear. Asa Hawks' original name was Asa Shrike in her short story "The Peeler." Obviously,

[5]   Martha Smith, "Georgian Pens 'Wise Blood,' A First Novel," *The Atlanta Constitution* May 1952.
[6]   Martin Greenberg, "Books in Short," *American Mercury* 75 (1952): 112.
[7]   Quoted in Jean Cash, *Flannery O'Connor: A Life* (Knoxville: University of Tennessee Press, 2002), 25.
[8]   Quoted in Kathleen Feeley, *The Voice of the Peacock* (New York: Fordham University Press, 1982), 19.
[9]   Asals, *The Imagination of Extremity*, 18.

this is an allusion to Miss Lonelyhearts' cruel editor, Shrike. Meanwhile Sabbath Lily Hawks' letter to Mary Brittle, a newspaper columnist, like West's protagonist, reads like something submitted to the Miss Lonelyhearts column. Yet, Brittle's response to Sabbath Lily's question, "Perhaps you ought to re-examine your religious values to see if they meet your needs in life. A religious experience can be a beautiful addition to living if you put it in the proper perspective and do not let it warp you," satirizes the objectivism pervasive in the era, providing a corollary to West's protagonist, Miss Lonelyhearts (*CW* 67). Interestingly, Brittle downplays the notion of religion as a subtle complement to suit the modern person, yet all of the characters who populate the book are, as Brittle would argue, warped by their religious persuasions. Sykes observes that in response to *Miss Lonelyhearts*, O'Connor reverses "West's irony, finding redemption in human suffering identified with Christ's sacrifice."[10]

Partly this is why *Wise Blood* shocked readers: it represented the religious O'Connor's first foray into brutality and Faulkneresque violence, themes she tackled regularly in her mature fiction. However, O'Connor's juvenilia such as "The Coat," "The Geranium," "The Turkey," "The Crop," and "Wildcat" did not include the violence found in *Wise Blood*, nor, for that matter, the depth of her anagogical vision.[11] O'Connor's depictions, reversals, and grotesque irony were all so shocking that they initially had the opposite effect: many read the novel as nihilistic precisely because it didn't fit into the confines of a conventional Christian novel. O'Connor often complained that "the writer who is a Catholic... will feel that any long-continued service to it [writing] will produce a soggy, formless, and sentimental literature, one that will provide a sense of spiritual purpose for those who connect the spirit with romanticism and a sense of joy" (*MM* 30–31).

In reaction to the aesthetic of typical religious fiction, O'Connor used her shocking violence as an experimental approach to Christianity in fiction. Through her biblical recapitulation, her backwoods prophets, and her ironic reversals, she avoids the sentiment and clichéd storylines which she found so trite. Yet, it was her divergence from the typical pious Christian fiction, beginning with *Wise Blood*, which caused such controversy as O'Connor complained: "Everybody who has read *Wise Blood* thinks I'm a hillbilly nihilist" (*HB* 81).

Frederick Asals has argued that *Wise Blood* has "become the whipping-boy of the O'Connor canon," a fact evidenced by Robert Giroux's introduction to Flannery O'Connor's *The Complete Stories*. Giroux wrote, "when *Wise Blood* was published in May 1952. I was disappointed by the reviews more than she was; they all recognized her power but missed her point."[12] In a sense, Giroux's comment mirrors the history

---

[10] John Sykes, *Flannery O'Connor, Walker Percy, and the Aesthetic of Revelation* (Columbia: University of Missouri Press, 2007), 25.

[11] *The New Yorker's* recently published exerts from Flannery O'Connor's prayer journals, forthcoming as a collection through Farrar, Straus and Giroux, attest to the fact that she was thinking about how to integrate her religious vision into her fiction: "Please let Christian principles permeate my writing and please let there be enough of my writing (published) for Christian principles to permeate" (26). See *The New Yorker* September 16, 2013 (26–30).

[12] Asals, *The Imagination of Extremity*, 61; Robert Giroux, Introduction to *The Complete Stories*, by Flannery O'Connor (New York: Farrar, Straus, and Giroux, 1971), xii.

of *Wise Blood*'s criticism, since it was so often misinterpreted that in the 1962 Farrar, Straus, and Giroux reprint, the novel included an author's note for the second edition, explaining that:

> The book was written with zest and, if possible, it should be read that way. It is a comic novel about a Christian *malgré lui*, and as such, very serious, for all comic novels that are any good must be about matters of life and death ... That belief in Christ is to some a matter of life and death has been a stumbling block for readers who prefer to think it is a matter of no great consequence. For them Hazel Motes's integrity lies in his trying with such vigor to get rid of the ragged figure who moves from tree to tree in the back of his mind. For the author Haze's integrity lies in his not being able to. (*CW* 1265)

O'Connor's insistence that Hazel be read as a Christian, despite himself, was meant to clear any uncertainty as to O'Connor's intentions. However, Ben Satterfield has criticized O'Connor's note, saying that "Only readers who have a sacramental view of life and who read fiction with the anagogical lenses provided by religious doctrine see Hazel as redeemed."[13] Satterfield's critique highlights a central problem with literary interpretation. As Ragen cautions, a *Wise Blood* reader "who is not attentive to the signs of the anagogical action—or who is unwilling to suspend any disbelief in the action of grace—will miss the point," which certainly characterizes O'Connor's defense of the novel, especially against critics who accused her of heresy.[14]

Despite the negative criticism for O'Connor's characters, whether justified or unjustified, *Wise Blood*'s importance in O'Connor's canon lies in the fact that it serves as an indicator of her later texts. As Bruce Gentry asserts, instead of the criticism for O'Connor's inchoate techniques, *Wise Blood* should be considered "O'Connor's most interesting and challenging text."[15] Although Asals claims that within O'Connor's corpus *Wise Blood* does not "have any real successors in her work," this chapter argues that quite the opposite is true: *Wise Blood* is paradigmatic of the themes that O'Connor continues to explore throughout her career.[16] Within the novel, "her characters are often driven—even tormented by the idea that they have been redeemed" and it is this torment of redemption that will continue to be a major motif in her fiction ranging from the Misfit in "A Good Man Is Hard to Find" to Tarwater in *The Violent Bear It Away*.[17] Hence, *Wise Blood*, as Brinkmeyer has noticed, must be read as "the starting point of her mature fiction."[18]

In a fitting memorial tribute, Charlotte Kelly Gafford recognized that "a careful and analytical reading of *Wise Blood* is imperative if one is ever to understand Flannery

---

13 Ben Satterfield, "*Wise Blood*, Artistic Anemia and the Hemorrhaging of O'Connor Criticism." *Studies in American Fiction* 17, no. 1 (1989): 33.
14 Ragen, *Wreck*, 3.
15 Marshall Bruce Gentry, *Flannery O'Connor's Religion of the Grotesque* (Jackson: University Press of Mississippi, 1986), 119.
16 Asals, *The Imagination of Extremity*, 5.
17 Ragen, *Wreck*, 1.
18 Brinkmeyer, *Art and Vision*, 100.

O'Connor. In it, she was explicit about her Christian theme. And in it is the genesis of most of her work which followed."[19] Following her logic, I contend that O'Connor's *Wise Blood* must be seen as an important text for more than just its use of grotesque and religious themes: it is an introductory primer to O'Connor's anagogical vision. Thus, by studying *Wise Blood* as a forecaster of her later work, this chapter argues that many of the religious approaches to writing which she continued to cultivate through her writing career originate from within her debut novel.

Biblical recapitulation

What is most striking about Flannery O'Connor's reliance on her biblical sources is not that she integrates biblical allusions into her stories, but that she rewrites several of these characters and stories in her fiction. Perhaps this explains why O'Connor rejoiced when George Clay claimed that her work "sounded like the Old Testament would sound if it were being written today" (*HB* 110). As O'Connor was writing *Wise Blood*, she certainly drew from several biblical sources, but most notable is her interest in the life of Paul—which is not unusual for her.[20] Yet, *Wise Blood*, I will argue, which centers around her portrait of Hazel Motes as a Pauline prophet, represents her earliest attempt at this method of biblical recapitulation. Within the novel, O'Connor's reprises and reimagines Paul's life, conversion, and ministry through the character of Hazel Motes. As Giannone suggests, "O'Connor stresses the wonder of Hazel's call by setting his story against that of St. Paul" since both stories tell of the transformation "of a Pharisee into an apostle."[21] While there has been some earlier speculation on the connection between Paul and Hazel Motes, I hope to show how Paul serves as the source material for her tortured protagonist and a primary example of her method of biblical recapitulation within the novel.

Catholic priest and noted O'Connor scholar George Kilcourse observes that *Wise Blood* "reverberates with biblical echoes of Paul of Tarsus, struck blind on the road to Damascus and healed with the new vision of faith."[22] It shouldn't be a surprise that O'Connor was so attracted to the story of Paul since "No single figure, except that of Christ himself, has more influenced the subsequent interpretation of Scripture and the formulation of biblical tradition" as well as "for Christian religion and culture."[23] Much the same way that Milton's *Paradise Lost* far supersedes its biblical origins in Genesis, O'Connor has rewritten Paul's conversion story in Acts into a contemporary and comic

[19] Charlotte Kelly Gafford, "Fiction of Flannery O'Connor Mission of Gratuitous Grace" (Part III). *The Catholic Week*, October 16, 1964.
[20] O'Connor's 1948 version of the New Testament included marks and annotations next to multiple verses in both I & II Corinthians and The Acts of the Apostles.
[21] Richard Giannone, "Paul, Francis, and Hazel Motes: Conversion at Taulkingham." *Thought* 59 (1983): 484.
[22] George A Kilcourse, *Flannery O'Connor's Religious Imagination: A World with Everything Off Balance* (Mahwah: Paulist Press, 2001), 43.
[23] David Lyle Jeffrey, ed., *A Dictionary of Biblical Tradition in English Literature* (Grand Rapids: William B. Eerdmans, 1992), 588.

bildungsroman tale of a Christian prophet. O'Connor herself acknowledged that *Wise Blood* was "a comic novel" and yet "very serious, for all comic novels that are any good must be about matters of life and death" (*CW* 1265).

The parallels begin with Paul's youth, since before he was one of the most influential figures in Christianity; Paul, then known as Saul, was a respected member of the Jewish community. Maritain notes that Paul was "born of a family of pure Jewish lineage at Tarsus in Cilica."[24] His father was both a Pharisee and a Roman citizen. As a result of his Roman citizenship, Paul received an excellent education in both Tarsus and Jerusalem, where he studied with the respected Rabbi Gamaliel, "the great Doctor of the Pharisees."[25] It was from his both classical education as a Roman citizen and Jewish education as a Shammaite Pharisee that Paul gained "an incomparable knowledge of Scripture, and that subtle and refined manner of argument."[26] N. T. Wright notes that Paul's first-century Jewish education includes a "zeal" for God, noting "'Zeal', as we shall see, is a key term to characterize the sort of Jew, and the sort of Jewish agenda, that the young Saul of Tarsus had pursued."[27] Saul of Tarsus, a well-known and respected Jew who is speculated to have been a member of the Sanhedrin, publicly aligned himself against the early Christian church. He was present for Stephen's martyrdom and "was in hearty agreement with putting him [Stephen] to death" (Acts 8:1). Stephen's death became the catalyst for persecution against the early Christian church as he later testified before King Agrippa: "And this is just what I did in Jerusalem; not only did I lock up many of the saints in prisons, having received authority from the chief priests, but also when they were being put to death I cast my vote against them" (Acts 26:10). As Fitzmyer observes, "Saul, who witnessed and consented to the death of Stephen, becomes the archpersecutor of the Jerusalem church."[28] Paul's own statements correspond with Fitzmyer's argument, as Paul writes, "I persecuted the church of God violently" (Gal 1:13).

Directly before his conversion, Saul was "still breathing threats and murder against the disciples of the Lord" and "went to the high priest[29] and asked for letters from him to the synagogues at Damascus, so that if he found any belonging to the Way[30] ... he might bring them bound to Jerusalem" (Acts 9:1–2). Yet, it is on his mission to persecute Christians that he undergoes his famous transformation:

> As he was traveling, it happened that he was approaching Damascus, and suddenly a light from heaven flashed around him; and he fell to the ground and

[24] Jacques Maritain, *The Living Thoughts of Saint Paul*, ed. Alfred O. Mendel (Philadelphia: David McKay Company, 1941), 11.

[25] Ibid., 12.

[26] Ibid., 12.

[27] N. T. Wright, *What Saint Paul Really Said* (Grand Rapids: William B. Eerdman's Publishing, 1997), 25; Wright cites Romans 10:2, highlighting Paul's comment: "I bear them witness that they have a zeal for God."

[28] Joseph A. Fitzmyer, *The Acts of the Apostles: A New Translation with Introduction and Commentary*, Vol. 31 of *The Anchor Bible* (New York: Doubleday, 1998), 397.

[29] While the unnamed high priest is most likely Caiaphus, Fitzmyer notes that it "may have been Caiaphas, the high priest from A.D. 18–36, or Jonathan, son of Ananus ... who was the high priest for a short time during A.D. 36–37" (422).

[30] The Early Christian church.

heard a voice saying to him, "Saul, Saul, why are you persecuting Me?" And he said "Who are You, Lord?" And He said, "I am Jesus whom you are persecuting, but get up and enter the city, and it will be told you what you must do." (Acts 9:3–6)

This encounter, which physically blinded Saul, serves as the catalyst for his paradigm shift, transforming him into an outspoken Christian evangelist and saint of the Christian church. Paul "began to proclaim Jesus in the synagogues, saying 'He is the Son of God'" (Acts 9:20). Thus, Paul changes completely from a self-proclaimed Christian persecutor to a Christian prophet.

The details of Paul's postconversion life are fairly well known. He became an active missionary, epistler, and a principle leader of the early Christian church. He is often credited with writing several books in the New Testament.[31] Furthermore, he was imprisoned multiple times for his Christian beliefs, before dying, what has speculated to have been, a martyr's death.[32]

Of these central events in the life of Paul, many are recapitulated through Hazel's own experiences in *Wise Blood*. The parallels begin with Hazel's own background which serves as an inverse to Paul's formal education. While Paul received the best education available to him, Hazel attends "a country school where he had learned to read and write but that it was wiser not to; the Bible was the only book he read" (*CW* 12). Maritain argues that "it is well known that the Pharisees burned with zeal for the integrity of doctrine and tradition, and for a precise and rigorous observance of the Mosaic law," yet O'Connor realizes that the religiosity of the first-century Judaism could only be matched by the passion and devotion of Southern Protestants.[33] In Hazel Motes, she constructs a man whose religious fervor is matched only by Saul of Tarsus himself. However, Motes does not have the formal education that Saul had—this could only be achieved by an Ivy League education—but what Motes' education lacks in formality, it makes up for in tenacity. Motes' grandfather was a circuit preacher who preached sermons from atop his car, a tradition Hazel follows. Hazel's grandfather was "a waspish old man who had ridden over three counties with Jesus hidden in his head like a stinger," which influences Hazel, who knew "he was going to be a preacher like his grandfather" (*CW* 9–10).

While Paul had a strict Jewish upbringing and was subject to the "spiritual and cultural forces of his youth," Hazel's own tutelage under his grandfather serves as an apt parallel.[34] Reflecting his religious vehemence, Hazel carries "a black Bible and a pair

[31] It is generally agreed that Paul wrote 1st and 2nd Corinthians, Romans, Galatians, Philippians, 1st Thessalonians, and Philemon. However, Colossians, Ephesians, 2nd Thessalonians, and 1st and 2nd Timothy are more problematic to verify Pauline authorship. Few still assert Pauline authorship of Hebrews, which is highly doubtful.

[32] Although his martyrdom "is not recorded in the NT itself, but along with other events listed yields a persistent aspect of Pauline iconography" (Jeffrey 588).

[33] Jacques Maritain, *The Living Thoughts of Saint Paul*, ed. Alfred O. Mendel (Philadelphia: David McKay Company, 1941), 12.

[34] H. J. Schoeps, *Paul: The Theology of the Apostle in the Light of Jewish Religious History* (Philadelphia: Westminster Press, 1962), 47.

of silver-rimmed spectacles" with him throughout the novel, reinforcing the religious and vision motifs (*CW* 12). Yet, Hazel is no allegorical figure; in fact, he serves as an inverse Paul.[35] He doesn't have the means, privilege, and respect that was afforded to Paul; rather he is poor, uneducated, and largely ignored by his peers. The fervor of Evangelical Christianity in the Protestant South is the rational counterpart for Saul's Pharisaical education. Consequently, Hazel's attachment to Eastrod, Tennessee, as the holy of holies seems comically like a young Saul, as O'Connor establishes Motes as "a backwoods Pharisee."[36]

A primary connection between the two figures lies in the fact that Motes, like a young Saul, achieved a Pharisaical understanding of the law. Unlike his grandfather, Motes never really accepts the tenants of Christianity. Instead he realizes that to follow Jesus is to invite uncertainty, as Motes views Christ as "a wild ragged figure motioning him to turn around and come off into the dark where he was not sure of his footing" (*CW* 11). Hazel believes that the "way to avoid Jesus was to avoid sin": if he can live strictly by the law, like Saul, and avoid sin, then there would be no need for redemption (*CW* 11). However, despite Hazel's attempts to run, the wild ragged figure of Jesus haunts his every move.

Up until his conversion, Hazel Motes' comprehension of Christianity is one lacking the Pauline message of grace. As Hazel ages, his conception of Christianity remains stagnant. During his childhood, he attempts to completely repudiate his sense of guilt by filling his shoes "with stones and small rocks," thinking "that ought to satisfy Him" (*CW* 36). Yet, once Hazel leaves for the army, he tries to adopt the atheistic sensibilities of his peers who tell him "nobody was interested in his goddam soul unless it was the priest" (*CW* 12). Much the way Hazel has avoided sin to avoid redemption, he now tries to mollify his inner turmoil by telling himself that he has no soul.

During the novel's opening scene, Hazel is trying to come to terms with his own theology—a theology he does not believe. Schoeps argues that evidence of Saul's Hellenistic Judaic education can be found by studying his logic in his epistles, since Saul's logic parallels that found "in Orphic circles," yet Hazel Motes' logic follows a similar pattern within his watered-down proofs against Christ's divinity.[37] Motes tells himself that he no longer has to avoid sin because he does not have a soul and sin cannot exist. Yet, throughout the novel he will be unable to convince anyone—including himself—of this belief. Seeking a spiritual appeasement, Motes boards a train to Taulkinham, "a small-time Corinth," asserting his own freedom from Jesus.[38] Throughout his trip, he distances himself by repeatedly asking strangers, "Do you think I believe in Jesus? ... Well I wouldn't even if He existed," and later arguing "there was no Fall because there was nothing to fall from and no Redemption because there was no Fall and no Judgment because there wasn't

---

[35] These differences reinforce the theme of reversals in O'Connor's fiction.
[36] Giannone, "Conversion," 492.
[37] Schoeps, *Paul*, 49.
[38] Giannone, "Conversion," 488.

the first two" (*CW* 7, 59). Ironically, Christianity is the one thing Motes cannot escape as he is continuously identified as "an elderly country preacher" (*CW* 9). After the porter escorts him to his berth, Hazel imagines it as a coffin: "it looked as if it were closing. He lay there for a while not moving," which makes him recall his grandfather's coffin:

> They had left it propped open with a stick of kindling the night it had sat in the house with the old man in it, and Haze had watched from a distance, thinking: he ain't going to let them shut it on him; when the time comes, his elbow is going to shoot into the crack. (*CW* 9)

This imagining a physical resurrection of his grandfather is, perhaps, the first Pauline allusion in the book. By introducing the idea that Hazel's grandfather will rise from his coffin, O'Connor is literalizing 1 Corinthians 15, Paul's theory of resurrection, "It is sown a perishable body, it is raised an imperishable body," an idea she would later revisit and expand upon in her short story "Judgment Day" (1 Cor. 15:42). Hazel's train ride ends with his imagining himself trapped in a coffin; thus, the novel begins with a Pauline allusion, which is probably what led O'Connor to declare her misanthropic protagonist "a Christian *malgré lui*" (*CW* 1265).

Hazel arrives in Taulkinham, still trying to convince himself that sin does not exist, which is why he visits a prostitute whose address he finds in the stall of the train station bathroom. "He felt that he should have a woman, not for the sake of pleasure in her, but to prove that he didn't believe in sin since he practiced what was called it" (*CW* 62). Yet typical of Hazel's ministry, this idea does not go as planned. On the way to Leora Watts' house, the taxi driver tells Hazel, "She don't usually have no preachers for company," and despite Hazel's insistence that he is not a preacher, the driver tells him, "You look like a preacher ... It's a look in your face somewheres," before telling Hazel, "It ain't anybody perfect on this green earth of God's, preachers nor nobody else. And you can tell people better how terrible sin is if you know from your own personal experience" (*CW* 16). Yet, on Hazel's third denial, the disgusted driver tells him, "That's the trouble with you preachers ... You've all got too good to believe in anything" (*CW* 17). Although he insists on visiting a prostitute, Hazel takes no pleasure in his actions and still carries a Judeo-Christian view on sin, despite his attempts to alleviate himself of such notions. For that matter, Hazel neither enjoys sex nor is good at it: "when he finished he was like something washed ashore on her and she made obscene comments about him" (*CW* 33). Instead, Hazel's views on sex seem directly opposed to those of other characters in the novel, specifically Sabbath Lily Hawks. Hazel practices sex to prove that it is not a sin, while Sabbath engages in sexual activity strictly because it is taboo. In a sense, both characters are looking for justification of their beliefs, which is why—believing that she is already damned—Sabbath writes to Mary Brittle for confirmation. Adversely, Hazel uses sex to reinforce his traditional notions of sin, yet he still maintains a "wordless conviction ... that the way to avoid Jesus was to avoid sin" (*CW* 11). However, if the corollary is true, by inviting sin, then he is inviting Jesus, which supports Gentry's assertion, "in going to visit Mrs. Watts, Hazel takes an important step toward Jesus."[39]

In keeping with this theme, it could be said that throughout Hazel's time in Taulkinham, he consistently searches out sin, thus, he is implicitly or explicitly seeking Jesus. However, during this same time, Hazel obsesses over the notion of freedom: freedom from social customs, freedom to control his own destiny, and freedom from the need for redemption.

In order to prove his own freedom from redemption, Motes starts his own church, the Church Without Christ. Yet even Hazel's desire to preach against the notion of redemption elicits Pauline associations. In a sense, Hazel's legalistic notion parallels preconversion Saul, as Hazel claims, "I AM clean … If jesus existed I wouldn't be so clean" (*CW* 52). Like Saul, Motes' church, which teaches "Nothing matters but that Jesus was a liar," is positioned in direct opposition against Christianity (*CW* 59). Of course, much to his dismay, Hazel's message falls on barren ground. Even the few that listen to his message completely misinterpret it. Throughout the novel, Hazel comically fails in almost all of his endeavors and the Church Without Christ is no exception: "If Haze had believed in praying, he would have prayed for a disciple, but as it was all he could do was worry about it a lot" (*CW* 83). He even fails miserably with his attempts to sin; his encounters with the emasculating Mrs. Watts fail to give Hazel the freedom he thought he would find.

Hazel imagines that true sovereignty can be found, not in sin, but in a car. Motes sees the automobile as emblematic of his own independence. He tells the salesman that he is "in a terrible hurry to get away in the car," adding "I wanted this car mostly to be a house for me," allowing a reprieve since "he didn't want to go back to Mrs. Watts" (*CW* 41). Yet, Hazel's vehicle is much more than just an apartment for him; it becomes the physical embodiment of his own worldview. As O'Connor claims, for Hazel, the Essex functions as "a kind of death-in-life symbol" since the car serves as Hazel's "pulpit and his coffin as well as something he thinks of as a means of escape" (*MM* 72). The car soon becomes the locus of Motes' theology.

However, even if readers are to believe Motes' claim that "No one with a good car needs to be justified," the sorry state of Hazel's Essex suggests that he is sorely in need of justification, since no one, other than Hazel, would describe the Essex as good (*CW* 64). When one mechanic "damns" his car, slamming the hood and telling Hazel that the vehicle cannot be fixed, Hazel tells the mechanic, "This is a good car," despite all the evidence to the contrary (*CW* 65). Yet, O'Connor is sure to note that Hazel "is mistaken in thinking that it is a means of escape" (*MM* 72). While Hazel insists saying, "It's a good car … That car'll get me anywhere I want to go," one that was "built by people with their eyes open," readers realize that it is Hazel who is blind (*CW* 71, 72).

---

[39] Gentry, *Religion of the Grotesque*, 129; The minor prophet Hosea is told to "take yourself a wife of harlotry" to shame Israel (Hos 1:1). Like Hosea, Motes "receives his redemption and purification in a way which seems unorthodox: he frequents the bed of a well-known prostitute" (Friedman 241). In both cases, this act "establishes the tone of unconventional prophecy" as both Motes and Hosea have sexual relationships with prostitutes which will become meaningful in their respective ministries (Friedman 241).

It is clear to readers that the automobile is not the mechanism of freedom that Hazel deludes himself into thinking it is; however, the Essex does not seem Pauline until associated with Hazel's ministry. It isn't until Hazel buys the car that he begins to identify himself as a preacher and the car quickly transforms into his pulpit as he moves from venue to venue. When evicted from the movie theater parking lot by a woman who shouts, "If you don't have a church to do it in, you don't have to do it in front of this show," Hazel responds by getting in his car and moving the Church Without Christ to another location (*CW* 59). Yet, the tone of Motes' sermons, which are all screeds against Christianity, becomes increasingly threatening. Motes, like Saul, begins ministry as the persecutor of the Christian church:

> "Where has the blood you think you been deemed by touched you?"
> "Rabble rouser," the little man said. "One thing I can't stand it's a rabble rouser."
> "What church you belong to, you boy there?" Haze asked, pointing at the tallest boy in the red satin lumberjacket.
> The boy giggled.
> "You then," he said impatiently, pointing at the next one. "What church you belong to?"
> "Church of Christ," the boy said in a falsetto to hide the truth.
> "Church of Christ!" Haze repeated. "Well, I preach the Church Without Christ. I'm member and preacher to that church where the blind don't see and the lame don't walk and what's dead stays that way." (*CW* 58–59)

Motes is obviously satirizing the basic tenants of the Christianity by claiming there is no need for redemption, no resurrection, no miracles, and so on. Through his attacks on these cardinal teachings of Christianity, "Motes takes on the role of Saul, the Church's persecutor."[40] Both Hazel and Saul become persecutors of Christians: just as "Saul began ravaging the church, entering house after house, and dragging off men and women,... [putting] them in prison," Hazel escalates his rhetoric from threats to murder (Acts 8:3).

Furthermore, these two figures, as a last great act of defiance against Christianity, play a major role in murder. Although Saul's participation in Stephen's death, the first Christian martyr, is unclear, however, whenever participants began stoning Stephen, they "laid aside their robes at the feet of a young man named Saul," who is "in hearty agreement with putting him [Stephen] to death," while Hazel Motes uses his car to kill Solace Layfield firsthand, re-enacting Stephen's death (Acts 7:58, 8:1).

Hazel, upset over Shoats' schism, follows Solace Layfield after he finishes preaching and confronts him saying, "You ain't true... What do you get up on top of a car and say you don't believe in what you do believe in for" (*CW* 114). As Brinkmeyer contends, Hazel sees Solace Layfield as "the embodiment of his own conscience, that part of him

---

[40] Ragen, *Wreck*, 109.

that knows Christ is true."[41] Hazel then orders Solace to "take off that hat and that suit"; ironically, the frightened Layfield "tore off his shirt" in the biblical tradition of tearing one's clothes as a means of expressing anguish (*CW* 114). Although the reactionary Hazel runs Solace over with his Essex, leaving the True Prophet, in extremis, on the side of the road, Motes' actions represent another one of his futile attempts to banish his own faith. Of course, he is shocked by his doppelganger's reaction as, dying, Layfield begs for forgiveness. Hazel leans "his head closer to hear the confession," but is disturbed by Solace Layfield's plea, "Jesus hep me," revealing, as Giannone argues, that "Layfield does believe in Jesus, and his belief costs him everything" (*CW* 115).[42] Through his death, Solace Layfield becomes a martyr similar to Stephen.

For all their similarities, the strongest parallel between Hazel Motes and Paul occurs within their respective conversions. While their mutual devotion to the law partially explains O'Connor's attraction to Paul, since "more than any other apostle, Paul had to come to terms with the law and its potential contradictions," it is their mutual paradigm shifts which occur after their respective conversions which interest her.[43] In fact, Steven Sparrow has written of "a letter I received in 1998 from Sally Fitzgerald (Fitzgerald was a close friend of O'Connor's), she told me that, the whole story, whatever modern turns it takes, is in fact a re-telling of the old, old—and ever new—story of Paul on the road to Damascus" and concludes saying, "I feel sure that Flannery intended him as a Pauline figure."[44] Of course this account occurs secondhand, yet looking at the two encounters, side by side, it is easy to see the parallels.

First, it is no coincidence that both conversions occur right after an execution; rather it demonstrates a freedom from Pharisaical legalism since both are offered grace, unasked, immediately preceding a violent death. Furthermore, in the two conversion stories, blindness serves as the catalyst. Similarly, both take place on the road, as each figure functions as a persecutor of Christ. Hazel's confrontation with the law comes as he leaves Taulkinham, on the highway passing mile-marker 666 and a sign reading "Jesus Died for You" (*CW* 117). Motes repeatedly claims that he does not need to be justified, yet his encounter with the policeman shows that he has neither a good car nor freedom from the need for justification (Romans 4:25, *CW* 64).

Hazel is pulled over by a patrolman, who explains to Hazel that he didn't pull him over for a legal violation, but rather because "I just don't like your face" (*CW* 117). The officer asks for Hazel's license, to which Motes responds, "I don't like your face either... and I don't have a license" (*CW* 117). The policeman removes Hazel from the car and then pushes Hazel's car over an embankment, destroying the entirety of the "Church without Christ."

---

[41] Robert Brinkmeyer, "'Jesus, Stab Me in the Heart!': *Wise Blood*, Wounding, and Sacramental Aesthetics." *New Essays on "Wise Blood,"* ed. Michael Kreyling (New York: Cambridge University Press, 1995), 81.

[42] Richard Giannone, *Flannery O'Connor, Hermit Novelist* (Urbana: University of Illinois Press, 2000), 57.

[43] Giannone, "Conversion," 496.

[44] Stephen Sparrow, "Wisdom: Simple or Idiotic Religious Vision and Free Will in Flannery O'Connor's Novel *Wise Blood," The Comforts of Home*, Last modified January 22, 2002, http://mediaspecialist.org/sswisdom.html.

Following the loss of his vehicle, Hazel is finally forced to confront reality. Although Hazel has been naively optimistic about the Essex, consistently trying to overlook its wretched condition, O'Connor suggests Hazel "does not really escape his predicament until the car is destroyed" (*MM* 72). Just before he leaves Taulkinham, Hazel tells one mechanic, "This car is just beginning its life. A lightening bolt couldn't stop it!" (*CW* 116). Yet the reference to a lightning bolt certainly furthers "the allusion to Paul's being struck on the road to Damascus," offering a foreshadowing of Hazel's fate and the inevitable striking down of both Hazel and his vehicle.[45] The destruction of his automobile, Hazel's last vestige of escape from Christ, represents the end of Hazel's heretical ministry and parallels the end of Saul's Pharisaical ministry, as the police intentionally takes Motes' car—and later his life—without explanation. By using policemen as emblematic of "the law," O'Connor reinforces Pauline theology:

> The patrolman who stops him now, and the policemen who bash his head in with a billy club at the end of the novel, do what they do without much reference to guilt or innocence. It seems an illustration of the idea that under the law all are condemned. (Ragen 149)

These incidents echo the central Pauline theological tenant: relief from the law, through grace.[46] The death of the Essex finally grounds Hazel, who is no longer able to run from his fate. He stares out into the "distance that extended from his eyes to the blank gray sky that went on, depth after depth, into space. His knees bent under him" (*CW* 118). Like Saul's encounter with God, Hazel is thrown to the ground, yet in Hazel's encounter, vision is foregrounded. Through Hazel's blinding of himself, a grotesque act of violence, Sykes claims that "the body becomes the means to spirit, the necessary point of access to that divine grace paradigmatically joined to nature in the person of Christ."[47]

Indicative of her methodology, O'Connor has inverted the story since "on the road to Damascus, Paul is jolted out of his rigid Pharisaism" while Hazel is stunned out of his rigid nihilism, literally, on the road leaving Taulkinham.[48] Furthermore, in Paul's encounter, he has a finite destination, whereas when the officer asks the shiftless Hazel, "Was you going anywhere," he aptly responds, "No" (*CW* 118). Paul is blinded during his experience on the road and told to head toward the city where he can be healed; similarly, Hazel is blinded immediately after he arrives in the city. Although Paul's blinding is only temporary, lasting only three days, Hazel's is permanent.

This vision motif emerges as a strong connection between Motes and Paul throughout *Wise Blood*. When Hazel tells his landlady, Mrs. Flood, that he intends to blind himself, she can't understand the act: "instead of blinding herself, if she had felt

---

[45] Kilcourse, *Flannery O'Connor's Religious Imagination*, 81.
[46] Romans 3:21–24.
[47] Sykes, *Aesthetic*, 47.
[48] Giannone, "Conversion," 496.

that bad, she would have killed herself," as she ponders "what possible reason could a person have for wanting to destroy their sight" (*CW* 119). Asals argues that Hazel's "final self-blinding and mortification of the flesh seem admissions ... that he has seen nothing all along," especially after Motes tells Mrs. Flood, "If there's no bottom in your eyes, they hold more" (*CW* 126).[49] Motes has, essentially, admitted his own blindness by blinding himself in order to receive sight. It is Mrs. Flood, a character who, at times, seems to speak for O'Connor, who befittingly points out, "You must believe in Jesus or you wouldn't do these foolish things" (*CW* 127).

Motes' admission of his own blindness has further biblical echoes when compared to Jesus' confrontation with the Pharisees. When challenged, Jesus responds, "For judgment I came into this world, so that those who do not see may see, and that those who see may become blind" (John 9:39). Yet, the Pharisees reply, "We are not blind too, are we?" to which Jesus rejoined, "If you were blind, you would have no sin; but since you say, 'We see,' your sin remains" (John 9:40–41). What Jesus suggests is the need to acknowledge blindness, something that Motes previously avoided throughout the novel, signified by the fact that Motes keeps his mother's spectacles "in case his vision should ever become dim" yet keeps them "at the bottom of his duffel bag" (*CW* 13). Innately, he knows his vision needs correcting, yet Motes spends most of the novel ignoring his own blindness. His conversion occurs when he realizes that he cannot redeem himself—especially since he no longer has a car to justify himself. His self-blinding, then, becomes the ultimate act of penance to acknowledge his own blindness and, in essence, regain his sight.

Long before Motes' self-mutilation, vision emerges as a central theme in *Wise Blood* through his antagonistic relationship with Asa Hawks, the counterfeit-blind street preacher. It is Hawks who, initially, sets the spiritual tone for the novel, telling Motes, "You got eyes and see not, ears and hear not, but you'll have to see some time" (*CW* 30). It is ironic that Hawks paraphrases the Old Testament: "They have eyes, but they do not see; They have ears, but they do not hear," since Asa will later align himself with Paul from the New Testament (Psalms 135:16–17).[50] Previously, Hawks even attempted to blind himself, as he "preached for an hour on the blindness of Paul," until his nerve failed and instead, he maimed his face with lime (*CW* 65). It is telling of O'Connor's own biblical intertextuality that she chooses this Psalm since it is also a refrain in Jesus' preaching: "You will keep on Hearing, but will not understand; You will keep on seeing, but will not perceive" (Matt 13:14).[51] Yet, this is the same message that Paul repeats to the Jews in Rome; thus, O'Connor has astutely chosen this message—the connection between the Old and New Testament, between Christ and Paul's ministry.[52]

Hazel's obsession with Hawks comes to a head when an entirely shocked Hazel finds out Sabbath Lily is a bastard. "'You couldn't be a bastard,' Haze said, getting

---

[49] Asals, *The Imagination of Extremity*, 35.
[50] This is first quoted in Psalms (115:5–6, 135:15–16), but later repeated in Isaiah 6:10, 42: 18–20 and Jeremiah 5:21. O'Connor repeats this quote in "An Exile in the East" and drafts of "Judgment Day."
[51] See also Mark 4:11, Luke 8:10.
[52] Acts 28:26–27.

very pale. 'You must be mixed up. Your daddy blinded himself'" (*CW* 68). Hazel, who takes everyone literally at their word, cannot fathom the concept that Hawks is merely a false prophet begging for money, not a genuine preacher, which leads Motes to question, "What kind of a preacher are you? ... not to see if you can save my soul?" (*CW* 61). However, Hazel's confrontation with Hawks reaches an ironic climax when Motes asks him, "If Jesus cured blind men, how come you don't get Him to cure you?" to which Hawks can only answer "He blinded Paul" (*CW* 63). Of course, the corollary response is that he restored Paul's sight and that this false prophet was never blinded to begin with. Yet, Ragen notes, "Although Motes and Hawks are in some ways versions of Oedipus and Teiresias, it is more significant that both are versions of Saul of Tarsus."[53] This comparison to Paul is especially relevant since O'Connor is sure to note Hawks as "the fake blind man," while Hazel, like Paul, becomes the genuinely blind man. Therefore, readers are forced to make the blind-prophet connection not with Hawks, but with Motes himself. Once Motes discovers Asa's secret—that is, feigning blindness—he realizes that the street preacher has much more in common with the prophets of Baal than with Paul. This repeated emphasis on vision "serves to show us that Haze is the seeing unbeliever [much like Asa Hawks or the unconverted Saul of Tarsus] who, at the novel's end, ironically becomes the blind seer."[54] Thus, the vision motif unfolds through O'Connor's attention to Hazel's own naivety (a social blindness) during his interactions with Hawks, the false-blind preacher.

In his letter to the Galatians, Paul describes his own physical ailments,

> You know that it was due to an illness of mine that I preached the gospel to you in the first place ... you welcomed me as an angel of God, indeed as Christ Jesus ... Had it been possible, you would have plucked out your eyes and given them to me! (Gal. 4:13–15)

Of course, Paul is not specific about his affliction, his "thorn in the flesh," so speculation ranges from poor vision to Malta fever (2 Corinthians 12:7).[55] Although Paul's vision remains conjecture, Motes' physical act of blinding itself is an extremely literal interpretation of Pauline theology.

After Motes blinds himself with lye, Mrs. Flood finds Hazel engaging in forms of self-mutilation, which she associates with Christian ascesis: "He might as well be one of them monks, she thought, he might as well be in a monkery" (*CW* 123). Giannone aptly notices that the "ascesis of his body keeps his will in line with the absolute," yet, his action goes beyond hermetic devotion.[56] Motes' self-mortification has Pauline implications, inasmuch as it is the material incarnation of Paul's claim: "For if you live according to the flesh, you shall die: but if by the Spirit you mortify the deeds of the

[53] Ragen, *Wreck*, 111.
[54] Kilcourse, *Flannery O'Connor's Religious Imagination*, 51.
[55] See Murray J. Harris' *The Second Epistle to the Corinthians: A Commentary on the Greek Text.* (Grand Rapids: Eerdmans, 2005), 171–172.
[56] Giannone, *Hermit*, 61.

flesh, you shall live" (Rom. 8:13).[57] Through Hazel's own mortification of the flesh, he becomes a grotesque rendering of postconversion Paul.

Through her recapitulation of the Pauline narrative, by rewriting Hazel as a Saul/Paul figure, O'Connor incorporates elements from both the gospels of Matthew and John. Ragen notes that "there are few references in *Wise Blood* to the converted Paul, the apostle to the gentiles and writer of the epistles," especially since "no scales fall from Motes's eyes after he has been blinded (Acts 9:18) and he never becomes a preacher for Christ."[58] O'Connor is not interested in a strict retelling of the Paul story; instead she weaves various biblical analogues into *Wise Blood*. Therefore, she does more than follow the spiritual advice found in the Bible by personifying it in the same way that Hazel literally crucifies his flesh: "The literalism of O'Connor's imagination is finally more extreme than the fundamentalism with which it has such evident affinities."[59] Both Paul and Motes embody the following commandment of Jesus: "If your right eye causes you to sin, gouge it out and throw it away. It is better for you to lose one part of your body than for your whole body to be thrown into hell" (Mt 5:29). O'Connor seems to have this verse in mind when Motes, quite literally, re-enacts Jesus' command. In context, recognizing Jesus' instruction in Matthew is crucial to understanding the novel since Hazel's extreme act of self-blinding is vital to his own redemption. This verse exemplifies O'Connor's method, serving as the central paradigm of biblical recapitulation in *Wise Blood*; Motes discards both of his eyes, realizing that he must sacrifice to be redeemed.

The novel ends with Hazel's conversion and drastic attitude shift, much like Paul's own conversion. His dynamic transformation can be seen through his interaction with Mrs. Flood. As Hazel leaves the room, Mrs. Flood asks, "[W]ere you planning to find you another rooming house? ... Maybe you were planning to go to some other city!"; yet, Hazel's response is poignant: "'That's not where I'm going,' he said. 'there's no other house nor no other city'" (*CW* 129). Hazel has spent most of his time running with no certain destination, but now he realizes he has a finite objective which explains his final words to the police officers who bash his head in, "I want to go where I'm going" (*CW* 131). Although he dies long before becoming a famous epistler—or its modern equivalent, a Christian apologist—Hazel Motes' conversion story is very much a retelling of Paul's conversion, which only affirms O'Connor's theory "that all good stories are about conversion" (*HB* 275).

The strength in O'Connor's method of biblical recapitulation within *Wise Blood*— and further evidence that her debut novel serves as a diagram for this method in her later works—is her multidimensional nature as a writer. She transforms Saul, ardently living by his Pharisaical system, into Hazel, the modern man with a no-system system, as "she shows him [Motes] judging the modern Pharisees pharisaically."[60] Both Saul and Hazel believed sin could be mastered while claiming to be the "I AM," God himself.

[57] Douay-Rheims edition.
[58] Ragen, *Wreck*, 112.
[59] Asals, *The Imagination of Extremity*, 78.
[60] Giannone, *Hermit*, 52.

Backwoods prophets

In large part, the success of the *Wise Blood* lies neither in its simplistic plot nor in its spartan attention to detail, but with the eccentric, yet striking characterizations found throughout the story. O'Connor's prophets serve as the most gripping and compelling figures in Taulkinham. Readers are privy to some of the most austere, yet memorable characters in her corpus as she uses her debut novel to develop the prophetic archetype, which would become another staple of her fiction: the backwoods prophet. The characters in *Wise Blood* are aberrant and erratic, so tortured and Jesus-crazed that it leads Mrs. Flood to notice that preachers "were all, if the truth was only known, a little bit off in their heads" (*CW* 119).

O'Connor's use of the backwoods prophet, as I have previously argued, demonstrates that she is not just interested in prophets but is also a very distinct type of prophet figure: the outliers and outcasts. Yet, *Wise Blood* allows readers to see "how O'Connor does value the biblical tradition preserved by her backwoods southern Protestants."[61] In many ways, O'Connor takes St. Thomas' declaration seriously as he wrote, "the revelation which is made by the demons may be called prophecy."[62] She is not interested in men of God who possess respectability and social standing. Her religious figures are not clean and respectable pillars of the community, as she avoids many of the typical clichés: the charismatic pastor of the mega-church, the scholarly seminarian, the affable priest; in fact, Hoover Shoats is a parody of these polished and likable religious leaders. Rather, O'Connor is interested in a radically different paradigm: the castaway prophets, those who live and preach on the fringes of society, or even the demons carrying God's message—an archetype with a strong biblical precedent.

Living in the Protestant South, O'Connor was intrigued with similarities between the Evangelical Christian fundamentalists who surrounded her and their connection to the biblical prophets, as Wood writes: "O'Connor honored the Bible-centered faith of fundamentalists because, as we have seen, it gave them a storytelling cast of mind."[63] Yet, until *Wise Blood*, these figures were largely absent from her early fiction. Of course, this partially explains why "early reviewers tended to misread *Wise Blood* as an attack upon southern religious fundamentalism."[64] Instead of producing a romantic Christian protagonist, Motes belongs to "the violent order of hewing down the tree which does not bring forth good fruit and casting it in the fire."[65] But through their eccentric faith and actions, the prophets serve to drive the storyline. Her archetype emerges, inchoate, throughout *Wise Blood* as O'Connor creates a world populated with the early incarnations of her backwoods prophets.

[61] Farrell O'Gorman, *Peculiar Crossroads: Flannery O'Connor, Walker Percy, and Catholic Vision in Postwar Southern Fiction* (Baton Rouge: Louisiana State University Press, 2004), 178.

[62] St. Thomas Aquinas, *Summa Theologica*. Vol. 4 (Part 3). (New York: Cosimo Classics, 2007), Q172, A5.

[63] Wood, *South*, 37.

[64] Kilcourse, *Flannery O'Connor's Religious Imagination*, 46.

[65] Albert Sonnenfeld, "Flannery O'Connor: The Catholic Writer as Baptist," *Contemporary Literature* 13 (1972): 447.

The prophets in her works are often terribly flawed—she did not always put the message in the heart of the righteous—but, much like characters such as Rufus Johnson and Manley Pointer, this message comes from the troubled, the sinners, or the nonbelievers, a fact lost on Solace Layfield, "The True Prophet." While the role of the prophet is to serve as the mouthpiece of God, Layfield is sorely mistaken by accepting the position: "He had consumption and a wife and six children and being a Prophet was as much work as he wanted to do. It never occurred to him that it might be a dangerous job" (*CW* 113). Clearly, as O'Connor develops this model in her later fiction, it *is* a dangerous job, with her prophets experiencing everything from rape to murder.

Although these preachers and street urchins do not seem to fit the mold of a traditional prophet figure, the narrator's parody of their names such as the True Prophet or the fake blind man lets us know the folly of their intentions. Some of her most memorable characters are not the prophets of grace, but the false prophets who still lead our characters to the divine, such as Manley Pointer or Mary Grace. This, more than anything, is obvious throughout the novel. In no other work can readers find so many bizarre and, ultimately false, prophets. If Hazel Motes is destined to be a Christian preacher, then these blasphemous prophets are destined to fail.

If Motes represents a recapitulation of Paul, then Hoover Shoats seems to have his biblical roots in the Bible's original conman-prophet, Simon. Simon, the magician, "heard Phillip preaching the good news about the kingdom of God and the name of Jesus Christ…Even Simon himself believed; and after being baptized, he continued on with Phillip as he observed signs and great miracles taking place" (Acts 8:12–13). Yet "when Simon saw that the Spirit was bestowed through the laying on of the apostles' hands, he offered them money, saying 'Give this authority to me as well, so that everyone on whom I lay my hands may receive the Holy Spirit'" (Acts 8:18–19). St. Irenaeus "argues that Simon's faith was not genuine but feigned"; the same could be said about Shoats, who attempts to exploit the Church of Christ Without Christ.[66] Like Simon, Shoats, who refers to himself as Onnie Jay Holy, a former radio preacher from Soulease, "a program that gives real religious experiences to the whole family," approaches Hazel with a for-profit venture (*CW* 88). As Hazel preaches outside a theater, Shoats joins in, telling the audience that the Holy Church of Christ Without Christ is "based on your own personal interpitation of the Bible, friends. You can sit at home and interpit your own Bible however you feel in your heart it ought to be interpited," adding "It'll cost you each a dollar but what is a dollar? A few dimes!" (*CW* 86–87). Even though Hazel protests, "If don't cost you any money to know the truth!"; Shoats spins Motes' statement, "You hear what the Prophet says, friends…a dollar is not too much to pay" (*CW* 87). After hearing Hazel preach, Shoats offers an impromptu business plan: "I never heard a idear before that had more in it than that one. All it would need is a little promotion" (*CW* 90). Ironically, he doesn't understand Motes' objections, assuring him, "You needn't to be afraid that if I seen this new jesus I would cut you out of anything" (*CW* 90). When Hazel, disheartened by Shoats' extension of

---

[66] Quoted in Jeffrey, *Biblical Tradition*, 714.

the Church Without Christ, tries to explain his ideas to Shoats: "there's no such thing or person ... It wasn't nothing but a way to say a thing," for which the veteran conman reacts much like the taxidriver: "that's the trouble with you innerleckchuls ... you don't never have nothing to show for what you're saying" (*CW* 90).

Asa Hawks, on the other hand, like Hoover Shoats, creates a self-centric theology. Part preacher, part showman Asa Hawks marketed his own martyrdom, advertising his act of blinding himself to draw attention to his tent revival. There were "two hundred people or more were there, waiting for him to do it" and he "preached for an hour on the blindness of Paul, working himself up until he saw himself struck blind by a Divine flash of lightning" (*CW* 65). Yet, when the time came, he lost his nerve, streaking his face with lye, but leaving his eyes and vision intact. Like Motes, Hawks imagines himself pursued by Christ: "he fancied Jesus ... was standing there too, beckoning to him; and he had fled out of the tent into the alley and disappeared" (*CW* 65). Although this young version of Hawks had not intended to con his parish, he embodies those self-serving preachers whom Shoats mimics. Whereas Hawks intends to sacrifice his vision, he does so, less as a testament to Paul than to his own legacy, which is why he still keeps the newspaper clippings advertising his own act. In this way, these two false prophets, who serve as antagonists to Hazel's own ministry, also serve as catalysts who lead Hazel to abandon the Church Without Christ. Shoats hears Hazel's message and recognizes the message as a potentially powerful gimmick, while Hawks meets Hazel and recognizes this prophet as a threat. Either way, both for-profit prophets see religion as a means to exploit others.

As prophets, both Shoats and Hawks are fairly simplistic characters in comparison to Motes, who represents an amalgamation of complex biblical allusions, yet one of the most obvious markers of a character's role as false prophet in *Wise Blood* is that they all share one marker in common: they are all associated with swine. In biblical mythology, the pig serves as a compelling and loaded image, associated with a lack of cleanliness. The negative connotations of this pig imagery will become a staple in O'Connor's fiction from Mr. Paradise, who according to Mrs. Connin favors a pig in "The River," to Mrs. Turpin, who runs a pig farm in "Revelation." Throughout the Bible, the swine becomes a symbol of the unclean and even the demonic. In *Wise Blood*, O'Connor creates explicit parallels between her false prophets and swine.

The most obvious example of a character marked with the sign of the swine comes from Onie Jay Holy (a.k.a. Hoover Shoats). His name, Shoats, is an explicit reference to a shoat, a young pig. Yet, though Hoover Shoats is named after a pig, the animalistic Enoch Emery, who works the gate at the zoo, "appeared on all fours at the end of the abelia" acting like a pig (*CW* 47). In fact, Enoch, who carries a change purse, which looks like "a hawg bladder," is even described in demonic terms, since "anyone who parted the abelia springs at just that place, would think he saw a devil" (*CW* 77, 45). Even Sabbath Lily embraces the association when she wonders "should I go the whole hog or not?" (*CW* 67).

This association with swine is no accident; O'Connor is simply following her source material since the "Bible often parodies images and motifs from other mythologies when the context is one of demonic parody."[67] This parody explains why the novel begins with the pastoral description: "the plowed fields curved and faded and the few hogs nosing in the furrows looked like large spotted stones" (*CW* 3).[68] Subconsciously, beginning with this opening image, readers can't help but associate Mrs. Wally Bee Hitchcock with the same pig imagery, seeing as how she is "a fat woman with pink collars and cuffs and pear-shaped legs that slanted off the train seat and didn't reach the floor" (*CW* 3). This, more than anything, should be seen as O'Connor's denunciation of the entire town of Taulkinham.

However, the most germane comparison between swine and human can be found in Hazel Motes' first car ride. As Motes drives his Essex down the highway "a string of pigs appeared snout-up over the ditch and he had to screech to a stop and watch the rear of the last pig disappear" (*CW* 42). This string of pigs is certainly reminiscent of Jesus' thrice-told encounter with the demon-possessed man:

> Seeing Jesus from a distance, he ran up and bowed down before Him; and shouting with a loud voice, he said "What business do we have with each other, Jesus, Son of the Most High God? I implore You by God, do not torment me! For He had been saying to him, "Come out of the man, you unclean spirit!" And He was asking him, "What is your name?" And he said to Him, "My name is Legion; for we are many." And then began to implore Him earnestly not to send them out of the country. Now there was a large herd of swine feeding nearby on the mountain. The demons implored Him, saying, "Send us into the swine so that we may enter them." Jesus gave them permission. And coming out, the unclean spirits entered the swine; and the herd rushed down the steep bank into the sea. (Mark 5:6–13)

Although Hazel does not encounter Jesus during his ride, he discovers a sign which reads "WOE TO THE BLASPHEMER AND WHOREMONGER! WILL HELL SWALLOW YOU UP?" (*CW* 42). This sign seems especially prophetic since Hazel had recently started the Church Without Christ (blasphemer) and lost his virginity with a prostitute, Leora Watts (whoremonger). His car, surrounded by the red gulleys, seems to be in the midst of being swallowed by Hell. It is this sign which forces Hazel to return to Taulkinham, and it is the repetition of the pig imagery which informs readers that despite Hazel's insistence "I AM clean," a direct response to the unclean swine he has encountered, he is clearly in need of redemption (*CW* 52).

This is why the demon-possessed man presents a modern-day analogue to Motes, who tries to use his car as a means to escape Jesus. Ironically, it is a "string of pigs," similar to those in which the demons are cast, which halts Motes' escape from God. O'Connor seems to be aware of the parallels as she informs readers that Hazel "had a hard time holding the car in the road" as he passed "stretches where red gulleys

---

[67] Frye, *The Great Code*, 149.

[68] This is a telling image since Hazel's grandfather preaches to his parishioners: "They were like stones! He would shout. But Jesus had died to redeem them!" (*CW* 10). Therefore, the novel begins with the juxtaposition of stones (people) and pigs (false prophets), which may accurately reflect the religious makeup of Taulkinham.

dropped off on either side" and "666 posts" (*CW* 41). Certainly this hellish imagery that surrounds Hazel, the same gulleys from which the swine emerge, corresponds with this account, as Hazel serves as the tortured man and the pigs which literally cross his path become the manifestation of the biblical account. In fact, O'Connor will later reference this same incident in her story "The River" as Mrs. Connin reads to young Harry Ashfield from her book, *The Life of Jesus Christ for Readers Under Twelve*. Thus, the discernible reference in *Wise Blood* serves as a precursor to her continued fascination with Christ's encounter with the demon-possessed man.

Of course, her false prophets are not the only characters who are "marked" in *Wise Blood*, O'Connor gives readers plenty of attributes to alert readers to Hazel's prophetic status, from his name to the repeated emphasis on vision, but it is God's constant presence, shadowing his every action, which affirms his status as a *Christian malgré lui*. Throughout the novel, Hazel imagines himself being pursued by the ragged and "soul-hungry" figure of Christ who "would have him in the end" (*CW* 11). However, O'Connor continues to use biblical archetypes both to indicate Motes' status as the *true* prophet as well as to extend the metaphor of Hazel being haunted by Christ.

As Hazel, seeking freedom from the haunting image of Christ, takes the Essex on the open road "to see how well it worked," he is followed not just by the stow-a-way Sabbath Lily but also by a single cloud in the sky, "a large blinding white one with curls and a beard" (*CW* 66). Not only is a cloud an archetypical symbol of divine presence, but this particular cloud with curls and a beard seems to typify stereotypical depictions of God, reminiscent of Renaissance works such as Michelangelo's *The Creation of Adam*. Yet, much like the Pauline markers, there is a biblical precedence for this depiction. Throughout Exodus, while the Israelites roamed the desert, God's presence is frequently indicated through the form of a cloud. As "The Lord said to Moses, 'Behold I will come to you in a thick cloud, so that the people may hear when I speak with and may also believe in you forever" (Ex 19:9). Just like the cloud's appearance to the Israelites, God's presence follows Hazel.

Further interactions between Moses and God are often signified with clouds as a marker of divine presence, as Moses "entered the mist of the cloud" in communion with God (Ex 24:18). Throughout their time in the desert, the cloud of God's presence followed the tabernacle: "for throughout all their journeys, the cloud of the LORD was on the tabernacle by day, and there was fire in it by night" (Ex. 40:38). While God's presence followed the Israelites in the form of a cloud, O'Connor goes out of her way to associate Hazel's drive with the image of God pursing him. This technique, marking her unconventional prophet with the sign from Moses, the original *prophet malgré lui*, will foreshadow her later work and is especially foregrounded in her short story "Parker's Back," where O'Connor will imbue O. E. Parker with several literary characteristics of both Paul and Moses.

As Hazel and Sabbath Lily ride in the Essex, "the blinding white cloud was a little ahead of them, moving to the left," and later "the white cloud was directly in front of them" (*CW* 68). In *Life of Moses*, a work of which O'Connor was not only familiar but which she quotes from in *Mystery and Manners*, St. Gregory of Nyssa expounds on the importance of the cloud as a symbol for God. If "Moses' ascent to Mount Sinai and his finding God in the dark cloud is symbolic of man's search for God in the world and his ultimate realization that God can only be found in the darkness of faith," then the cloud following Hazel must foreshadow his ultimate encounter with God in the novel's end.[69] If the cloud serves as a symbol of Motes' search for God, then Sabbath's description that the car runs "as smooth as honey" seems to allude directly to Moses' destination, the promised land, described as a land flowing "with milk and honey" (*CW* 72, Num. 13:27).

Yet, perhaps, more telling is the disappearance of the cloud. Soon after his encounter with a mechanic who fixes the Essex pro bono, "the blinding white cloud had turned into a bird with long thin wings and was disappearing in the opposite direction" (*CW* 72). The transformation of God's image from one archetypical image (cloud) to another (bird) provides a fascinating rhetorical juxtaposition. The bird is most often associated with the Holy Ghost, a symbol to which she will return in her later story "The Enduring Chill." Ironically, the Holy Ghost only appears after the mechanic's gesture of grace (free gas), actions for which Motes does not want to feel indebted, saying, "I don't need no favors" (*CW* 72). However, recognizing this marker takes on an added significance, since, throughout the novel, the fact that Hazel is pursued by the entire Trinity (God, Jesus, and the Holy Ghost) must surely be a sign of his election and ultimate prophetic destiny.

O'Connor's use of such overt biblical imagery is clearly meant to capture the reader's attention. In much the same way that O. E. Parker will later stand barefoot in front of a burning tree as a correlative to Moses, Motes, surrounded by pigs in this hellish imagery or being pursued by a cloud, is as much a reference to Christ's encounter with Legion and God's connection to Israel as it is a marker of Hazel's importance. O'Connor presents the reader with a deluge of biblical imagery in hopes that they will recognize the importance of what is in front of them. In this case, the demon-possessed man or the cloud as divine presence, as her biblical model, highlights this parallel to her backwoods prophet.

Typical of her fiction, it is not always the righteous (or the believers) who bring God's message. The Bible is filled with instances, such as Balaam and his talking donkey, of those outside the cult of belief recognizing God. Following in St. Thomas' footsteps, O'Connor notes, "In the gospels it was the devils who first recognized Christ and the evangelists didn't censor this information. They apparently thought it was [*sic*] pretty good witness" (*HB* 517). Clearly O'Connor, like St. Thomas, believed that demons could serve as prophets, yet her explicit allusion to this account provides an early connection between the biblical prophets to whom she was drawn and the backwoods prophets who haunt her fiction. As Rufus Johnson, who proclaims "Satan has you in his power...Not only me. You too," demonstrates, it was not always the believers who proclaimed Christ (*CW* 627). Perhaps this is best summarized by Young Tarwater's consciousness when he realizes "It ain't Jesus or the devil. It's Jesus or *you*," a message that her prophets frequently bring (*CW* 354). Hence, the cloud imagery only

---

[69] Quoted in Herbert Musurillo, "History and Symbol: A Study of Form in Early Christian Literature," *Theological Studies.* 18 (1957): 371.

solidifies Hazel's consecrated status. Like Saul/Paul, he tries his best to both deny and run from God, yet despite his best efforts, to the contrary, Hazel winds up subject to the same spiritual forces he seeks to deny.

While I have previously argued that Motes is a modern retelling of Paul, Edmondson contends, "*Wise Blood* most resembles the story of Jonah, an allegory teaching the consequence of man's flight from God," highlighting the reluctant prophet motif which would be a mainstay in O'Connor's fiction.[70] Although, Edmondson overlooks the Pauline allusions in *Wise Blood*, O'Connor's backwoods prophets are often reluctant to bring their message—in which case, Motes seems to be a literary prototype for her later prophet, O. E. Parker. Both Motes and Parker, physically marked, remain reluctant to spread their message. Like O. E. Parker, Motes avoids bringing a message to the people, but is focused on a single person. O. E. Parker brings Jesus, literally, to Sarah Ruth, just as Motes intrigues Mrs. Flood, who views him as a spiritual enigma. She rationalizes, "If she was going to be blind when she was dead, who better to guide her than a blind man? Who better to lead the blind than the blind?" (*CW* 130). Motes, the commonplace prophet, who experiences an extreme transformation based on an extreme act, is sent to bear witness to a single individual, roughly following the same story arc of O. E. Parker.

Motes may represent an early incarnation of O. E. Parker, yet many of the bizarre characters in *Wise Blood* seem like anomalies among O'Connor's fictions; there are no more Enoch Emerys or Asa Hawkses in her later works. However, the most influential preacher to appear in *Wise Blood*—the man who serves as the earliest incarnation of her backwoods prophetic archetype—is the very character who never appears in the novel: Hazel's grandfather.

Although only present in flashbacks, Motes' grandfather is the predecessor to Old Tarwater in *The Violent Bear It Away*. Motes' grandfather, a shiftless nomadic evangelist, rides "over three counties with jesus hidden in his head like a stinger" (*CW* 10). Like the biblical models before him, he brings a message not of peace or love but of salvation from damnation: "Every fourth Saturday he had driven into Eastrod as if he were just in time to save them all from Hell" (*CW* 10). The grandfather, a circuit preacher from Eastrod, Tennessee, stands in direct opposition to the prophets found in Taulkinham such as Shoats, who tells onlookers, "You don't have to believe nothing you don't understand and approve of. If you don't understand it, it ain't true" (*CW* 86). In contrast, Hazel's grandfather provides the antithesis of Shoats' subjective religion as the grandfather tells his followers that "Jesus was so soul-hungry that He had died, one death for all, but He would have died every soul's death for one. Did they understand that? Did they understand that for each stone soul, He would have died ten million deaths?" (*CW* 11). As Hazel tries to convince himself and others that there is no need for redemption, the grandfather preaches that humans are inevitably "mean sinful unthinking" creatures whom Jesus died to redeem (*CW* 11). This backwoods prophet who brings a message of a savior who "would chase him over the waters of sin" and "would never let him forget he was redeemed" is a shocking and unpleasant

---

[70] Edmondson, *Return to Good and Evil*, 35.

figure (*CW* 11). To the grandfather, confrontation with Christ is inevitable, yet Hazel intends to avoid a confrontation with Christ, which is why he searches for "the way to avoid Jesus" (*CW* 11).

Through her early development of Hazel's relationship to his proselytizing grandfather, O'Connor establishes a pattern that will reoccur in her next novel, *The Violent Bear It Away*. The antagonistic relationship between the established prophet and the unwilling disciple, developed in *Wise Blood*, becomes the focal point of the Mason–Tarwater relationship in *The Violent Bear It Away*. Much like Hazel's grandfather, Old Tarwater's appearance in the novel is very brief, yet his influence haunts both Young Tarwater and Rayber. Of course, the biblical connection is made explicit for readers as Mason "compared their situation to that of Elijah and Elisha" (*CW* 356). Although it is not clear whether Hazel's grandfather realizes it, it is his influence that serves as the basis for Hazel's obsession with Christ. Even when Hazel is drafted into the army, he plans on injuring himself to receive a 4-F deferral from conscription: "He had thought at first he would shoot his foot and not go ... a preacher can always do without a foot. A preacher's power is in his neck and tongue and arm" (*CW* 10). Pre-dating the Mason–Tarwater dynamic, Hazel's own reluctant ministry has its roots in his grandfather's preaching. Hazel's car serves as the entirety of the Church Without Christ, much like his grandfather, who "would climb onto the top of [his car] and shout down at them" (*CW* 10). Many of Hazel's sermons are developed as a response to his grandfather's own hillbilly theology. His grandfather stressed that no matter what "Jesus would have him in the end!"; which is why Hazel preaches, "What you need is something to take the place of Jesus ... The Church without Christ don't have a Jesus but it needs one! It needs a new jesus! (*CW* 11, 80).

As O'Connor's preface states, Hazel's ministry is a foregone conclusion from his initial denials until he finally accepts the fact that "he was going to be a preacher like his grandfather" (*CW* 10). Yet, after Hazel experiences a Pauline shift and believes in his own need for redemption, he imagines Jesus based on his grandfather's image, resorting to the aesthesis of his youth. Motes, like his predecessor, becomes a nontraditional prophet in his own right as he walks on stones and wraps his chest in barbed wire, all of which lead Mrs. Flood to vocalize what readers are already thinking: "You must believe in Jesus or you wouldn't do these foolish things" (*CW* 127). It is in these footsteps that her later prophets will follow. Their message may be strange and their means destructive, as they, like Motes, remain both Christ-haunted and seemingly foolish.

Reversals

In his monumental literary study of the Bible, *The Great Code*, Northrop Frye notes that "there are, of course, many different rhetorical styles in the Bible."[71] It was these genre-spanning styles and literary techniques of the Bible which seemed to forever

---

[71] Frye, *The Great Code*, 204.

imprint themselves on O'Connor's own fiction. Yet, as a predecessor for her more mature fiction, *Wise Blood* serves as the precursory work in which she developed and perfected themes common to her corpus, specifically, the literary staple which would long be associated with Flannery O'Connor: ironic reversals. However, I will show how many of the reversals found throughout the novel contain biblical echoes. As Frederick Asals observes, "in O'Connor's work, the incarnation of biblical language in fictional action reverses the relation between literal and metaphorical: as the Bible's metaphors become her literal actions."[72] Finally, I will show that *Wise Blood* should be seen as significant not only as the genesis of this technique but for the multiplicity of differing types of reversals she utilizes throughout the novel.

For those familiar with O'Connor's wry sense of humor, it should come as no surprise that her debut novel, like her later fiction, is filled with ironic reversals. *Wise Blood* reverses many things: through her use of ironic juxtaposition, she reverses the literal and metaphoric; through her repeated emphasis on dualities, she reverses Hazel's way of seeing the world; and through her paradigmatic reversals, she reverses readers' expectations. Recognizing the reversals is important, but by understanding their biblical origins, we get a better understanding of why O'Connor uses these reversals.

While she uses many different ironic devices, one of the most interesting is her use of ironic juxtapositions—pairing opposites together—found, most often, within her use of ironic naming, especially since "for O'Connor, names in fiction are sacramental."[73] Throughout her fiction, she would often pair ironic names together to lead to a greater understanding of the character; she would continue to use this strategy of reconciling opposites with characters such as Thomas and Sarah Ham in "The Comforts of Home," or Obadiah Elihue and Sarah Ruth in "Parker's Back," or Mary Grace in "Revelation." It would soon become clear that in O'Connor's fiction, names are important and *Wise Blood* represents, perhaps, her earliest attempt of using paradoxical logic within character names.

There are several biblical significant name combinations throughout *Wise Blood* following the pattern of biblical reversals, the most obvious of which, as others have noted, is the ironic juxtaposition of Hazel Motes. Critics such as Satterfield have pondered over her use of naming in *Wise Blood*, trying to make sense of this method, as he notes that Hazel stands for "one who sees God."[74] The etymology of the Hebrew origin of the name is extremely significant throughout the novel to reinforce the vision motif. Hazel is likely a reference to the biblical Hazel, the Syrian King.[75] Margaret Whitt notes that while the biblical "Hazel sought power...the fictional Hazel, ultimately, and ironically, sought God's empowerment."[76] Doubly significant is Hazel's last name, Motes, which also references vision. As several scholars have previously observed, Motes is an obvious reference to the Gospel of Matthew:

---

[72] Asals, *The Imagination of Extremity*, 78.
[73] Paul Ferguson, "Onomastic Revisions in Flannery O'Connor's *Wise Blood*," *Literary Onomastics Studies* 13 (1986): 109.
[74] Satterfield, "Artistic Anemia," 35.
[75] See 2 Kings Chs. 8–13.
[76] Whitt, *Understanding O'Connor*, 17.

And why seest thou the mote that is in thy brother's eye, but seest not the beam that is thy own eye? Or how sayst thou to thy brother: Let me cast the mote out of thy eye; and behold a beam is in thy own eye; and then shalt thou see to cast out the mote out of thy brother's eye.[77] (Mt. 7:3–5)

Whitt emphasizes that "In this name selection, O'Connor calls attention to the eyes," yet more importantly, this reference that O'Connor uses is taken from Jesus' teaching on judgment, specifically a lesson in which he condemns judging others.[78]

The reference is ironic since the novel begins with judgment, not by Hazel, but *of* Hazel through the eyes of Mrs. Hitchcock, who notes that Hazel's "suit had cost him $11.98. She felt that that placed him" (*CW* 3). This is only appropriate for a novel filled with judgment: Hazel's judgment of others ("Where has the blood you think you been redeemed by touched you? ... Nothing matters but that Jesus was a liar"), Hazel's judgment of himself ("I AM clean," he repeats), the judgment of Mrs. Flood ("'I'm as good, Mr. Motes,' she said 'not believing in Jesus as a many a one that does'"), and the judgment of God, which looms silently in the background of this novel (*CW* 58–59, 52, 125).

Hazel Motes, then, is an extremely significant—and ironic—name highlighting one of the central motifs: vision. Thus, the name serves as an exemplar of O'Connor's method of reversals. If Hazel is one "to see God," clearly this is impossible throughout most of the novel because of "the mote" that is in his eye—or even the self-righteous impulse to point out the 'mote' in someone else's eye. It isn't until Hazel blinds himself with lye, disabusing himself of this impulse, that he is able to see, embodying O'Connor's reversal. While her protagonist should be representative of vision, he is unable to see until he becomes physically blinded. Yet, a blind Hazel is able to see what others, such as Mrs. Flood, cannot comprehend.

O'Connor utilizes this same method of ironic juxtaposition for both Asa and Sabbath Lily Hawks. Satterfield notes that Asa stands for "healer" and Hawks is representative of a bird of prey. However, there is certainly more to this combination. While O'Connor references the Syrian king Hazael with her title character, Asa is most likely a reference to Asa, King of Judah. Asa was praised for clearing idols from Judah, but he later allied himself with Syria, "instead of placing his trust in God."[79] The name carries a duality of both pleasing and misguiding, or lacking in faith. However, O'Connor pairs Asa, posing as a blind prophet, with the image of the hawk, known for its keen vision, to further this irony since Asa (as well as Sabbath) is misguided.

Sabbath's first name is a reference to the Sabbath day and the fourth commandment[80] as she tells Hazel, "My mother named me that just after I was born because I was born on the Sabbath and then she turned over in her bed and died" (*CW* 66). As Ferguson suggests, "the name is ironic since the sluttish young woman who bears it is not at all holy, is in the service of a false and worldly religion, and ultimately becomes the

---

[77] Douay-Rheims Version.
[78] Whitt, *Understanding Flannery O'Connor*, 17.
[79] Ferguson, "Onomastic Revisions," 101.
[80] "Remember the Sabbath day by keeping it holy" (Exodus 20:8).

Madonna for Motes' nihilistic church."[81] Her middle name, Lily, could be a guarded reference to Lilith, but it also echoes Jesus' teaching on faith in his sermon on the mount. "Observe how the lilies of the field grow; they do not toil nor do they spin, yet I say to you that not even Solomon in all his glory clothed himself like one of these" (Mt. 6:28–29). O'Connor pairs these images of faith, the Sabbath, and lilies with an image of a bird of prey, which is symbolic, since Sabbath Lily's relationship with Hazel is largely based on how she manipulates him. Yet, again, her name functions as an ironic reversal since it marks her as a character of faith and vision. Sabbath is faithful to the "Church without Christ" and its new jesus, but ironically, she is completely blind to the futility of her devotion. This irony is extended further by her own logic, which forces Hazel to doubt his own church. As she confides that she is a bastard, this anti-Ave Maria questions her own status within the Church Without Christ. Hazel, in turn, assures her saying, "There's no such thing as a bastard in the Church without Christ... Everything is all one. A bastard wouldn't be any different from anybody else" (*CW* 69). Yet, it is this very statement which sows the seeds of discontent, as Hazel wrestles internally with this very question, secretly believing "that a bastard couldn't be saved in the Church Without Christ" and this sentiment haunts him (*CW* 69).

Through confessing her own illegitimate birthright, Sabbath Lily Hawks attempts to subtly signal her own sexual maturity. Yet, it is this very question which exposes Hazel's own cognitive dissonance, a question that simultaneously dooms both any hope of a future with Hazel Motes as well as the future of the Church Without Christ. It is through her misguided attempts at sexual seduction that she actually, ironically, seduces Hazel to belief in Christ. By the novel's end, it is only appropriate that her character is "sent to a detention home" by Mrs. Flood because Sabbath "hadn't counted on no honest-to-Jesus blind man" in Hazel Motes (*CW* 121).

Yet the juxtaposition found in Enoch Emery's name is certainly the most complex allusion in the story (perhaps even in O'Connor's corpus), serving as an indicator of his importance. Although some are quick to dismiss him, Gentry correctly argues that "Enoch is one of the major critical issues" in *Wise Blood*.[82] Some scholars have noticed that Enoch is an allusion to the biblical Enoch, the father of Methuselah, and that "Enoch walked with God; and he was not, for God took him" (Gen. 5:24). Of course, this is somewhat ironic considering that the Book of Hebrews praises Enoch as supremely faithful stating, "By faith Enoch was taken up so that he would not see death; and he was not found because God took him up; for he obtained the witness that before his being taken up he was pleasing to God." (Hebrews 11:5). Generally, most will concur that Enoch Emery is a direct reference to the Enoch who walked with God, the one previously alluded to, yet "the Hebrew expression 'walked with God' denotes a devout life; the allusion to prefallen Adam and Eve with whom God walked in the cool of the day (Gen. 3:8) points to Enoch as one who maintained something like the original communion with God."[83] However, this description does not fit Enoch Emery,

[81] Ferguson, "Onomastic Revisions," 100.
[82] Gentry, *Religion of the Grotesque*, 124.
[83] Jeffrey, *Biblical Tradition*, 237.

as Edmondson suggests, "The Enoch of *Wise Blood* walks not with God, but with the beasts."[84] However, what *Wise Blood* critics have overlooked—the way to understand the fullness of this allusion—is that there is another biblical figure named Enoch: the son of Cain.

Obviously, Enoch is a very loaded name which could refer to the Enoch of the Sethite line, the paradigm of virtue and who was in such close communion with God that he ascended into Heaven without dying a natural death. However, it could also be a pointer to Enoch of the Cainite line, the son of the first murderer who carries the sins of his father, the mark of Cain. If it is an allusion to Enoch the Cainite, it may explain Enoch Emery's numerous references to his overbearing father. By naming her character "Enoch," O'Connor presents readers with a stunning binary opposition through her use of biblical reversals; nowhere in the Bible is there a name so loaded with double-entendre. It reflects both the sins of Cain and the devout nature of one who walks with God.

This name, Enoch, is appropriate for the character since it signifies the primary dilemma of this would-be disciple. He is a man divided between the carnal (Enoch, son of Cain) and the spiritual (Enoch, the Sethite). O'Connor notes that "Enoch's brain was divided into two parts," just as Enoch himself is divided between two paradigmatically opposing biblical positions, yet understanding Enoch's bifurcation helps readers to understand Enoch's ultimate choice toward the physical (Enoch, son of Cain), an explanation for his exit from the novel in a gorilla suit (*CW* 49).

Rhetorically, however, *Wise Blood*'s significance lies in more than O'Connor's use of ironic juxtapositions; rather, it represents a very different type of reversal that would be found in her later work: dualism. O'Connor's later fiction makes repeated use of doppelgangers in an attempt to demonstrate "an ineluctable human dualism, the divided self that is the inheritance of fallen man."[85] This use of doubling, which first appears in *Wise Blood*, would become a stock trait in O'Connor's fiction, whether for minor purposes, for example, Susan and Joanne in "A Temple of the Holy Ghost," or major purposes, such as Julian's mother and her African-American doppelganger who serves as the catalyst for her story "Everything that Rises Must Converge." Ralph Wood even argues that the Misfit is the grandmother's own double.[86] Yet, this technique can be traced back to Enoch Emery as well as other variations of doppelgangers found in *Wise Blood*, the frequency of which led Lewis to discover that "the characters seem to be grotesque variations on each other."[87]

Although Enoch's own dichotomy, the schism between his carnal and spiritual side, might represent a minor use of this technique of reversals, Enoch's relationship with Hazel highlights this theme of dualistic reversals in *Wise Blood*. Lacking in physical similarities, Enoch is Motes' spiritual doppelganger:

---

[84] Edmondson, *Return to Good and Evil*, 48.
[85] Asals, *The Imagination of Extremity*, 121.
[86] Wood, *South*, 39.
[87] Lewis, "Eccentrics Pilgrimage," 150.

Enoch is a grotesque parody of Hazel Motes. As Motes moves toward a spiritual rebirth—as he goes 'backwards to Bethlehem'—Enoch the wholly physical creature, in a 'satiric inversion of the evolutionary process' becomes a gorilla. (Shinn 63)

Like Cain and Abel, the two brothers of the same flesh who take completely different paths, or Jacob and Esau, Hazel and Enoch are brought together by more than fate; through Hazel and Enoch, O'Connor "presents complementary extremes: there is Enoch or Haze, the monkey or the monkery."[88]

Both Enoch and Hazel possess remarkable similarities when they meet. Both are new to Taulkinham, running away from Christian upbringings. Hazel's grandfather was a circuit preacher and Hazel "knew by the time he was twelve years old that he was going to be a preacher," having "a strong confidence in his power to resist evil" (*CW* 11). Although readers are told very little about Enoch's family history, Enoch himself divulges both that "My daddy looks just like Jesus," and that he previously attended Rodemill Boys' Bible Academy (*CW* 28). In both circumstances, their move to the city from the country follows a contemporary pattern: "Christ went into the wilderness to be tempted; modern man goes into the city."[89]

More importantly, both characters experience duality. Hazel's dual nature is grounded in the spiritual, divided between his Christian upbringing and his search for a new jesus. On the one hand, Hazel is obsessed with the spiritual; on the other, he is the "King of Beasts" who seeks to indulge his carnal nature (*CW* 96). Like Hazel, Enoch is divided between animal instinct and spiritual instinct. His "wise blood" impels his instinctive and animal-like actions. Throughout the novel Enoch claims to have wise blood and tells Hazel, "You act like you think you got wiser blood than anybody else...but you ain't! I'm the one has it" (*CW* 33). There is a precedent for Enoch's claims, as throughout the Bible, "there is a strong emphasis on the blood as the 'life' of the animal."[90] It is this life-blood that drives Enoch's actions, since for him, knowledge is not empirical; he knows "by his blood. He had wise blood like his daddy," which dictates his behavior throughout the novel (*CW* 44). Yet, Enoch is not the only character with the gift of wise blood. O'Connor claimed that "Haze is saved by virtue of having wise blood; it's too wise for him ultimately to deny Christ. Wise blood has to be these people's means of grace—they have no sacraments" (*HB* 350). For Motes, who claims "my blood has set me free," it is a spiritual reference, while for Enoch, it is purely physical, which explains the carnal imagery associated with his character (*CW* 82).

Motes and Enoch's duality is demonstrated by their respective actions throughout the novel, specifically their individual treatment of the new jesus. For Hazel, the new jesus "ain't anything but a way to say something," a metaphor to express a concept, yet Enoch searches for the carnal, a mummified man to serve as a new jesus (*CW* 90). Motes' attraction to the idea of freedom from a redeemer, rather than a literal new redeemer, explains why the new jesus upsets him because Enoch brings a concrete reminder of Christ, the mummified man, which Enoch claims to be the new jesus.

---

[88] Asals, *The Imagination of Extremity*, 57.
[89] Shinn, "Violence of Grace," 69.
[90] Frye, *The Great Code*, 148.

Although they have similar character traits, Hazel and Enoch are prototypically opposed in sensibilities. Enoch is associated with the bestiality of the secular world, whereas Hazel is, ultimately, a failure in the realm of the carnal, since "he had not been very successful with Mrs. Watts... and she had made obscene comments about him" (*CW* 33). In fact, Hazel takes no comfort in the corporeal since, for him, sin was "not for the sake of pleasure," but rather "to prove that he didn't believe in sin" (*CW* 62). On the corollary, Enoch is animalistic in his instinctive nature and even works as a guard at the zoo, reinforcing his primal connection (*CW* 33). O'Connor details Enoch's rituals, which are so common that everyone at the zoo knows his patterns; in fact, Hazel tells Enoch: "the guard said I'd find you at the swimming pool... He said you hid in the bushes and watched the swimming" (*CW* 48). Enoch constantly associates himself with the bestial, frequenting the animal cages, the museum, and movies about Gonga the ape. Enoch's obsession with "making obscene" comments to the animals is not a form of disdain, but of jealousy, as Enoch envies the animals he is supposed to guard. Stephens complains about the "gross animalism of the whole book," yet this imagery reinforces Enoch's secular nature and, by its corollary, Hazel's numinous awareness, since Motes abhors the physical, yet is captivated by the religious.[91] It is their bifurcation which forces each character to adopt a side by the end of the novel.

Originally inveigled by street preachers into starting his own heretical church, Motes, obsessed with the nature of original sin, eventually embraces his sacred side and rejects the physical by blinding himself, removing the mote from his eye; the barrier solidifying his internal division. Ultimately, it is Hazel's epistemological search which brings him back in touch with his spiritual self as he accepts his fate as a "*Christian malgré lui*" (*CW* 1265). However, for Enoch, who "didn't want to justify his daddy's blood," he, ultimately, does just that. He rejects his spiritual self (Enoch the Sethite) with an inclination toward the carnal (Enoch the Cainite) as he literally becomes an animal by the novel's end (*CW* 76). Emory exits the story running off into the jungle in a gorilla suit, burying his clothes in the jungle because "he only knew he wouldn't need them any more" (*CW* 111). His choice is less a reverse evolution as has been suggested, but rather evidence of Enoch's own internal schism. His ultimate decision, becoming a gorilla, serves as a response to Hazel's own proclivity toward the spiritual. By the novel's end, these two doppelgangers represent an ironic reversal since they are two different sides of the same paradigm.

Hazel and Enoch may be spiritual doppelgangers; however, Enoch is not the only double in the novel. In fact, Asals argues that "the entire world of *Wise Blood* is one of ironic duality."[92] Solace Layfield, whom Shoats dubs the "true prophet," serves as Hazel's physical double. Although they are quite different, they look extraordinarily similar, so much so that upon seeing Layfield for the first time, Hazel is so enchanted "that he stopped preaching" (*CW* 94). Their physical resemblance is so striking that it leads the woman next to Motes to inquire "Him and you twins?" (*CW* 94). The two share several other similarities: they are both described as consumptive, both drive

[91] Martha Stephens, *The Question of Flannery O'Connor* (Baton Rouge: LSU Press, 1973), 68.
[92] Asals, *The Imagination of Extremity*, 41.

high rat-colored cars, and both lose their cars in a ditch. Hazel is haunted by this figure, as Solace Layfield (the prophet) mirrors Hazel's own failures. By coming face to face with Layfield, Motes cannot run from the reality that is reflected by this caricature; it is Hoover Shoats' absurd parody of Motes' message. Furthermore, Layfield's name is fairly indicative of his inevitable fate. After Hazel chases down Layfield in the Essex, running him over in a field, Layfield gives Hazel his confession: "Stole theter car. Never told the truth to my daddy" (*CW* 115). As if administering a bizarre last rites sacrament, Hazel leaned "his head closer to hear the confession" (*CW* 115). Thus, through this act, the murdered Layfield, who admits belief in Christ, is absolved—finding solace lying dead in a field. Layfield's death in some ways mirrors Hazel's own, as he is found face down in a ditch. Thus, not only do they both look alike, but both prophets receive grace in death.

Hazel's own radical *volte-face*—a Pauline shift—from muttering threats against Christ and martyring Christians to accepting his role as a Christian prophet represents the novel's final reversal: Motes' own paradigm shift. By the novel's end, Hazel is set in motion, not by a desire to run from Christ, but to redeem his previous mistakes, a world in which Hazel admits he can no longer preach because "I don't have time" (*CW* 125). With this final motion, Brinkmeyer insists, Hazel undergoes "a plunge into the wounded body wherein matter and spirit are yoked together—typif[ying] the motion underlying almost all of O'Connor's fiction," which is sacramental reconciliation.[93] Hazel, who has consistently rejected his role as Christian prophet, a role that he has been running from since he was 12 years old, in his final act of blinding, has undergone a complete transformation. Hazel converts from a nihilistic evangelist who declares, "I don't believe in sin" to a man who seeks repentance for his transgressions (*CW* 29).

Hazel's complete reversal, from heretic to martyr mirrors the radical shifts that O'Connor will imbue in her later characters. Using the biblical Pauline model, O. E. Parker transforms from shiftless outcast to a man with a message, while Young Tarwater, like Motes, tries to run from his prophetic destiny until he finally accepts the inevitable and embraces sanctification. As Wood maintains, Hazel Motes' final acts of *ascesis* "are not self-justifying sacrifices meant to earn Motes's salvation; they are deeds of radical penance offered in gratitude for the salvation" he has already received.[94] Hence, by the novel's end, Hazel becomes the very essence of what he was running from: redeemed.

O'Connor's debut novel follows the same system of reversals found in both the Old and New Testament, a system which Northrop Frye attempts to reconcile by arguing "in the Old Testament the New Testament is concealed; in the New, the Old revealed."[95] In this context, O'Connor's own "fiction miraculously duplicates this feat," using reversals to merge Old Testament and New Testament source material into modern fiction.[96] This merger explains her attraction to both Old and New Testament source

---

[93] Brinkmeyer, *Art and Vision*, 88.
[94] Wood, *South*, 169.
[95] Frye, *The Great Code*, 79.
[96] Joanne McMullen, *Writing Against God: Language as Message in the Literature of Flannery O'Connor* (Macon: Mercer University Press, 1996), 142.

material, just as her satirical humor explains her attraction to biblical irony; as *Wise Blood* and her later fiction show, she was extremely fond of these dualities. Of course, her use of ironic reversals represents more than her sense of humor: it shows her earliest desires to communicate her own religious precepts in her fiction. O'Connor believed that "writers who see by the light of their Christian faith will have, in these times, the sharpest eyes for the grotesque, for the perverse, and for the unacceptable," elaborating that "Redemption is meaningless unless there is cause for it in the actual life we live, and for the last few centuries there has been operating in our culture the secular belief that there is no such cause" (*MM* 33). Her point is that by using the grotesque and the perverse associated with modern life, she is able to do more than follow the Pauline model: she subverts readers' expectations by reversing the polarity, but does so to offer redemption and to make this redemption believable. Through this approach, reversals, pairing opposing names, figures, and images, she integrates her own religious vision into her fiction.

Although readers may be tempted to focus on the novel's reliance on the grotesque, O'Connor's use is not meant to be gratuitous; rather, she uses it as a tool to reaffirm her own sacramental approach to her art since "the value of the grotesque so often lies into its reversals."[97] For O'Connor, this blending of the absurd and the surreal was a means to capture the readers' attention while incorporating a religious framework to her fiction—a framework overshadowed by the disturbing violence found in her stories. Yet *Wise Blood* parallels its biblical antecedent since Jesus' command to tear out your eye if it "makes you stumble" is both grotesque and shocking, much like the violence found in the novel (Mt. 5:29). As the axiom of O'Connor's approach to fiction, *Wise Blood* is ultimately successful since her artistic intentions for integrating a Christian aesthetic in her fiction set the tone for the rest of her writing career.

---

[97] Gentry, *Religion of the Grotesque*, 94.

3

From Dishonor to Glory:
Biblical Recapitulation in "A Good Man Is Hard to Find" and "Judgment Day"

Toward the end of Marilynne Robinson's novel *Home*, a 2008 National Book Award nominee, set in the same year and town as her Pulitzer Prize–winning 2004 novel *Gilead*, Glory Boughton looks at her brother Jack and sees "a man of sorrows and acquainted with grief, and as one from whom men hide their face."[1] The allusion is a reference to Isaiah 53:3[2] and one of several biblical allusions in a novel that follows a prodigal son theme. Yet, Robinson, known for her use of Christian themes in her writing, takes almost as much from Calvin and Dickinson as she does from any other text. Of course, turning to the Bible is no recent trend for writers, as Detweiler and Jasper "emphasize the bible as probably the single most important literary influence on Western culture."[3] For many writers, this sacred text serves as inspiration for literary exploration and explication, the nature of which can range from the parabiblical to the allegorical, such as Bunyan's famous *A Pilgrim's Progress*. Yet, Flannery O'Connor's approach to rewriting or recapitulating biblical texts represents an entirely different strategy. Her fiction does not offer a reimagining of the biblical source texts in the style of Milton's *Paradise Lost*; nor are her works sermons incognito, such as Blake's *The Marriage of Heaven and Hell*. Unlike Mark Twain's humorous *The Diary of Adam and Eve* or Julian Barnes' *A History of the World in 10 ½ Chapters*, she does not use this source material in its original period or context. Rather her approach, though unprecedented, most closely mirrors something like Elizabeth Bishop's "A Miracle for Breakfast" or, perhaps, a more dogmatic version of Borges' "The Gospel According to Mark."

O'Connor was fond of rewriting biblical narratives by grounding them into contemporary settings, capturing both the grotesqueness of humanity and the grittiness of life in the twentieth-century South. Yet, O'Connor contemporizes these texts to give the old stories a "new" feel. She hopes that readers will get the same message as the original, in a different setting. Similarly, in Elizabeth Bishop's poem, she rewrites

---

[1] Marilynne Robinson, *Home* (New York: Farrar, Straus and Giroux, 2008), 318.
[2] He was despised and forsaken of men, a man of sorrows and acquainted with grief; And like one from whom men hide their face.
[3] Robert Detweiler and David Jasper, eds., *Religion and Literature: A Reader* (Louisville: Westminster John Knox Press, 2000), xii.

Jesus feeding the 5000 and sets the poem in the New York City "Depression-era soup lines."[4] By doing so, "the poem takes quite seriously the Gospel's call. 'Come to me and eat.'"[5] Unlike Borges, whose gospel rewrite becomes a parody of the crucifixion, Bishop leaves no room for satire. Yet, even Bishop's approach in poems such as "A Miracle for Breakfast" and "Squatter's Children" is not necessarily following the same method as O'Connor's, since the two have completely different intentions. In Bishop's poetry, the poet "hears the words, understands the promise behind them, but can only repeat that promise in secular terms. Wrestling with how to respond to human need"; in essence, by transforming "the words of Jesus into a flash of quiet inquiry," readers encounter a non-Christian poet who tries to make Christianity "work" in the modern world.[6] Whereas both O'Connor and Bishop, in this instance, use a very similar technique, for very different reasons.

Thus, there are few, if any, writers who take a similar approach in their fiction. Although often quoted, O'Connor's letter to John Hawks is appropriate as she informs him, "I write the way I do because and only because I am a Catholic. I feel that if I were not a Catholic, I would have no reason to write" (*HB* 114). For O'Connor, the Bible is not an inspiration for her fiction; it is the *reason* for it, which explains her use of this intentional device of biblical recapitulation, using Christian themes for a mainstream audience. For readers, recognizing these biblical allusions serves as a pointer toward evaluating the range of theological explorations throughout O'Connor's fiction. By incorporating specific theological dilemmas, grounded in often extreme situations, O'Connor seeks to wake both the theologically informed and uninformed reader alike to the possibility of grace. Therefore, it is this technique of retelling biblical stories which helped her accomplish her mission of sharing her vision "in a territory held largely by the devil" (*MM* 113).

If the benchmark of good fiction is, as Flannery O'Connor claimed, a story that "hangs on and expands in the mind," then "A Good Man Is Hard to Find" has passed the litmus test since the definitive meanings have yet to be exhausted more than 50 years later (*MM* 108). In many ways, it serves as a watershed story: some readers are horrified by the violence, while others are mystified by O'Connor's ability to balance the theological with the absolute callousness of the serial killer, the Misfit. For O'Connor, the frequently anthologized "A Good Man Is Hard to Find" is meant to serve as the magnum opus of her anagogical vision, as she instructed readers: "You should be on the lookout for such things as the action of grace in the Grandmother's soul, and not for the dead bodies" (*MM* 113). Of course, this work, one which casual readers are most likely to encounter, has not only provoked first-time O'Connor readers, but it has also had the same effect upon many critics who fixated on the grotesqueness. O'Connor, herself, even complained, "I am mighty tired of reading reviews that call *A Good Man*

---

4   Thomas Gardner, *John in the Company of Poets: The Gospel in Literary Imagination* (Waco, TX: Baylor University Press, 2011), 79.

5   Ibid., 81.

6   Gardner, *John in the Company of Poets*, 134; Readers will find several secular writers who, like Bishop, interact with Christianity from a nonbeliever's viewpoint; most recently, Jonathan Franzen's *Freedom: A Novel* (New York: MacMillan, 2010), 369–370 does this quite well.

brutal and sarcastic. The stories are hard but they are hard because there is nothing harder or less sentimental than Christian realism" (*HB* 90). Yet, "A Good Man Is Hard to Find" has remained one of her most popular short stories simply because it provides an introduction to O'Connor's fiction: an easily accessible piece that is representative of themes and techniques common within her work.

Frederick Asals notices that "'A Good Man Is Hard to Find' is among the first of O'Connor's mature stories"; written in 1953 and published in 1955, it certainly demonstrates her development as a writer.[7] Although the account of a family trip to Florida gone awry after a car wreck—and the grandmother's unintentional recognition of the felon who arrives offering assistance—is, perhaps, her most violent work, it demonstrates O'Connor's mastery of foreshadowing and humor. The story begins with the grandmother's warning: "I wouldn't take my children in any direction with a criminal like that aloose in it," which is exactly what she does, leading her child and grandchildren to their own demise (*CW* 137). A foreboding tone overshadows the darkly humorous short story as the grandmother dresses in a "navy blue straw sailor hat with a bunch of white violets on the brim and a navy blue dress with a small white dot in the print. Her collars and cuffs were white organdy trimmed with lace" (*CW* 138). Following in Southern genteel fashion, she dons the costume of her station: "in case of an accident, anyone seeing her dead on the highway would know at once that she was a lady" (*CW* 138). On their way, they pass by a small graveyard "with five or six graves" which is oddly appropriate for Bailey, his wife, the grandmother, June Star, John Wesley,[8] and the unnamed baby, all of whom drive through the eerily named town of Toombsboro (*CW* 139). All of these things prepare readers for the worst, but most telling is when Bailey wrecks the car as his children joyously proclaim, "We've had an ACCIDENT!"—just the occasion for which the grandmother had been preparing (*CW* 144).

In a letter to John Hawkes, O'Connor acknowledges the interpretations of those "who tell their students that the Grandmother is evil" since she is the catalyst for the meeting, yet O'Connor tells Hawkes she is glad that his students do not view the grandmother "as pure evil" and realize she "may be a medium for grace" (*MM* 110, *HB* 389). Years later Asals argued, "Even if we grant that the old lady bears responsibility for the accident, is she also responsible for the fact that this dirt road, of all the dirt roads in Georgia, is the one that harbors the Misfit"; but the foreshadowing leads readers to agree with Hawkins' conclusion that "It seems, in fact, as if these two characters were meant to meet, as if they had *to*."[9]

The story further demonstrates O'Connor's mastery of her trademark dry, Southern irony. The action begins with the grandmother trying to dissuade her son from taking a family vacation to Florida, but instead she tries to assure him of the benefits of educational travel: "You all ought to take them somewhere else for a change so they

[7] Asals, *The Imagination of Extremity*, 152.
[8] Although not a biblical reference, the name John Wesley (1703–1791) is a historical allusion to the Christian theologian and cofounder of the Methodist movement.
[9] Asals, *The Imagination of Extremity*, 150; Hawkins, *The Language of Grace*, 40.

could see different parts of the world and be broad" and suggests, "They never have been to east Tennessee" (*CW* 137). Few think of East Tennessee as a cultural hub for world travelers, especially since John Wesley believes that "Tennessee is just a hillbilly dumping ground" (*CW* 139). There is also a much darker ironic tone to the Misfit's casual comments as he tells the grandmother, "We buried our clothes that we had on when we escaped ... We borrowed these from some folks we met"; the implications for the Misfit and his gang are much more ominous than his tone suggests (*CW* 148–149).

Yet, while the story is an excellent example of O'Connor's evolution as a writer, it is heavily indebted to *Wise Blood*. Following suit of her debut novel, "A Good Man Is Hard to Find" tells the story of a man who is tortured by his unbelief. He grew up in a strict Christian fundamentalist family and is very introspective about his own nihilism. Running from the law in his car, he is being actively pursued. The narrative is filled with subtle animal imagery—Bobby Lee gains the dreaded swine association as June Star complains, "He reminds me of a pig," while O'Connor connects the Misfit to a serpent when he reacts "as if a snake had bitten him" (*CW* 150, 152). In many ways, the Misfit, then, is Hazel Motes recast, although "A Good Man Is Hard to Find" ends before the Misfit's conversion.

The Misfit, an escaped criminal, is anxious after spending an unspecified time detained in prison. Much like Motes, who was forced to serve in the U.S. Army when drafted, the Misfit describes having his freedom stripped away: "Turn to the right, it was a wall ... Turn to the left, it was a wall. Look up it was a ceiling, look down it was a floor" (*CW* 150). Both characters, after spending time in exile, feel the need to exercise their freedom, especially after having a confrontation with the law. Furthermore, while both are described in terms of their eyeglasses, Hazel kept his buried, while the Misfit "wore silver-rimmed spectacles that gave him a scholarly look" (*CW* 146). Even more telling is that mobility becomes a motif in both stories. From the beginning to the end in *Wise Blood*, whether it is on a train or in a car, Hazel spends most of his time on the run. Although he appears only briefly, stepping out of a "hearse-like automobile" with plans to steal Bailey's car, the Misfit puts Hiram to work servicing it: "It'll take a half a hour to fix" (*CW* 148). Both the Misfit and Hazel spend most of their time running from their fundamentalist past; they seem haunted by Christ as the Misfit tells the grandmother that "somebody is always after you" (*CW* 149).

However, the strongest link between these two—Hazel Motes, the "Christian *malgré lui*," and the Misfit, the man who is "pleased in spite of himself to be known"—lies in their joint reaction to Christ, since both characters do not suffer from a traditional lack of faith as much as they seem to occupy an eternal limbo, immersed in religiosity (*CW* 1265, 147). The Misfit's belief in Christ is so fanatical that Bellamy correctly notices, "The Misfit is a Bible Belt Fundamentalist in spite of himself," mirroring Hazel's own status.[10] Hazel Motes hears the gospel and reacts with disdain; taking this message literally he asks, "Where has the blood you think you been redeemed by touched you?" (*CW* 58). The Misfit, as Bellamy claims, like "many literal interpreters of the

---

[10] Michael O. Bellamy, "Everything Off Balance: Protestant Election in Flannery O'Connor's 'A Good Man Is Hard to Find,'" *Flannery O'Connor Bulletin* 8 (1979): 116.

Bible ... has an inordinate respect for the written word," but is much the same way.[11] The Misfit, for instance, takes the Freudian psychiatrist's Oedipal explanation literally: "It was a head-doctor at the penitentiary said what I done was kill my daddy but I know that for a lie" (*CW* 150). Following in the footsteps of Hazel Motes, Wood notes that in the Misfit, O'Connor "creates an ex-fundamentalist who is not embarrassed but scandalized by the supernatural."[12] When both are presented with the gospel, both violently rebel. Hazel reacts by making strange public displays, asking if others are redeemed and claiming, "I AM clean" (*CW* 52). The Misfit may hold the pose of the gentleman killer, politely addressing others and even apologizing for Bailey's outburst "don't you get upset. Sometimes a man says things he don't mean"–yet when confronted about Christ's resurrection, he reverts to child-like anger: "It ain't right I wasn't there because if I had of been there I would of known ... if I had of been there I would of known and I wouldn't be like I am now" (*CW* 152). The Misfit, the "bringer of death[,] is profoundly offended that the Giver of Life cannot be dismissed as a mere holy man or eminent ethical figure."[13] In this case, both nihilists blame their current situation, their torture over unbelief, based on Christ's claim of resurrection.

The Misfit has been equated with everyone from Christ[14] to the devil to the Antichrist—luckily poor Hazel Motes never suffered a similar fate. Yet, if the Misfit, "a prophet gone wrong," is another version of Hazel Motes, id unleashed, he must also reflect shades of Saul, the original *Christian malgré lui* (*MM* 110).

Following Saul, the Misfit rebels against belief in Christ; his murder of the grandmother is most certainly the physical embodiment of the Pauline theology to which O'Connor was drawn. Furthermore, the Misfit is hardened against Christ, and like Saul he executes a believer (although if the grandmother is indeed a Christian martyr, she is perhaps the most annoying in history). Ironically, this murder is as much of a spiritual transformation for the grandmother as it is for the Misfit; he realizes the emptiness of sin, which is why O'Connor views the Misfit as a potential prophet:

> I don't want to equate the Misfit with the devil. I prefer to think that, however unlikely this may seem, the old lady's gesture, like the mustard-seed, will grow to be a great crow-filled tree in the Misfit's heart, and will be enough of a pain to him there to turn him into the prophet he was meant to become. (*MM* 112–113)

Of course, accepting this optimistic interpretation can be difficult since readers may not be inclined to see this theologically troubled killer as a modern-day Lazarus who will be resurrected through the grandmother's touch. In fact, there is a fitting anecdote O'Connor used to repeat: "A lot of people get killed in my stories, but nobody gets hurt."[15] Perhaps this explains the theological dimension of the Misfit's casual remark,

---

[11] Bellamy, "Everything Off Balance", 118.
[12] Wood, *South*, 38.
[13] Ibid.
[14] One teacher famously asked, "the Misfit represents Christ, does he not," to which O'Connor replied, "He does not" (HB 334).
[15] Quoted in Wood, *South*, 42.

after shooting the grandmother: "She would have been a good woman ... if it had been somebody there to shoot her every minute of her life" (*CW* 153).[16] Yet the tension caused by O'Connor's violence is difficult to reconcile; as Michaels notes, "I suspect that even (or especially?) readers with a high tolerance for violent literature and film are uncomfortable with O'Connor for the same reason they are uncomfortable with violence in the Bible—not because of the violence per se, but because of its religious dimension."[17] While his criminal history may be difficult to overlook, in an exchange with one reader, O'Connor discusses the potential of the Misfit's future: "The Misfit, of course, is a spoiled prophet. As you point out, he could go on to great things" (*HB* 465).

Yet, the biblical dimension has been entirely overlooked in the criticism of "A Good Man Is Hard to Find." In his essay, "Reading the Map in 'A Good Man Is Hard to Find,'" Hallman Bryant claims that the only biblical allusion in the story is the reference to the town of Timothy.[18] Her brief Pauline allusion aside, "A Good Man Is Hard to Find" shows evidence of her development as a writer, which is why the biblical allusions are far more subtle than in *Wise Blood*, and this is why writers such as Bryant and Fike are grossly mistaken, as they overlook the Misfit's central reference to the gospels. Through my reading of "A Good Man Is Hard to Find," I intend to show how the story is not merely an allusion to, but a radical re-writing of Christ's encounter with the rich young ruler, with the Misfit serving as a recapitulation of the ruler.

Highlighting the key parallel between O'Connor's Misfit and the story of the rich young ruler[19] clarifies her approach to the explicit theological issues within the story by explicating her method of biblical recapitulation. In order to awaken readers to the nature of grace, O'Connor has the Misfit directly allude to the story she is retelling, as he plainly explains to the grandmother, "If He did what He said, then it's nothing for you to do but thow [*sic*] away everything and follow Him," echoing Jesus' command to "sell all you possess and give to the poor ... and come, follow Me" (*CW* 152, Mk. 10:21). Ironically, the Misfit, a serial criminal, serves as the source for the story's major biblical allusion. Hence, understanding this interaction opens up a new theological dimension to reading "A Good Man Is Hard to Find."

The story of the rich young ruler is recounted in Matthew, Mark, and Luke, all in analogous fashion:

> As He was setting out on a journey a man ran up to Him and knelt before Him, and asked Him, "Good Teacher what shall I do to inherit eternal life?" And Jesus said to him, "Why do you call Me good? No one is good except God alone. You know the commandments, Do not Murder, Do not commit adultery, Do not steal,

---

[16] Even this comment seems to recapitulate Paul's famous dictum: "I affirm, brethren, by the boasting in you which I have in Christ Jesus our Lord, I die daily" (1 Cor. 15:31).

[17] J. Ramsey Michaels, "Eating the Bread of Life: Muted Violence" in "*The Violent Bear It Away,*" *Flannery O'Connor in the Age of Terrorism: Essays on Violence and Grace.* ed. Avis Hewitt and Robert Donahoo (Knoxville: University of Tennessee Press, 2010), 66.

[18] Bryant speculates that the town is a reference to 1st Timothy, while Matthew Fike's essay "The Timothy Allusion in 'A Good Man Is Hard to Find'" argues that the name is a reference to the pastoral letters, 1st and 2nd Timothy.

[19] Found in Mt. 19:16–30, Mk 10:17–30, Lk. 18:18–23.

Do not bear false witness, Do not defraud, Honor your father and mother." And he said to Him, "Teacher, I have kept all these things from my youth up." Looking at him, Jesus felt a love for him and said to him, "One thing you lack: go and sell all you possess and give to the poor, and you will have treasure in heaven; and come, follow Me." But at these words he was saddened, and he went away grieving, for he was one who owned much property. (Mk. 10:17–22)

Within the rich man's encounter with Jesus, the young magistrate approaches Jesus and asks, "Good Teacher, what must I do to inherent eternal life?" (Mk. 10:17). Sanders notes that in the Hebrew tradition, "A rabbi, or a teacher of the law, derived authority from studying and interpreting the bible. Jesus did both," yet it is not a scriptural interpretation the ruler is seeking in his query.[20] Jesus, by declaring himself as God's agent, asserts that he is more than merely an interpreter of the law. Thus, in approaching Jesus, it is clear that the ruler, much like the Misfit, seeks knowledge of the afterlife rather than a scriptural interpretation. It is apparent by the fact that the ruler goes out of his way to find Jesus that he is sincere in his questioning and not merely trying to test Jesus. His query seems legitimate because (1) it is a question that has piqued the curiosity of humankind throughout the ages, and (2) the ruler recognizes Jesus as the "Good Teacher" who could provide him with an answer.[21] Thus, this first interaction, in which the young ruler acknowledges Jesus and asks what he must do to inherit eternal life, indicates a type of belief. This idea of Jesus as "good" signifies the ruler's initial openness to the possibility of seeing Jesus as the Messiah, the same possibility that the Misfit considers. This ruler, like the Misfit, is not completely skeptical and, on some level, is willing to consider that Jesus might be who he claims to be.

However, Jesus challenges the young man's assumption by deconstructing the question by responding, "Why do you call me good?" (Mk. 10:18). At the heart of his question, Jesus is challenging the young man's idea of goodness, a strategy Flannery O'Connor will later use in her short story "Good Country People." The young ruler sees "goodness" as something obtainable through deeds, but Jesus' response is that "no one is good except God only" and, thus, according to Jesus, goodness can only be achieved through God (Mk. 10:18). In a sense, Jesus tells the young man "A Good Man Is Hard to Find."

Jesus' response to the ruler to follow the commandments is not only "a generic answer which any teacher of the Law in his day would have given" but also a method to entice the ruler to re-evaluate his own legalistic belief system.[22] The ruler is asserting his own righteousness when he tells Jesus he has kept the commandments "from my youth up" (Mk. 10:20). In his answer, the ruler highlights his attempt to seek eternal life through works, by scrupulously keeping the commandments.

At this point, Jesus tells him, "one thing you lack: go sell all you possess and give to the poor, and … come, follow Me" (Mk. 10:21). This watershed moment is not

---

[20] E. P. Sanders, *The Historical Figure of Jesus* (New York: Penguin Books, 1993), 238.
[21] Sanders, *The Historical Figure of Jesus*, 269.
[22] Joseph A. Fitzmeyer, *The Gospel According to Luke X–XXIV: A New Translation with Introduction and Commentary*. Vol. 28A of *The Anchor Bible* (New York: Doubleday, 1985), 1197.

meant, necessarily, as a test, but instead it is Jesus offering grace to the young ruler as he beckons him to disregard the law and become one of his disciples. It signifies Jesus' foresight that "what the man needs is something other than knowledge of what is good."[23] The ruler's questions about the law echo the Misfit's questions about the law since both are disheartened by the discrepancies they have found.

The interaction ends with a somewhat ironic twist: instead of being overjoyed at the prospect of joining Jesus, as some readers might initially suspect out of this "good" man who follows the law, the ruler "was saddened and he went away grieving, for he was one who owned much property" (Mk 10:22). As Kierkegaard suggests in *Fear and Trembling*, "if the rich young man whom Christ met on the road had sold all his possessions and given them to the poor, we would praise him as we praise all great deeds."[24] In fact, Kierkegaard asserts there is no doubt that the ruler would have heard the words, "you shall get every penny back," as many biblical characters, such as Abraham, were rewarded not only for their sacrifice but for their resignation and willingness to sacrifice.[25] Although Jesus reaches out in love to the ruler, the young man is not able to escape his own system of legalism.

Yet, there is more linking the Misfit to the rich young ruler than just a direct quotation. Although O'Connor presents readers with an obvious reversal, much the same way she rewrites the privileged Saul through the life of a backwoods fundamentalist, Hazel Motes, O'Connor gives us the inverse of the ruler obsessed with goodness, a nihilistic serial killer. The ruler's question for Jesus, the nature of the afterlife, is essentially the same question the Misfit asks. Yet, while the ruler tries to take comfort in perceived "goodness," the Misfit, who believes himself unredeemable, seeks consolation in meanness—presenting an interesting reversal. O'Connor's story hinges not on the Misfit's allusion to Christ's encounter with the ruler, but on his own theological dilemma:

> Jesus was the only One that ever raised the dead... and he shouldn't have done it. He thown everything off balance. If He did what He said, then it's nothing for you to do but thow away everything and follow Him, and if He didn't, then it's nothing for you to do but enjoy the few minutes you got left the best way you can—by killing somebody or burning down his house or doing some other meanness to him. (*CW* 152)

This inability to believe in resurrection lies at the very heart of the Misfit's spiritual crisis, serving as the catalyst which leads to his life of crime. In a sense, Susan Srigley correctly categorized the Misfit when she notes that his "outward violence is a sign of the refusal to accept a divinely ordered world."[26] Thus, O'Connor presents

---

[23] Daniel Patte, *The Gospel According to Matthew: A Structural Commentary on Matthew's Faith* (Philadelphia: Fortress Press, 1987), 270.

[24] Søren Kierkegaard, *Fear and Trembling*, trans. Alastair Hannay (New York: Penguin Classics, 1986), 58.

[25] Ibid., 78.

[26] Susan Srigley, *Flannery O'Connor's Sacramental Art* (Notre Dame: University of Notre Dame Press, 2004), 102.

readers with a much more complex character than a cursory reading would imply. This introspective antagonist, finding no suitable answer to the grand theological questions which haunt him, has rebelled through criminal activity, the easiest outlet available to him.

In order for readers to realize the depths of her character, O'Connor chronicles the Misfit's own spiritual crisis through the progression of his conversation with the grandmother. The nucleus of the story, for all intents and purposes, is centered around the grandmother's interactions with the Misfit, specifically in how the Misfit "allows the conversation to affect him much more than he had expected it to."[27]

Throughout the story, the grandmother proves to be a master manipulator. She is able to control the children, John Wesley and June Star, through the promise of adventure and finding a hidden treasure. She manipulates Red Sam through general flattery: "Because you're a good man!" she tells him, to which he readily agrees (*CW* 142). She exploits her own son, Bailey, by using his kids against him as they convince their father to make a detour, while the grandmother promises that the side-trip will be educational. However, when the grandmother meets the Misfit and makes an obvious attempt to save her own life by saying, "I just know you're a good man ... You're not a bit common," she meets the first person immune to her charms (*CW* 148). The grandmother, in her frenzied state, even tries to urge the Misfit to renounce his ways, telling him that he "could be honest" and begs him to "settle down and live a comfortable life" without "somebody chasing you all the time" (*CW* 149).

Of course, O'Connor's Misfit is much too clever for the grandmother's frantic logic. O'Connor writes the Misfit as a wholly jaded character, a man who has "been most everything" ranging from gospel singer to undertaker and has even "seen a man burnt alive" and "a woman flogged" (*CW* 149). However, it is not the Misfit's own past which creates this theological dilemma; rather the Misfit is unsettled because he knows that the law doesn't work and that there is no way he can "settle down and live a comfortable life" (*CW* 149). As Wood argues, "Having felt the Abrahamic knife at his own throat, he has become a mass murderer."[28] The gospels all lay claim to Christ's resurrection, yet the Misfit cannot find the ability to believe in such an event, having never witnessed anything similar. The Misfit explains, "crime don't matter. You can do one thing or you can do another, kill a man or take a tire off his car, because sooner or later you're going to forget what it was you done and just be punished for it" (*CW* 150). This typifies the Misfit's innate and Pharisaical understanding of the law. Echoing the rich young ruler's religious literalism, the Misfit follows the letter of the law rather than the spirit. His own spiritual literalism parallels his understanding of the law as he assures the grandmother, "I said long ago, you can get a signature and sign everything and keep a copy of it. Then you'll know what you done and you can hold up the crime to the punishment to see if they match" (*CW* 151). It is through this legalistic understanding and devotion that the Misfit realizes there are limitations to the law, yet the Misfit

---

[27] Gentry, *Religion of the Grotesque*, 37.
[28] Wood, *South*, 38.

reveals he is not only a legalist but "a good historicist, though he's far from knowing it: he will not credit ancient events that he cannot empirically verify."[29]

This is where the crux of Flannery O'Connor's story lies. The Misfit, with all of his life experience, has realized that the punishment can never fit the crime, which is how the Misfit receives his name, "because I can't make what all I done wrong fit what all I gone through in punishment" (*CW* 151). His name is more than a reference to the two similar criminals in the Atlanta area around the time the story was written: he embodies his own moniker.[30] He realizes that there is a "mis"-fit between the law and the punishment, which is why he signs everything himself, including his criminal acts, and keeps a copy to "know what you done and you can hold up the crime to the punishment and see do they match" in an attempt "to prove you ain't been treated right" (*CW* 151). In reaction to what he perceives to be the inequity of original sin, the Misfit has developed his own rudimentary moral accounting system to try to counterbalance his actions with the consequences. Yet, deep down, he realizes the futility of such a system. In the same way that he may have been wrongfully imprisoned, there is no way he can be justly punished for taking six lives on the side of the road. He realizes that since legalism and grace can never be reconciled, the law cannot work exactly. Hence, the Misfit acts out through violence.

At the locus of the Misfit's ambivalence is a familiar theme within O'Connor's corpus: the polarity of absolutes—"there is no middle ground between absolute belief in Christ's messianic function and a belief that life is nasty, brustish, and short."[31] The Misfit has created a false dichotomy in his mind, which is why he gravitates to base instinct. To believe in the possibility of resurrection would require a faith unavailable to the Misfit since he would need to witness such events firsthand. This false dilemma, as well as his attachment to his own system of violence, is why the Misfit continuously spurns the grandmother's proselytizing. He rebuts her command to "Pray," by telling the grandmother, he "don't want no help" since he's "doing all right" by himself (*CW* 151, 150).

This is not to suggest that the grandmother's ceaseless command for him to pray doesn't upset the Misfit; on the contrary, it profoundly affects him. As if taking a cue from the grandmother's antagonism, the Misfit curses Jesus because he throws everything off-balance: "For the Misfit, Christ is the great stumbling block, the one whose presence completely disrupts the order of human life and endeavor."[32] Since Jesus was unjustly punished, yet indiscriminatingly offers grace to everyone, he would return the Misfit to a world in which "one is punished a heap and another ain't punished at all" (*CW* 151). This is precisely the world the Misfit's system of record-keeping seeks to eliminate.

This is the crux of the Misfit's philosophical and theological dilemma, his lack of faith and inability to believe in resurrection, unsettling his tendency toward "killing somebody or burning down his house or doing some other meanness to him," and

[29] Wood, *South*, 41.
[30] See McCartney, Keeler, "Search for Kidnap-Robbery Trio Centers in Atlanta and Vicinity," *The Atlanta Constitution*. October 25, 1952. 1; "'The Misfit' Robs Office, Escapes with $150," *The Atlanta Constitution*. November 6, 1952.
[31] Bellamy, "Everything Off Balance," 119.
[32] Brinkmeyer, *Art and Vision*, 33.

essentially the driving force behind the entire story (*CW* 152). It is not the existence of God that bothers the Misfit, but rather what he perceives to be a great injustice. Following in the ruler's frustration of Christ's command to sell everything, the Misfit is upset by this great equalizer. By raising the dead, Christ claims to offer a new system, a system of grace that overrides the law. Incertitude plagues the Misfit as he claims, "It ain't right I wasn't there because if I had of been there I would of known . . . I would of known and I wouldn't be like I am now" (*CW* 152). The Misfit finds himself, like several in the gospels who encounter Jesus' message and are unable to accept it, "rebuking Jesus for having reversed everything."[33]

The flaw in the Misfit's system is that it is difficult for him to comprehend the foreign idea of grace. His lack of understanding leads to the grandmother's gesture as "she reached out and touched him on the shoulder" (*CW* 152). When she reaches out in love and offers him something he hasn't earned, she is echoing Jesus and this is unbearable to him. Since the Misfit lives in a meritocracy with an established legalistic system, he cannot accept a new system which would offer grace to those who are undeserving. This is why the Misfit "sprang back as if a snake had bitten him and shot her three times through the chest" since "his shooting her is a recoil, a horror at her humanness" (*CW* 152, *HB* 389). However, like it or not, the Misfit's system has been overridden by the introduction of grace, which is why her death—his own act of meanness—brings him "no real pleasure in life" (*CW* 153).

In the wake of tragedy, with a gun pointed at her head, her false faith and piety evaporate and she finally sees clearly: "she tells the truth: she is not a good woman; he is not a good man; they both are in terrible trouble, and they both need radical help."[34] The grandmother, who is identified only as such, in the end, does fulfill her purpose and becomes a "grand" mother as her maternal actions lead her to tell the Misfit, "Why you're one of my babies. You're one of my own children" (*CW* 152). Through her selfless actions, her embrace, and forgiveness, she becomes a conduit of God's grace.

Throughout the story, the Misfit views life in binaries; hence, "The choice is finally a stark either/or, which to The Misfit takes the form of Jesus or meanness" and the Misfit has chosen meanness.[35] Spending his life living out Hobbes' dictum that man is a wolf to man, the Misfit seems to have no redeeming moral value, yet the conclusion of the story is startling because it suggests a change: with the grandmother's offering of grace and the Misfit's reaction, killing her, but adding, "It's no real pleasure in life" (*CW* 153). His words echo just how much the gesture has affected him, as he realizes that there is no pleasure in life, not even in meanness:

> The Misfit is touched by the Grace that comes through the old lady when she recognizes him as her child, as she has been touched by the Grace that comes through him in his particular suffering. His shooting her is a recoil, a horror at her humanness, but after he has done it and cleaned his glasses, the Grace has worked

---

[33] Gardner, *John*, 124.
[34] Wood, *South*, 39.
[35] Asals, *The Imagination of Extremity*, 151.

in him and he pronounces his judgment: she would have been a good woman if *he* had been there every moment of her life. True enough. (*HB* 389)

Ironically, the Misfit realizes the efficacy of the grandmother's final act as he deems her "good." Once again, alluding to Christ's interaction with the rich young ruler, the subtext of the story seems to be O'Connor's rephrasing of Christ's question: Why do you call me good? Yet, through the grandmother's sacrifice, readers finally encounter a character worthy of such a title since she lies at rest in a crucifixion pose, "her face smiling up at the cloudless sky," suggesting the final discovery of grace (*CW* 152). Through her death, she "provides an analogue to Christ's innocent death, despite the sin of pride that marked her previously."[36]

Through his invitation to the ruler to throw away everything and join him, Jesus offers the same grace that the grandmother offers the Misfit as she reaches out and touches him on the shoulder. Much like the Misfit, the ruler lets his foolish obstinacy stand in the way of acting on faith. Yet, when examining the two stories side by side, there are several major differences which immediately rule out any possibility of allegory. Perhaps this is why the connections have been overlooked; after all, the Misfit is "a hypocritical liar who has no faith in a moral purpose in the universe," while the ruler clings wholeheartedly to the law of Moses.[37] O'Connor has written the Misfit, ostensibly, to be the exact opposite of his biblical counterpart; however, inwardly they are identical—they are spiritual doppelgangers. While the Misfit has broken all of the commandments the young man keeps, both men realize that the law cannot work, that there is a "misfit" between punishment and crime or between a desire to be good and standing before the law. The similarity lies in the fact that both believe one can either sacrifice "for the greater good" or reject "that goodness by inflicting as much outward violence as possible to sustain it"; while the ruler chooses the former, the Misfit chooses the latter, yet neither one is satisfied.[38] The two men share the same sensibility: when challenged both the Misfit and the ruler "don't want no hep," and both implicitly claim, "I'm doing all right by myself" (*CW* 150).

Both men, through great effort, have put together their own systems in which they seek to save themselves: a legalistic checklist, of sorts. Hence, after being confronted by Jesus, the two, respectively, realize that the law does not work for them. One realizes the limits of good works, the other of evil deeds. By approaching Jesus, despite having followed the letter of the law, the rich young ruler realizes it does not work, but he cannot move beyond the law. In both cases, "mere belief is not enough," given that the Misfit and the ruler both walk away from certain salvation disheartened because neither can resign himself to give up his own way of life and accept a new one.[39] O'Connor even parallels the ending of the story, since the ruler "went away grieving," while the Misfit mutters, "It's no real pleasure in life" (Mk 10:22, *CW* 153).

---

[36] Sykes, *Aesthetic*, 85.

[37] Hallman Bryant, "Reading the Map in Flannery O'Connor's 'A Good Man Is Hard to Find,'" *Studies in Short Fiction* 18, no.3 (1981): 305.

[38] Srigley, *Sacramental Art*, 102.

[39] Matthew Fike, "The Timothy Allusion in 'A Good Man Is Hard to Find,'" *Renascence* 52, no.4 (2000): 314.

This is why, in these parallel accounts, Jesus is such an affront: he throws their lives off balance. The gospels' claims of Jesus' resurrecting the dead, offering life as a thing unearned, undermines both systems since faith requires complete dependence on God. Yet this dependence is a concept too difficult for either man to accept. Jesus, with his command, means to show the ruler that it is impossible for humans to save themselves, but with his summons to "come, follow Me," Jesus presents the ruler with grace (Mk. 10:17). Of course, this grace is not reserved for just the rich; in fact, this is why Jesus asks the ruler to throw away his possessions, presenting himself as the great leveler who will throw the social hierarchies off-balance. In offering grace to the rich and the poor, Jesus shows that it is not about merit or justification. Both men react in a similar fashion as Hazel Motes: this system of undeserved mercy that Christ presents is too much for either the ruler or the Misfit to comprehend.

Theologically, this is where the story gets tricky. O'Connor uses the Misfit, not the grandmother, as the spiritual barometer and the means of the grandmother's redemption. In fact, Gentry rightly notices that "The grandmother herself does almost nothing" to bring about her own atonement; rather it is thrust upon her by the Misfit.[40] It is through the grandmother's death that O'Connor tells readers that "in this story you should be on the lookout for such things as the action of grace in the grandmother's soul and not for the dead bodies" (*MM* 113).

While the dead bodies may be difficult to ignore, death, particularly the grandmother's death, becomes the author's vehicle to deliver the message of grace. Yet, reading the story without O'Connor's interpretation tends to be much less compelling. By retelling the story of the rich young ruler in the modern-day South, O'Connor writes from a standpoint of Christian orthodoxy like no other writer before her, with the hope that—as she has often claimed—the thematically Christian message might have an impact upon her readers.

Judgment Day

Although O'Connor has the Misfit intentionally allude to the story of the rich young ruler, the parallel—that is, her method of biblical recapitulation—in this early story is somewhat subtle. Yet, the biblical resonances could not be more striking in her final story, "Judgment Day." While it does not include the same level of violence—or the subsequent popularity—of "A Good Man Is Hard to Find," "Judgment Day" is possibly the most theologically explicit story within O'Connor's corpus.

The story, as many know, is a reworking of her earlier story "The Geranium,"[41] part of the collection of which was used for her MFA thesis. She explains: "It's a rewrite of a story I have had around since 1946 and never been satisfied with, but I hope I have it

---

[40] Gentry, *Religion of the Grotesque*, 161.
[41] Karl-Heinz Westarp details this story's transformation from "The Geranium" (1946) into early drafts, "An Exile in the East" (1954) and "Getting Home" (1964) before it became "Judgment Day" (1964), which he asserts is "perfect in style and structure" (52).

now" (*HB* 588). Many have noticed the complexity, the theological and narratological depth, she develops within its many draft stages. Her final version of "Judgment Day," which she had briefly titled "Getting Home," is filled with several biblically thematic elements ranging from T. C. Tanner's hometown of Corinth, Georgia, to his obsession with his own demise. As Whitt observes, O'Connor succeeded by transforming "The Geranium" from a simplistic tale into a "theologically pungent" masterpiece.[42]

Read alongside her earlier works, "Judgment Day" illustrates O'Connor's maturity as a writer, diverging from her typical narrative fare. Unlike any other story in her corpus, it is set in New York City—her only work located above the Mason-Dixon line—while the opening scene occurs shortly before Tanner's heavily foreshadowed death and features a series of five interlocking flashbacks. Along with "Parker's Back," readers can clearly see the evolution of O'Connor's own aesthetic in "Judgment Day," since it is one of her few nonlinear tales and demonstrates her growth as a writer from her earlier, simplistic plot structures to a much more complex structure.

Compared with her earlier works such as "A Good Man Is Hard to Find" and *Wise Blood*, it is easy to see that, although her art began to explore new and experimental territory, her anagogical vision only deepened. By noting the connection between Tanner's obsession with resurrection and the final judgment with Paul's account of resurrection in 1 Corinthians 15, O'Connor presents her most candid version of biblical recapitulation. Throughout "Judgment Day," her dependence on Pauline doctrine serves as a means to transform Tanner into a vehicle for grace, epitomizing both Paul's and Christ's message and vision of resurrection.

The story highlights the last days of T. C. Tanner, a man who, after spending his entire life in the South, is forced to move to New York City, a town he hates, with his daughter and her son-in-law. For readers, the narrative begins with Tanner living in New York City, conserving his strength for his journey back to Georgia: "he meant to walk as far as he could get and trust the Almighty to get him the rest of the way"; however, when told chronologically, it begins 30 years prior to the opening scene (*CW* 676).

In the past, T. C. Tanner managed a sawmill outside Corinth, Georgia, overseeing the operations of a crew of African-American laborers. When a mysterious stranger appears in the form of Coleman,[43] a man who begins lounging around the sawmill in plain sight of his fellow workers, Tanner feels threatened. Fearful of the influence of the slothful figure, he is forced to confront the stranger. Oddly, Tanner, who is impetuously carving a block of wood, approaches the man, ready to threaten him with his knife. Yet, at this very moment, he feels "some intruding intelligence that worked in his hands"; it was "an invisible power" (*CW* 683). As Tanner draws closer, instead of anger, he pities the stranger and asks, "you can't see so good, can you boy?" (*CW* 683). Tanner, then, hands Coleman the pair of spectacles he had been half-consciously whittling, instructing him to "put these on ... I hate to see anybody can't see good" (*CW* 683).

---

[42] Margaret Whitt, "Letters to Corinth; Echoes from Greece to Georgia in O'Connor's 'Judgment Day,'" *Flannery O'Connor and the Christian Mystery*, ed. J. P. Murphy et al. (Provo: Brigham Young University Center for the Study of Christian Values in Literature, 1997), 62.

[43] The name "Coleman" is likely a play off the term "coal man," a reference to Coleman's racial identity.

Ironically, this scene where Tanner helps a man to see echoes a theme familiar to O'Connor's work: vision. Like Hazel Motes or the Misfit, the story explores the need for corrective vision as O'Connor rewrites and alludes to Jesus' healing of the man born blind. When the blind man is brought to Jesus:

> [Christ] spat on the ground, and made clay of the spittle, and applied the clay to his eyes, and he said to him, "Go wash in the pool of Siloam." So he went away and washed and came back seeing. Therefore the neighbors, and those who previously saw him as a beggar, were saying, "Is not this the one who used to sit and beg?" (John 9:6–9)

As Tanner hands over the glasses he had been whittling, Coleman, appreciating the gesture, accepts them. At this moment, Tanner immediately "saw the exact instant in the muddy liquor-swollen eyes when the pleasure of having a knife in this white man's gut was balanced against something else" (*CW* 683). Although he was unconsciously whittling the glasses, his gift of sight transforms Coleman. In him, Tanner sees before him "a negative image of himself, as if clownishness and captivity had been their common lot" (*CW* 683). From that point on, Tanner and Coleman remain lifelong friends.

This image of clownishness and foolishness foreshadows the theological underpinning of the entire story: the folly of the messenger and, perhaps, the message that he delivers. However, this scene introduces another theologically cogent motif popular in O'Connor's fiction: prophecy (in this case she uses vision as a means to discuss prophecy). Tanner, half-conscious of his own actions, represents a different type of prophet *malgré lui*. Although he never struggles with belief, like Hazel Motes or the Misfit, it is as if Tanner is destined to serve as a bizarre prophet, in spite of himself. This scene not only echoes Christ's healing of the blind man but Paul's conversion at Damascus and gives readers the first of several Pauline–T. C. Tanner parallels.

This strange and unexplainable event is the catalyst for Tanner's unlikely prophetic journey. The "Invisible power" that leads him to carve the glasses seems to be the Holy Spirit working through him. As Tanner gives Coleman the new glasses that enable him to see, it is like a "clownish" version of Jesus looking at the blind man. Tanner, handing the wooden spectacles to Coleman, echoes Jesus, as both use unconventional objects as means to correct vision.

When Tanner sees Coleman as his "negative image," he is identifying with Coleman, since both are "clownish and captive" in this broken world (*CW* 683). They are both imprisoned in different ways; yet through this action, Coleman is released, wearing the wooden spectacles that have no glass, but which restores his vision of a world that is whole rather than broken. Thus, as Wood argues, "these glasses that are not glasses become the means ... and the symbolic center of the story," marking his transformation into an O'Connor prophet.[44]

---

[44] Ralph Wood, "Obedience to the Unenforceable: Mystery, Manners, and Masks in 'Judgment Day,'" *The Flannery O'Connor Bulletin* 25 (1996–1997): 163.

Tanner's impish nature is a trademark of O'Connor rhetorical device. He is an atypical prophet, a clownish figure who brings the truth to New York City, a place where no one is interested (in a sense mirroring Taulkinham). O'Connor doesn't divulge the circumstances that lead to his dislocation—readers do not know how he lost his business and personal property—rather, the story moves forward 30 years later, when Tanner and Coleman are living in a dilapidated shanty, working an illegal still in the woods. When the property is purchased by Dr. Foley, a biracial doctor who agrees to let the two live on his land if they work the still for him, Tanner decides to move to New York City with his daughter—a decision he lives to regret. When he arrives in New York, his eschatological beliefs bother everyone around him, including his daughter, and he becomes obsessed with two things: Corinth and judgment. Hence the story's title.

Like Paul, Tanner leaves Corinth, but quickly grows despondent in New York City, a town he claims is "no kind of place" in his letter to Coleman (*CW* 676).[45] An exile, Tanner thinks of nothing more than his own death, continuously insisting that he be buried back home in Corinth, Georgia. Throughout "Judgment Day," he has a reoccurring dream of his own death, in which he returns home in a coffin, only to be resurrected in Corinth, screaming "Judgment Day!" (*CW* 692). It is this dream—which supernaturally draws him South—that leads him to the conclusion that he must return to Georgia, dead or alive. Tanner's obsession with his own death and resurrection echoes Paul's thesis of bodily resurrection (1 Corinthians 15); thus, it is during his time in New York City that T. C. Tanner truly becomes a recasting of Pauline theology.

It is interesting, though not surprising, that O'Connor would turn to this chapter, which many claim to be the most important chapter in 1 Corinthians, where "doctrinal instruction seems to be Paul's primary aim."[46] It was a chapter that O'Connor was not only familiar with but also interested in, since inside her copy of the New Testament,[47] she has clearly marked 1 Corinthians 15:3. Within 1 Corinthians 15, Paul outlines three essential tenets: Christ resurrected (1–11), the resurrection of man (12–34), and absolute resurrection (35–58).

In the first part of Paul's letter, he reiterates the importance of the resurrection of Christ, stressing "Christ died for our sins according to the Scriptures, and that He was buried and that He was raised on the third day" (1 Cor. 15:3–4). He also asserts his own authority by reminding the church "last of all, as to one untimely born, he [Christ] appeared to me" (1 Cor. 15:8). Paul then applies the idea of Christ's physical resurrection to the people of Corinth saying, "so we preach and so you believed" (1 Cor. 15:11). Thus, the first tenet seeks to establish, unequivocally, his belief in the resurrection of Christ as common ground for all those who preach Christ as well as for followers of Christianity. Paul argues that the incontrovertible authenticity of Christ's

---

[45] The fact that Tanner writes two letters to Corinth (a postcard, plus the letter pinned inside his jacket) is an obvious allusion to Paul's letters to Corinth, Greece (1st & 2nd Corinthians).

[46] Victor Paul Furnish, *New Testament Theology: The Theology of the First Letter to the Corinthians* (New York: Cambridge University Press, 1999), 105.

[47] *The New Testament of Our Lord and Saviour Jesus Christ: A New Translation.* New York: Sheed & Ward, 1948 (BS 2095. K6 1944 A in the Flannery O'Connor Special Collections).

resurrection is of utmost importance in his ministry and the undercurrents of this argument surfaces in Tanner's own proclamations of resurrection.

In the penultimate section of this chapter, Paul engages those who doubt the resurrection of believers as he argues, "Now if Christ is preached, that He has been raised from the dead, how do some among you say that there is no resurrection of the dead?" (1 Cor. 15:12). Paul asserts that if there is no resurrection and the dead are not raised, then Christ, himself, never rose, and hence, Christianity is illogical.

Traditionally, the Greek citizens of Corinth would have found the concept of resurrection confusing, especially considering many of the original members of the Corinthian church were converts from mystery religions. Paul addresses the doubts and skepticism of many that the resurrection was not a physical reality. At its heart, this chapter essentially argues that since Christianity centers around the axiom that Christ resurrected from the dead, then they must trust in God's ability to resurrect believers. By following the logical implications that arise from this claim, Paul believes it is doctrinally essential to acknowledge Christ's ability to resurrect the members of the church. Hence, he "argues for the inevitability of a resurrection of believers from the dead."[48] In fact, in a well-recited and cogent metaphor, Paul writes, "I affirm, brethren, by the boasting in you which I have in Christ Jesus our Lord, I die daily" (1 Cor. 15:31). Although this verse seems to embody the grandmother's death in "A Good Man Is Hard to Find," this metaphor, too, is an apt way of describing T. C. Tanner, who, after moving to New York, daily fantasizes about his own death and resurrection. In fact, Tanner is the very embodiment of Paul's claim. O'Connor uses Tanner's somewhat deluded beliefs about the resurrection as a pointer toward the rich mystery of Paul's metaphors about a spiritual resurrection beyond present human understanding. This underlying eschatological tenet is crucial in O'Connor's understanding of Christianity; thus, this verse serves as a nexus to link these two stories.

The final section of 1 Corinthians 15 centers around Paul's concern with "how the dead are raised."[49] He insists that "there are also heavenly bodies and earthly bodies, but the glory of the heavenly is one, and the glory of the earthly is another" (1 Cor. 15:40). At the crux of this entire chapter is Paul's message that "the resurrection of the dead" occurs when the body "is sown a perishable body, it is raised an imperishable body; it is sown in dishonor, it is raised in glory" (1 Cor. 15:42–43). In a sense, this is the message that Tanner brings: the gospel turns things from perishable to permanent, from dishonor to glory. Paul emphasizes that as the earthly body falls victim to decay and "is sown a natural body," a heavenly body is raised in its place (1 Cor. 15:44). While fighting growing misinterpretations about the idea of resurrection, Paul argues that there is "a glorious resurrection-transformation of both the dead and the living wherein the final enemy, death, is swallowed up in victory."[50] Paul's claim parallels what he wrote earlier: "may your spirit and soul and body be preserved complete without blame at the coming of our Lord Jesus Christ" (1 Thessalonians 5:23). Essentially, in

---

[48] Gordon D. Fee, *The First Epistle to the Corinthians* (Grand Rapids: Eerdmans, 1987), 714.
[49] Ibid.
[50] Ibid.

both letters he "suggests that the difference between soul and spirit means something" and that Jesus' resurrection is "not the soul or abstract essence of the body but a 'spiritual body'" which is contrasted with "the natural body."[51] However, by having T. C. Tanner's insistence that he will literally resurrect in Corinth, Georgia, on his own accord, O'Connor invites a comic parallel to Paul's missive to the Corinthians.

That we are led to these issues by the town's name (Corinth, GA)—which brings to mind Corinth, Greece, and, more importantly, Paul's letters to the Corinthian church—should come as no surprise to O'Connor's audience. Readers need look no further than *Wise Blood* to notice her penchant for biblically evocative names. As Margaret Whitt points out, "We know the setting of the story was selected by design. After all, Corinth does not appear in 'The Geranium,' but enters the manuscript in a later version."[52] However, while the name Corinth is an obviously symbolic name, it is also modeled after the actual town northwest of Milledgeville: "How convenient for O'Connor that a town with this name existed, literally, within the confines of her own territory."[53] In a sense, "Judgment Day" explores what happens when an idea native to O'Connor's "territory"—resurrection of the body—is introduced to a setting where it is not at home. Corinth is both a literal home for Tanner as well as the final home for his body. He yearns for both, which provides the basis of this story's biblical transformation. Hence, it provides an ideal exemplar of O'Connor's tendency to rewrite biblical stories set in the modern-day South.

Upon his migration North, Tanner is quick to denounce the city and is afraid to step foot outside the apartment. His new neighbor, an African-American actor, who Tanner is convinced is a kindred soul from South Alabama, finally piques his curiosity. As the actor moves in next door, Tanner, in his clownish way, tries to identify with him. Tanner, waiting out in the hall, greets his neighbor, "Good morning, Preacher," since "it had been his experience that if a negro tended to be sullen, this title usually cleared up his expression" (*CW* 689). Although his approach is ignorant, Tanner has only the best intentions in mind. He refers to the new neighbor as "Preacher" and asks him if he would be interested in fishing—an action rife with biblical allusion and brings to mind this comic prophet's attempt to be a fisher of men[54] (*CW* 689). However, Tanner's awkward and confused attempts at friendship quickly agitate the neighbor; he violently confronts Tanner by grabbing his shoulders and says, "I don't take no crap... off no wool hat red-neck son-of-a-bitch peckerwood old bastard like you" and finally telling Tanner, "I'm not a preacher! I'm not a Christian. I don't believe in that crap" (*CW* 690). The neighbor responds in horror at the thought that such a person could try to identify with him telling Tanner, "There ain't no Jesus and there ain't no God," to which Tanner responds, "And you ain't black... and I ain't white!" (*CW* 690). Tanner's logic is revealed in this reversal, as he comments that if the actor is correct and there is no God, then we can't be who we think we are. Tanner's absolute certainty echoes Paul's logical reversal as he tells the people of Corinth who doubt the idea of resurrection,

[51] Frye, *The Great Code*, 20.
[52] Whitt, "Letters," 63.
[53] Ibid., 64.
[54] An allusion to Mt. 4:19, Mk 1:17.

"if the dead are not raised, not even Christ has been raised; and if Christ has not been raised, your faith is worthless" (1 Cor. 15:16–17). This connection between the two is important as both Tanner and Paul attempt to resolve obvious contradictions. Hence, O'Connor uses the same rhetorical reversals found in Paul's own arguments.

Tanner genuinely, yet awkwardly, reaches out to the actor, sincere in his desire for companionship in a new place. He views the neighbor as a suitable replacement for Coleman, but his attempt at friendship is forcefully denied. This event not only serves to reinforce Tanner's condemnation of the big city but also triggers his first stroke, which leaves him confined to a chair. Yet, it is not until he overhears his daughter's plans to bury him, against his will, in New York City rather than his native Georgia that he becomes obsessed with returning home to Corinth, the locus of his prophecy.

There are complexities for modern readers, who may have a hard time accepting T. C. Tanner as a prophet. It is hard to dismiss Tanner's derogatory attitudes toward African-Americans and his refusal to work for Dr. Foley, in order to avoid becoming "a nigger's white nigger" (*CW* 685). It is difficult to overlook Tanner's racist and bigoted attitudes, especially to believe in his call to prophecy or notice the Pauline inference, but even Paul himself admits his own former prejudice as he states, "For I am the least of the apostles, and not fit to be called an apostle, because I persecuted the church of God" (1 Cor. 15:9). Before his conversion, Paul was a known persecutor of Christians. Thus, Tanner's previous attitudes, before his stay in New York, only strengthen the parallels to Paul's ministry and exude the richness of O'Connor's prophetic metaphor.

The unnamed actor is not the only one who dismisses Tanner's message; both his daughter and son-in-law completely ignore his warnings. Paul's address in 1 Corinthians 15 is intended for those who do not believe in the possibility of resurrection, and this includes Tanner's daughter, who complains, "don't throw hell at me. I don't believe in it"; the son whom Tanner lost "to the devil"; his son-in-law; and the actor who claims, "there ain't no Jesus and there ain't no God" (*CW* 678, 679, 690). Although one of the primary purposes of Paul's letter to the Corinthian church is to assert Christ's resurrection to believers, the letter is also addressed to nonbelievers who doubt the possibility of such an event. To skeptics, Paul's insistence on believing in the resurrection seems foolish, just as Tanner appears the foolish messenger bringing a truth to nonbelievers, rejected by everyone he encounters, including his own daughter. She can't—or won't—accept that "the Judgment is coming," as Tanner tells her, "the sheep'll be separated from the goats. Them that kept their promises from them that didn't" (*CW* 686).[55] His message falls upon deaf ears, since everyone ignores his warnings, believing him to have a perverse fascination with death. Yet, through this generational conflict, "Judgment Day" offers a paradigmatic example that, in O'Connor's fictional world, it "is often a younger generation scowling at the instinctive religion of their parents or social inferiors."[56] In this case, it is not only Tanner's daughter but the entire city that rejects his message, which "is also what O'Connor imagined her typical reader to resemble,

[55] A direct reference to Mt. 25:32.
[56] Hawkins, *The Language of Grace*, 26.

the generation of wingless chickens for whom God is dead."[57] This rejection serves as a catalyst for Tanner's death since no one in New York is receptive to his ministry; he feebly tries to bring his message of resurrection back to Corinth. Tanner's dilemma parallels, almost exactly, Paul's as he addresses all of those who "say that there is no resurrection" (1 Cor. 15:12).

It is not until the day his daughter leaves him alone, under terrible weather conditions, that Tanner decides to make his getaway, with an ill-conceived plan to walk to a train station and catch a freight train to Georgia. Yet, while he begins his journey repeating Psalms 23, he fears "he would never get there [Corinth] dead or alive" (*CW* 693). Tanner only makes it halfway down the apartment's staircase before losing his balance and landing "upsidedown in the middle of the flight" (*CW* 694). His positioning, being turned upside down, is a perfect physical representation of O'Connor's method of reversal—since she has in many ways written Tanner to be a reversal, and a recapitulation, of Paul and his message.

Delusional from his fall, Tanner relives his waking dream; believing he is in his coffin, he cries "in a weak voice, 'Judgment Day! Judgment Day! You idiots didn't know it was Judgment Day, did you?'" (*CW* 694). Instead he is greeted by the face of the actor, who mocks, "There's not any judgment day, old man. Except this. Maybe this here is judgment day for you" (*CW* 694). Tanner replies, "Hep me up, Preacher. I'm on my way home!" (*CW* 694).[58] When his daughter finds him, his head and arms are "thrust between the spokes of the banister; his feet dangled over the stairwell like those of a man in the stocks" (*CW* 695). She quickly has him buried, against his wishes, in New York City. However, her troubled conscience leads her to exhume his body and send him back home. Hence, the story ends, not only with Tanner's foreshadowed death but also with his resurrection and reburial in Corinth.

This ending, ironically, reflects Tanner's own very literal interpretation, believing that he will be resurrected as he pleases, as soon as he arrives in Corinth, Georgia. Tanner imagines arriving home in a coffin, giving "a thrust upward with both hands and spring[ing] up in the box" and crying out, "Judgment Day! Judgment Day! ... Don't you two fools know it's Judgment Day?" (*CW* 692). Yet, his vision is paradigmatic of Paul's, a body "sown in dishonor but raised in glory; it is sown in weakness, it is raised in power" (1 Cor. 15:43). Tanner's body exists in a state of dishonor, since his life—especially its last stage—has been less than an honorable one; he dies in a state of weakness, yet through Tanner, O'Connor exemplifies Paul's teachings. Tanner offers the actor grace, but the actor refuses to listen but tells him, "there's not any judgment day" (*CW* 694). As he lies in the stairwell, dying, the actor still can't accept his message; the actor can't believe that Tanner is a potential reflection of himself, unlike Tanner, who recognized Coleman as a negative version of himself. Tanner's last gesture is to show the neighbor that they are both clownish and captive, but the neighbor can't accept such a thing and wants nothing to do with his message. The neighbor, emblematic of

---

[57] Hawkins, *The Language of Grace*, 26.
[58] This is the exact opposite of the Misfit, who claims "I don't want no hep ... I'm doing all right by myself" (*CW* 150).

everyone Tanner encounters in New York City, inevitably, crucifies the person bringing that message—a possible reinterpretation of Paul's own death.

Indicative of O'Connor's narrative approach, her protagonist follows a rhetorical strategy based on biblical precedent. He is a strange and seemingly unfit prophet, an unlikely candidate to bring God's message of victory over death to the "no place" of New York City, yet this is often true of God's elected. Tanner is clearly the most religious character within "Judgment Day," especially since most dismiss his message as "hardshell Baptist hooey"; however, he is difficult to ignore (*CW* 678). Even his daughter realizes her father's complexity as she tells her husband, "he was somebody when he was somebody. He never worked for nobody in his life but himself" (*CW* 677). While he resides in New York City, Tanner never encounters another self-identified Christian; hence through his eyes, the Big Apple is rotten to its core, inhabited only by those who believe that "there ain't no Jesus and there ain't no God" (*CW* 690). It seems, then, that conflict is inevitable when he moves from Corinth, Georgia, to New York City. The message that he brings, the message that gets him killed, is the message that Paul preaches in 1 Corinthians 15: through the gospel, everyone will be changed, both now and at the Judgment day. It seems a foolish message, carried by a foolish messenger. As Whitt argues, his death "gives us a comic example of Paul's ideas."[59] Through Tanner, O'Connor presents a fool spreading Paul's foolish message.

On an anagogical level, Tanner is more than merely a Pauline figure. O'Connor uses him to literally embody Paul's message to the Corinthians, as he writes, "the word of the cross is foolishness to those who are perishing, but to us who are being saved it is the power of God" (1 Cor. 1:18). Paul realizes that his message must sound foolish, but he asks, "has not God made foolish the wisdom of the world? For since in the wisdom of God the world through its wisdom did not come to know God, God was well-pleased through the foolishness of the message preached to save those who believe" (1 Cor. 1:20–21). Paul is aware of how strange his message must sound to outsiders, although this is an irony lost on T. C. Tanner.

At the heart of O'Connor's story is a foolish and clownish man who delivers a life-changing message. While she subverts the expectations of the prophet, she does not change the prophecy. O'Connor's protagonist is the incarnation of Paul's message as he states, "let no man deceive himself. If any man among you thinks that he is wise in this age, he must become foolish, so that he may become wise" (1 Cor. 3:18). O'Connor's fool, T. C. Tanner, is the perfect courier to the directive since he is not only foolish, but his attempts to talk to his neighbor reveal his good intentions masked within a coarse nature. The strangeness of Tanner, the way he apparently reverses the polarity of Paul's exalted vision and makes it an old man's foolishness, is, oddly, Paul's point—that this message of resurrection is foolishness to the no place, in this case, the perishing world of New York City.

In this way, Tanner, ignorantly directed by "some intruding intelligence," is much like the grandmother in "A Good Man Is Hard to Find," whose "head cleared for an instant" as she, unknowingly, reaches out to the Misfit with love (*CW* 683, 152). Brad

---

[59] Whitt, "Letters," 72.

Gooch's biography, *Flannery: A Life of Flannery O'Connor*, speculates on the direction that her fiction might have taken had she not succumbed to such a premature death. The topic is a popular one on which many have varying opinions; James Whitlark, for instance, often speculated that O'Connor would move toward Eastern religious practices and ecumenicalism, similar to Thomas Merton. Yet, by looking at her early fiction, "A Good Man Is Hard to Find," and one of her final stories, "Judgment Day," we see one analogous pattern emerging: the use of biblical recapitulation from the beginning of her literary career to the end. Although O'Connor integrates Christian referents into many of her stories, these two are perhaps the most explicit examples of literal retelling. T. C. Tanner may not understand his calling, but he follows it, while the grandmother acts on instinct, offering grace to the Misfit, which in turn is O'Connor's way of offering the same message to the reader; she makes the judgment literal and places it in the mouth of a fool from Corinth, Georgia, or a cackling grandmother from the hills of Tennessee. Her point is the same as Paul's: through the gospel, people can be changed; they can be transformed from "dishonor" to "glory," both now and on Judgment day. O'Connor speaks this grace through the only way she feels is likely to catch the reader's attention—an exaggerated foolishness.

4

The Terrible Speed of Mercy:
Flannery O'Connor's Backwoods Prophets

According to St. Thomas, prophetic vision is not a matter of seeing clearly, but of seeing what is distant, hidden. The Church's vision is prophetic vision; it is always widening the view. The ordinary person does not have prophetic vision but he can accept it on faith. St. Thomas also says that prophetic vision is a quality of the imagination, that it does not have anything to do with the moral life of the prophet.

HB 365

If Flannery O'Connor had stayed in the North after graduate school, perhaps the South would have been robbed of one of its principle figures. Her stories are so quixotic, bizarre, and strange that they often leave a lasting impression upon readers. Geographically, O'Connor could not have found more fertile ground for both her theological and artistic vision since "She was drawn to the Bible Belt for the same reason that H. L. Mencken was repelled by it—because most Southerners still take seriously the God whom the smart secular world has largely dismissed."[1] While her eccentric characters would not fit in any other setting, Walker Percy aptly noted, many "non-Southern Americans are still baffled by O'Connor and generally can't make heads or tails of what she was about."[2] In crafting her fiction, she was able to take advantage of a rich theological tradition as well as a familiar framework which was already in place since "the South still lives in a world steeped in Bible stories that belong to everyone."[3] O'Connor herself acknowledges that her bizarre caricatures found fertile ground in her Southern setting: "The Hebrew genius for making the absolute concrete has conditioned the Southerner's way of looking at things" (*MM* 202).

The American South's fascination with prophets is one that neither begins with O'Connor nor ends with the Southern Renaissance. In *The Mind of the South*, W. J. Cash notes the backwoods prophets serve as a tradition predating O'Connor's fiction. The backwoods preacher descends from the Southern religious tradition,

---

[1] Wood, *South*, 88.
[2] Walker Percy, *How to Be An American Novelist In Spite of Being Southern and Catholic* (Lafayette: University of Southwestern Louisiana, 1982), 1.
[3] Christiana Bieber Lake, *The Incarnational Art of Flannery O'Connor* (Macon: Mercer University Press, 2005), 31.

which demands a "passionate, whimsical tyrant, to be trembled before, but whose favor was the sweeter for that. A personal God, a God for the individualist, a God whose representatives were not silken priests but preachers risen from the people themselves."[4] Affirming this idea, Andrew Lytle in his essay "The Hind Tit," which is his contribution to the influential *I'll Take My Stand*, writes, "prophets do not come from cities... They have always come from the wilderness."[5] This tradition continues in Southern literature, as nearly 30 years after O'Connor's death, Dennis Covington's *Salvation on Sand Mountain* echoes these themes while documenting snake handling in Southern Appalachia. In his empathetic portrait of these backwoods prophets of the postmodern South, Covington writes, "Snake handling, for instance, didn't originate back in the hills somewhere. It started when people came *down* from the hills to discover they were surrounded by a hostile and spiritually dead culture," adding "The South hasn't disappeared. If anything, it's become more Southern in a last-ditch effort to save itself."[6] Covington's nonfiction profile reads like an updated version of O'Connor's Powderhead, as he highlights snake handlers equating themselves with their biblical exemplars. One handler claims, "'The Bible says you're gonna suffer for your faith,' he said in his soft Georgia accent... 'Look what happened to Stephen. I'd rather die of snakebite than get stoned to death.'"[7] Although the prophets in O'Connor's fiction must seem like an extreme fundamentalist caricature, Covington shows that there is certainly a precedent for such characters in the South, even decades after her death. As Lake insists, "The crazy backwoods Protestants in her fiction (such as old man Tarwater) who actually believe the Bible is true are her allies, not her antagonists. It is largely because of their fanatical commitment to the Bible that the South is different."[8]

The South offered her the context and ideal setting for her deeply rooted biblical stories—tales of prophets and prophecies, modern-day Moses and Pauline figures, religious visions, and damnations. However, O'Connor's eccentric messengers are not intended to be satirical, but rather part of an honest inclination toward her biblical source material since she has her characters "discover the literal language of God already in their own Southern slang."[9] Furthermore, these figures offer a striking correlation to their biblical ancestors. Unlike her ability to distort biblical materials, her backwoods preachers stay true to form. She does not write about the beloved disciples of the New Testament or the kings and virtuous messengers of the Old Testament; rather she is attracted to the eccentric figures of the Bible associated with austerity and fear—those who are so esoteric that they are avoided, at all costs, by preachers and amateur theologians. As True argues, O'Connor "brought a vision as accurate and piercing as any Old Testament prophets; and her work, like the prophets', was aimed at

4   W. J. Cash, *The Mind of the South* (New York: Vintage Books, 1960), 56.
5   Andrew Nelson Lytle, "The Hind Tit," *I'll Take My Stand: The South and the Agrarian Tradition* (New York: Harper, 1930), 206.
6   Dennis Covington, *Salvation on Sand Mountain: Snake-Handling and Redemption in Southern Appalachia* (New York: Penguin, 1996), xvii–xviii.
7   Ibid., 134.
8   Lake, *The Incarnational Art*, 31.
9   Ronald Schleifer, "Rural Gothic: The Stories of Flannery O'Connor," in *Critical Essays on Flannery O'Connor*, ed. Melvin J. Friedman and Beverly Lyon Clark (Boston: Hall, 1985), 89–90.

quickening the conscience and calling an estranged people to the tragic glory of God's chosen."[10] Thus, these prophet figures who appear throughout her fiction serve as literal renderings of their biblical counterparts (e.g., Elijah, Elisha, Shadrach, Meshach, Abednego, among others).

This unique vision comes from the way in which O'Connor viewed her own authorial role. Throughout her work, she considered herself to be a type of prophet, an artist whose work foregrounded such violent figures and acts as a means of pointing her readers toward redemption. O'Connor essentially stated as much when, discussing her own work, she writes, when "a writer has a freak for his hero, he is not simply showing what we are, but what we have been and what we could become. His prophet-freak is an image of himself" (*MM* 118). Certainly a purely biographical reading of O'Connor's backwoods prophets seems inappropriate here; however, it is interesting to note that O'Connor, if not directly declaring herself a prophet, does consider her own prophet figures to be an extension of her authorial function. However, other scholars have argued that O'Connor wrote her prophets as a reflection of herself and she "did so not simply by portraying prophetic characters, but by declaring herself, as writer, to be a prophet."[11]

It seems only appropriate that an unconventional author would present her readers with such an unconventional rendering of spiritual leaders since, unlike traditional depictions, O'Connor's prophets present their audience with a message of divine retribution. Mirroring their biblical counterparts, these spiritual emissaries bring an edict of certain doom, such as Lucette Carmody of *The Violent Bear It Away*, who proclaims "I've seen the Lord in a tree of fire! The Word of God is a burning Word to burn you clean!" (*CW* 414). O'Connor's "A Circle in the Fire" provides a similar analogue. As its title indicates, the story foregrounds the image of fire in the role of prophecy. This method is part of what Susan Srigley has coined as O'Connor's "purgatorial vision."[12] Much like Elijah, who lets "fire come down from heaven and consume" Ahaziah's messengers, or the fire which threatens to swallow Shadrach, Meshach, and Abednego, this story follows in the biblical tradition of associating fire with the message of God (2 Kings 1:10).

Beyond her purgatorial vision, O'Connor seems to pick up on the longstanding association between prophets of God and fire. In fact, God first appears to Moses in the form of fire: "the angel of the Lord appeared to him in a blazing fire from the midst of a bush … and behold the bush was burning with fire, yet the bush was not consumed" (Ex. 3:2). O'Connor re-creates this scene in her story "Parker's Back," in which Obadiah Elihue Parker becomes a modern-day Moses standing in front of a tree which "burst into flame. The first thing Parker saw were his shoes, quickly being eaten by the fire" (*CW* 665). Coincidentally, the biblical Obadiah is also associated with fire. When Obadiah and Elijah meet, Elijah is confronted by the prophets of Baal, so he challenges these false prophets on Mount Carmel: "Call on the name of your god,"

---

[10] Michael D. True, "Flannery O'Connor: Backwoods Prophets in the Secular City," *Papers on Language and Literature* 5 (1969): 212.
[11] Asals, *The Imagination of Extremity*, 217.
[12] Srigley, *Sacramental Art*, 135.

Elijah tells them, "and I will call on the name of the Lord and the God who answers by fire, He is God" (1 Kings 18:24). Elijah prays to God, "O Lord, answer me, that this people may know that You, O Lord, are God ... the fire of the Lord fell and consumed the burnt offering and the wood and the stones and the dust," as Obadiah, stunned, stands witness to this miraculous event (1 Kings 18:44).

Within *The Violent Bear It Away*, a title which emanates violent connotations, two of the principle characters, Mason and Tarwater, imagine themselves in terms of Elijah and Elisha. Ironically, both Tarwater and Elijah associate their ministry with fire imagery since even Elijah's ascension into heaven is associated with the imagery of fire: "Behold, there appeared a chariot of fire and horses of fire which separated the two of them. And Elijah went up by a whirlwind to heaven" (2 Kings 2:11). This fire imagery even appears in prophecies of the Earth's end: "the day of the Lord will come like a thief, in which the heavens will pass away with a roar and the elements will be destroyed with intense heat, and the earth and its works will be burned up" (2 Peter 3:10). In fact, this verse inspired a phrase from an old slave song, which James Baldwin's *The Fire Next Time* made famous:

> God gave Noah the rainbow sign,
> No more water, the fire next time!

The prophetic destruction, which is frequently associated with fire throughout the Bible, seems to fit into a pattern: regeneration through violence, as cultural critic Rickard Slotkin calls it. As Slotkin outlines, throughout history, especially American history, people try to use violence to justify their intentions. This theme is interwoven into the fabric of American history beginning with the colonists who:

> saw in America an opportunity to regenerate their fortunes, their spirits and the power of their church and nation; but the means to that regeneration ultimately became the means of violence, and the myth of regeneration through violence became the structuring metaphor of the American experience. (Slotkin 5)

Similarly, this theme is not limited to history; it has enmeshed itself in our culture, including our literature. Slotkin explains that "myths are archetypal or universal to the extent that certain conditions of life or psychological states or concerns are universal among men" and that narratives such as "the death and resurrection of a nature-god" or "the hero's quest in the kingdom of death for the boon of life ... are common to all cultures."[13] However, Slotkin applies this theory to the foundations of Early Western American Literature, yet it certainly has application to both Southern literature (with works ranging from Faulkner's *Absalom! Absalom!* to McCarthy's *Blood Meridian*) and Southern history.[14] As Charles Regan Wilson points out, Southerners "saw their

---

[13] Richard Slotkin, *Regeneration Through Violence: The Myth of the American Frontier, 1600–1860* (Norman: University of Oklahoma Press, 1973), 10.

[14] See Slotkin's *Regeneration Through Violence* (1973), *The Fatal Environment* (1985) and *Gunfighter Nation* (1992).

culture, rather than their society, as enduring. The reality of Southern culture's alleged sacredness was less important than the Southerner's conviction that his regional values and cultural symbols were holy."[15] This intrinsic holiness led to the myth of the Lost Cause. After the "Confederate defeat, the Southern civil religion offered confused and suffering Southerners a sense of meaning, an identity in a precarious but distinct culture."[16] These Southerners confused the failed nation-state with their own version of Christianity, leading to the belief that, like Christ, the South would rise again, as they sought regeneration after the destruction of the Civil War. Nearly 100 years later, Martin Luther King Jr.'s famous 1963 eulogy for the tragic victims of the Sixteenth Street Baptist Church bombing in Birmingham contains this same theme. King reminds mourners:

> The innocent blood of these little girls may well serve as a redemptive force that will bring new light to this dark city. The holy Scripture says, "A little child shall lead them." The death of these little children may lead our whole Southland from the low road of man's inhumanity to man to the high road of peace and brotherhood.

King's insistence that the act would lead to Birmingham's redemption not only proved to be correct—the Civil Rights Act was passed in 1964—but also provides another example of the South's legacy of regeneration coming through violent acts.

Furthermore, the idea of regeneration through violence certainly predates the American experience and can be found in biblical stories such as the Genesis flood account or the Egyptian captivity narratives of Exodus. These parallels, Slotkin points out, drew comparisons from "Puritans [who] hoped their communities and social, religious, and political institutions would be purified through trial in *America deserta*."[17] Throughout the Bible, there are numerous instances of regeneration or renewal following violence and often this violence is forecasted or even incited by a prophet of God, such as Isaiah, who phrophesies:

> From the wildness, from a terrifying land. A harsh vision has been shown to me; The treacherous one *still* deals treacherously, and the destroyer *still* destroys. Go up, Elam, lay siege, Media; I have made an end of all the groaning she has caused. For this reason my loins are full of anguish; Pains have seized me like the pains of a woman in labor. I am so bewildered I cannot hear, so terrified I cannot see. (Isaiah 21:3)

Isaiah delivers a message of renewal through destruction, which is so terrifying that it physically traumatizes the messenger.

Nowhere is this method of holy renewal through destruction re-created more faithfully than in O'Connor's backwoods prophets. Her archetypical prophets descend

---

[15] Charles Regan Wilson, *Baptized in Blood: The Religion of the Lost Cause (1865-1920)* (Athens: University of Georgia, 1983), 15.
[16] Wilson, *Baptized in Blood*, 13.
[17] Slotkin, *Regeneration*, 39.

"out of a tradition older than even any in the South" with "the biblical prophets" serving as her models.[18] It is out of this *tradition* that her backwoods prophets emerge, creating Christ-obsessed figures like the Misfit, who brings grace to the grandmother through violence. His terrible acts of destruction serve as a catalyst for the grandmother's spiritual awakening—and perhaps even his own—as "she reached out and touched him on the shoulder" (CW 152). Although she commits no major crimes, Mary Grace, in O'Connor's "Revelation," brings grace through acts of violence. She accosts Mrs. Ruby Turpin throwing a book at her head and whispers, "Go back to hell where you came from, you old wart hog," as if this were a divine curse (CW 646). The prophets in both "The Lame Shall Enter First" and "The River" bring both annihilation and death. The club-footed Rufus Johnson engages Sheppard in a test of wills over his own belief in Jesus and, ultimately, succeeds in converting Sheppard's neglected son, Norton. Yet the story ends with Sheppard's discovery of Norton's body, which "hung in the jungle of shadows, just below the beam from which he had launched his flight into space" (CW 632). Norton has killed himself, in order to join his mother in heaven. This death, coupled with Rufus Johnson's criminal activities, explode Sheppard's own tightly controlled world. In her short story "The River," Bevel Summers's message strikes a chord with young Harry Ashfield and, ultimately, brings a similar annihilation as Summers preaches:

> All the rivers come from that one River and go back to it like it was the ocean sea and if you believe, you can lay your pain in that River and get rid of it because that's the River that was made to carry sin. It's a River full of pain itself, pain itself, moving toward the Kingdom of Christ, to be washed away, slow, you people, slow as this here old red water river round my feet. (CW 162)

Young Ashfield literalizes Bevel's message: "you'll be able to go to the Kingdom of Christ. You'll be washed in the river of suffering, son, and you'll go by the deep river of life ... You'll count" by drowning himself in the river (CW 165). This message brings annihilation not only for Harry, who drowns, but for Mr. Paradise, the religious skeptic, who attempts to save Ashfield's life, but ends up as an "ancient water monster" standing "empty-handed, staring with his dull eyes as far down the river line as he could see" (CW 171). Even "Good Country People" includes a prophet figure who does not bring physical violence, but certainly a message of destruction. The shiftless Pointer seduces Hulga Hopewell into a barn loft and then steals her wooden leg, shattering her worldview as he tells her, "you ain't so smart. I been believing in nothing ever since I was born!" (CW 283). This tradition of prophetic/purifying violence foregrounds judgment reserved for the ultrarighteous (or in Hulga's case, militantly nihilistic) Christian protagonists. These prophets bring a message meant to humble the proud and literalize the advice found in Ecclesiastes: "Do not be excessively righteous and do

---

[18] Gary M. Ciuba, *Desire, Violence & Divinity in Modern Southern Fiction: Katherine Anne Porter, Flannery O'Connor, Cormac McCarthy, Walker Percy* (Baton Rouge: Louisiana State University Press, 2007), 123.

not be overly wise. Why should you ruin yourself? Do not be excessively wicked and do not be a fool. Why should you die before your time?" (Ecclesiastes 7:16–17).

Following in this biblical model, the same way that T. C. Tanner lives in the woods and operates an illegal still before taking his message of resurrection to New York City, O'Connor's harbingers of destruction defy traditional expectations. They are neither respectable nor affable. Instead, the backwoods prophets of her fiction often share at least one (or perhaps all) of three of the following biblical-based characteristics.

First, O'Connor's prophets are often marginalized from society, living on the fringes, isolating themselves either physically or through their bizarre and eccentric behavior. This, of course, has a strong biblical precedent, as O'Connor remarked, "the prophet is a man apart. He is not typical of a group" (*HB* 517). Throughout the Bible, "prophets bring a message that often causes their contemporaries to regard them as traitors, fools, or madmen" including many of the most prominent.[19] Isaiah was told, "Go and loosen the sackcloth from your hips and take your shoes off your feet" and walk around "naked and barefoot three years" in order to shame the king of Assyria for taking "the captives of Egypt and the exiles of Cush, young and old, naked and barefoot" (Is. 20:2–4). If walking around naked for three years wasn't strange enough, Ezekiel was told, "lie down on your left side and lay the iniquity for the number of days that you lie on it," lying on his left side for 390 days, then rolling over and lying on his right side for 40 days (Ez. 4:4). Others distance themselves from their parishioners: Elijah lived outside of civilization where "ravens brought him bread and meat in the morning and bread and meat in the evening" (1 Kings 17:6). The followers of Elisha lived outside of society on the Jordan: "so he [Elisha] went with them; and when they came to the Jordan, they cut down trees" (2 Kings 6:5). Amos was a shepherd living on the outskirts of town who "was called, he says, directly from his flocks to prophesy to the people of Israel."[20] Hosea is told to marry a harlot to show the Israelites that "the Lord loves the sons of Israel, though they turn to other gods"; and John the Baptist emerged from the wilderness wearing "camel's hair" and "his diet was locusts and wild honey" (Hosea 3:1, Mark 1:6). These prophets were often peculiar and strange, subject to the will of God, living on the outskirts of society a pastoral lifestyle which is commonly associated with Jesus Christ. In fact, Howarth argues that Christ himself was a rural prophet:

> The [Roman] empire's nemesis is an itinerant pastor, Jesus of Nazareth. Born in a stable and trained as a carpenter, Jesus travels the countryside to preach to farmers and fishers. His parables use simple rural images to attack official corruption, while his miraculous deeds transform soil and food into spiritual emblems. (16)

These reoccurring figures in O'Connor's fiction (T. C. Tanner living in a shack, Bevel Summers being the iterant preacher, Manley Pointer being a nomadic conman) are a modernized version of this biblical archetype. These messengers are still subject to the same will of God and do not (or will not) conform to the social norms of the twentieth century.

[19] Frye, *The Great Code*, 218.
[20] Jeffrey, *Biblical Tradition*, 35.

The second trait found in O'Connor's rewriting of biblical prophets is that they are often reluctant to carry the message, much like Moses, who is commissioned to speak to the Pharaoh in Egypt, but hesitantly asks, "Who am I that I should go to Pharaoh and that I should bring the sons of Israel out of Egypt?" (Ex. 3:11). Moses continued to deflect this divine calling asking, "What if they will not believe me or listen to what I say?" adding, "Please, Lord, I have never been eloquent, neither recently nor in the time past, nor since You have spoken to Your servant; for I am slow of speech and slow of tongue" (Ex. 4:1, 4:10). However, Moses does eventually embrace his calling, praying, "Please, Lord, now send the message by whomever You will" (Ex. 4:13). Similarly, when Jonah is told, "Arise, go to Nineveh the great city and cry against it," he "rose up to flee to Tarshish" (Jonah 1:2–3). However, Jonah does, eventually, go to Nineveh to preach against it. In the New Testament, even Jesus' disciples were reluctant after Jesus tells them, "they will hand you over to the courts and scourge you in their synagogues" and "You will be hated by all because of My name, but it is the one who has endured to the end who will be saved" (Mt. 10:17, 22). Following in this tradition, O'Connor's backwoods prophets are often uncertain, like O. E. Parker, who refuses to show his friends his tattoo of the Byzantine Christ, lest they persecute him saying, "O.E.'s got religion and is witnessing for Jesus" (*CW* 671). Echoing Jonah, O. E. is cast out by his friends in much the same way "Jonah had been cast into the sea" (*CW* 672).

The final biblical trait found in O'Connor's backwoods prophets is the prophetic message itself. They bring the message from God of "THE TERRIBLE SPEED OF GOD'S MERCY," which is both destructive and regenerative (*CW* 478). Both the biblical prophets and O'Connor's backwoods prophets often bring a message of violence and annihilation to their intended audience. Unlike Hoover Shoats, the for-profit prophet who preaches a message of sweetness, "Every person that comes onto this earth … is born sweet and full of love" and uses sophistry to try to lure members to his church, O'Connor's backwoods prophets bring a message of terrifying judgment (*CW* 86). Even the sacrament of baptism has violent connotations in O'Connor's "The River," as Bevel Summers grabs young Harry Ashfield and "without more warning, he tightened his hold and swung him upside down and plunged his head into the water. He held him under while he said the words of Baptism" (*CW* 165). Yet, following the biblical antecedent, there are no shortage of prophets bringing violent and destructive prophecies—divine curses. Elijah, known for his unconventional ways, prophesized to Ahab, "Thus says the Lord, [i]n the place where the dogs licked up the blood of Naboth the dogs will lick up your blood" (1 Kings 21:19). Amos, whose name "means either 'burdensome' or bearer of a burden'—i.e., bad news," was synonymous for his message, which "was one of strong judgment."[21] Even John's Revelation is so full of death and destruction that many readers and theologians alike completely avoid it. However, no other work in O'Connor's corpus better illustrates this tradition of destructive prophecies than "A Circle in the Fire," in which three young men arrive on Mrs. Cope's farm, thus re-enacting the story of Shadrach, Meshach, Abednego, bringing a message of annihilation.

---

[21] Jeffrey, *Biblical Tradition*, 35.

A purifying violence in "A Circle in the Fire"

O'Connor's profoundly prophetic narrative begins with an eerie description of the landscape of Mrs. Cope's farm: "the last line of trees was a solid gray-blue wall a little darker than the sky" CW 232). This image of the gray–blue wall, which is more than a subtle Civil War reference, and the image of smoke surrounding trees foreshadow the fire imagery explicit in the title of the story as well as its ending. This opening account offers the perfect corollary to the story's ending, as the narrative converges on a "column of smoke rising and widening unchecked inside the granite line of trees" (CW 251).

"A Circle in the Fire" centers around Mrs. Cope, another of O'Connor's complacent females—following in the steps of Ruby Turpin of "Revelation," Mrs. May of "Greenleaf," Mrs. Fox of "The Enduring Chill," Mrs. Hopewell of "Good Country People," and Mrs. McIntyre of "The Displaced Person." In a striking parallel of Mrs. McIntyre, Mrs. Cope, who runs her own farm, is accompanied by a naïve sidekick, Mrs. Pritchard, a lady whom Mrs. Cope views as inferior. Mrs. Cope's interactions with Mrs. Pritchard serve to illustrate her own smugness.

Things change for Mrs. Cope when she is visited by three boys—Powell Boyd, Garfield Smith, and W. T. Harper. Powell Boyd is the son of a former farmhand, Mr. Powell, who used to work on Mrs. Cope's farm, but died after moving to Florida. In a telling exchange, Mrs. Cope remembers, "Your father was Mr. Boyd and you're J.C.?" (CW 236). Of course, he corrects her, "Nome, I'm Powell" (CW 236). O'Connor has argued that the Bible had more cultural currency in the South than anywhere else: "in the South the Bible is known by the ignorant as well" as the educated, adding that "Its center of meaning will be Christ" (MM 203, 197). Hence, O'Connor believed that modern Southern readers will recognize the use of J. C. as an obvious allusion to Jesus Christ. Through her exchange with Powell, O'Connor establishes that Mrs. Cope is not the spiritual barometer of the story since, unfortunately, she is unable to recognize J. C. or his messengers.

For all of his time away from the farm, Powell has described Mrs. Cope's land in Edenic terms. W. T. Harper complains that "All the time we been knowing him he's been telling us about this here place. Said it was everything here ... Said he had the best time of his entire life right here," while Garfield Smith affirms that Powell "Never shuts his trap about this place" (CW 237). Yet, despite his affinity for this pastoral paradise, Powell and his friends are unwelcomed additions.

Mrs. Cope, a single mother, frequently boasts of her responsibility in dealing with problems: "I thank the Lord all these things don't come at once" as well as telling those around her, "We have a lot to be thankful for" (CW 234). Like many of the characters in the Bible—and O'Connor's own work—who seem to tempt fate, Mrs. Cope claims, "We might all be destroyed by a hurricane. I can always find something to be thankful for" (CW 234). O'Connor allies Mrs. Cope with all of those sanctimonious characters who brag of their own virtues—such as Ruby Turpin of "Revelation" or Julian of "Everything That Rises Must Converge"—since Mrs. Cope is not as thankful (or righteous) as she claims. In fact, it is Powell, more than any other character, who appreciates this farm.

In what seems like a bizarre parallel to the servant from Christ's message of the talents, Mrs. Cope is more interested in the preservation of her farm rather than its use, as she continues to obsess over all the possibilities of potential disaster on the farm. Hence, she is like the servant who, upon receiving a talent from his master, "dug a hole in the ground and hid his master's money" and told him, "I was afraid, and went away and hid your talents in the ground" (Mt. 25:18, 25). The purpose of the parable is to encourage readers to make use of their talents, while Mrs. Cope merely sits on her farm, fretting over its eventual demise.

Powell, on the other hand, emerges as the antithesis of Mrs. Cope. Although he has spent less time on the farm, Powell expresses a much deeper appreciation for its beauty. As Mrs. Cope repeatedly proclaims her thanksgiving, Harper later tells Mrs. Cope, that young Powell "aint ever satisfied with where he's at except this place here" (*CW* 239).

Due to Mrs. Cope's anxiety, this image of fire emerges as a reoccurring theme within the story. Every time readers encounter Mrs. Cope she "was always worrying about fires in her woods," repeatedly grumbling, "Oh Lord, do pray there won't be any fires" (*CW* 232, 233). When the boys arrive, Mrs. Cope forces them to sleep outside because she is convinced they will accidentally set the barn ablaze with one of their cigarettes (*CW* 239). In fact, Mrs. Cope's fear of fire is accentuated when she learns that Powell, a latchkey kid, once "locked his little brother in a box and set it on fire" (*CW* 241). Even O'Connor's descriptions reinforce the idea of fire as they stare out at the "swollen and flame-colored" tree-line (*CW* 241). In an ironic instance of foreshadowing, the frenzied Mrs. Cope humorously attempts to scold Garfield Smith for smoking: "'Ashfield!' she said, 'Please pick that up. I'm afraid of fires'" (*CW* 238). Much like her inability to recognize J. C., her misidentification of Garfield as Ashfield seems ominous, especially since the story ends with her farm set ablaze.

These young rapscallions, who sleep in Mrs. Cope's field, bathe in her pond, and run naked around her farm, fit soundly into O'Connor's archetype of the backwoods prophet. Although they do not display reluctance, these boys *do* live on the fringes of society since their "backwoods origins is a source of their strength," as they make camp in her barn.[22] For them, Jesus lives in the country rather than the city, which is why they leave Atlanta for Mrs. Cope's small farm. Those prophets who lose their faith in O'Connor's fictional world [Hazel Motes, Mr. Head, Tarwater] do so in the city, rather than those who find him "in the primitive surroundings of a Southern revival."[23] This is why the boys feel so comfortable in the agrarian setting of Mrs. Cope's farm. Furthermore, the three bring a message of destruction and vengeance. Echoing the grandmother in "A Good Man Is Hard to Find," Mrs. Cope is successful in controlling almost everyone around her, including workers like Hollis, yet the boys seem oddly immune to Mrs. Cope's demands. When Mrs. Cope displays a hypocritical piousness, asking the boys, "Do you boys thank God every night for all He's done for you? Do you thank Him for everything?," they, comically, like Mary Grace in "Revelation," are somehow able to ignore her sanctimonious display, staying "as silent as thieves hiding" (*CW* 241). Even

22 True, "Secular City," 216.
23 Ibid.

when she attempts to banish them from her farm, W. T. Harper responds, "We ain't bothering nothing of yours" (*CW* 242). In fact, the boys arrive with a distinct message for Mrs. Cope: "Gawd owns them woods and her too" (*CW* 243). Their refusal to submit to her will offers the parallel to Shadrach, Meshach, and Abednego.

The prophetic analogues between the two narratives begin not with fire imagery, but with the boys' repudiation of her food. While in Babylonian captivity, Shadrach, Meshach, and Abednego follow Daniel's example, after each man decided not to "defile himself with the king's choice food or with the wine from which he drank" (Dan. 1:8). Just as Shadrach, Meshach, and Abednego refused to eat of King Nebuchadnezzar's food, these three boys rebuff the food Mrs. Cope offers: "We got plenty of our own food ... We don't want nothing of yours" (*CW* 242).

The self-righteous Mrs. Cope parallels Nebuchadnezzar, the king who "made an image of gold" of himself, an image for others to worship (Dan. 3:1). Mrs. Cope is quick to tell others about her many great deeds: "I have the best kept place in the country and do you know why? Because I work. I've had to work to save this place and work to keep it" and continues, "I don't let anything get ahead of me" (*CW* 235). Mrs. Cope, resembling Nebuchadnezzar, not only thinks highly of herself, but expects others to defer to her. She is condescending to Mrs. Pritchard, views her employees as incompetent since she believed her "Negroes were as destructive and impersonal as the nut grass," and treats her daughter, Sally Virginia, with contempt (*CW* 233). These three boys, much like their biblical counterparts, are the only characters in the story who renounce her tyrannical attitude.

This prophetic connection becomes clear as the foreboding fire imagery becomes a reality when Mrs. Cope ignores their ominous warning "Gawd owns them woods" (*CW* 243). In the biblical narrative, despite the king's edict, Shadrach, Meshach, and Abednego refuse to worship Nebuchadnezzar and are thrown into a blazing fire. However, Nebuchadnezzar exclaims, "Look! I see four men loosed and walking about in the midst of the fire without harm, and the appearance of the fourth is like a son of the gods!" (Daniel 3:25). Recalling this famous incident, O'Connor has the boys "set the brush on fire," as the three "began to whoop and holler and beat their hands over their mouths" as the fire widened (*CW* 250). O'Connor leaves the readers with the image of Mrs. Cope standing "taut, listening" as she sees "in the distance a few wild high shrieks of joy as if the prophets were dancing in the fiery furnace, in the circle the angel had cleared for them" (*CW* 251).

Foregoing the ominous foreshadowing and reoccurring fire motif, she chooses to end the story with an overt reference to her biblical source material: the story of Shadrach, Meshach, and Abednego. For O'Connor, this fire symbolizes the "unquenchable fire" prophesized by John the Baptist, the internal "blazing flame" that "will not be quenched" (Mt. 3:12, Ez. 20:47). These prophets dancing in the fire bring a similar message of judgment and destruction, echoing the prophet Jeremiah, who warned that disobedience will produce a fire that "will devour the palaces of Jerusalem and not be quenched" (Jer. 17:27).

The image of fire as a means of purification appears throughout O'Connor's fiction. Tarwater sets the woods on fire on his way back in to the city, Sarah Ham's question to Thomas, "Jesus... where's the fire?" becomes the mantra of "The Comforts of Home," and these three prophets bring both judgment and destruction through fire, an important characteristic of the prophetic archetype (*CW* 581). These prophets bring the same message as another young O'Connor evangelist, Lucette Carmody, who exclaims, "The Word of God is a burning Word to burn you clean, burns man and child, man and child the same, you people! Be saved in the Lord's fire or perish in your own!" (*CW* 415). Optimistic readers can only hope that these flames are, ultimately, regenerative, as Slotkin suggests. However, Asals posits, "while the imagery of fire in O'Connor's fiction may be demonic, it is most often purgatorial... and what it signals is the infliction of a searing grace."[24] Thus, through their actions, offering both hope and humility, "the author obviously means for us to see the boys' burning of the farm as Mrs. Cope's and Sally Virginia's opportunity for grace."[25] This purgatorial cleansing, the inevitable razing of her farm, will, perhaps, bring a transformation for Mrs. Cope and all of those who surround her.

A message of annihilation in "The Lame Shall Enter First"

Although these three prophets arrive, uninvited, on Mrs. Cope's farm, this is not true of all of O'Connor's prophets. In fact, Rufus Johnson, who brings a message of both judgment and annihilation, is invited to stay with Sheppard and his son, Norton, in O'Connor's story "The Lame Shall Enter First." The title, like both "Revelation" and *The Violent Bear It Away*, seems to make a veiled biblical allusion, suggesting that "the last shall be first" (Mt. 20:16). Many have noted the similarities between this story and her second novel, *The Violent Bear It Away*, since both stories are about a messenger who prophesizes against an academic humanist, while attempting to make a convert out of the humanist's child. Although "The Lame Shall Enter First" focuses on Rufus Johnson's evangelizing of young Norton, *The Violent Bear It Away* centers on Tarwater's attempts to baptize Bishop. In both stories, the young child becomes the focal point of each respective prophet figure. In fact, "The Lame Shall Enter First" seems to serve as an extension of *The Violent Bear It Away* since both narratives concentrate on the prophets themselves as well as their respective academic antagonists. Yet, the difference between the two lies not in plotline, but in the prophets themselves.

In "The Lame Shall Enter First," Sheppard, a father who is ironically named because he provides no guidance for his son Norton, a clever reversal, is disappointed with his son's lack of intelligence. He invites Rufus Johnson, a club-footed delinquent who has tested a 140 on his IQ test, to stay with him and Norton. Similar to Tarwater, who is raised by his great-uncle Mason in the woods, Rufus has been raised on the fringes of society by his grandfather "in a shack without water or electricity" (*CW* 596). Sheppard is surprised to find that a boy with such a turbulent upbringing could have a high

---

[24] Asals, *The Imagination of Extremity*, 225–226.
[25] Sarah Gordon, *Flannery O'Connor: The Obedient Imagination* (Athens: University of Georgia Press, 2000), 167.

IQ, yet still be such a strong believer in the Bible. Throughout the story, Sheppard tries to ridicule away Rufus' religious tendencies: "That book is something for you to hide behind ... It's for cowards" and adding, "You don't believe it. You're too intelligent" (*CW* 627). However, despite Sheppard's attempts to assuage him of such notions, Rufus claims, "I believe it!" repeatedly exclaiming, "Even if I didn't believe it, it would still be true" (*CW* 627).

Sheppard's attempt to expose Johnson's foolish belief in Christianity begins with his attempt to buy him a special shoe for his club-foot. He continually attempts to win over Johnson with his good deeds, telling his son, Norton, "I'd simply be selfish if I let what Rufus thinks of me interfere with what I can do for Rufus," yet Johnson is able to see through Sheppard's humanitarian façade, claiming, "He thinks he's Jesus Christ!" (*CW* 609). Sheppard views himself "as the savior of Rufus Johnson" and explicitly tells Johnson as much; however, it is Rufus who responds, "Save yourself... Nobody can save me but Jesus" (*CW* 624). In both situations, Rufus' response is certainly ironic because he has the capability to outsmart Sheppard, rather than vice-versa.

Whereas this would-be philanthropist takes Rufus Johnson into his house, feeding and clothing him, he does so with a motive of shaping Johnson into another version of himself. In response, the young prophet reciprocates the only way he know how: he does "not so much accept charity from Sheppard, as share what he knows—the gospel—with the hungry and the poor in spirit," in this case, offering grace to both father and son.[26]

O'Connor highlights the battle of wills persisting between the two figures, yet by the story's end, it is Sheppard, not Rufus, who must concede defeat. Although Sheppard has already claimed responsibility for the deviant's actions, serial burglary, he quickly regrets his decision and begins wishing that "he had never laid eyes on the boy" (*CW* 625). After he learns of Rufus' criminal past, a past he had vouched for to the policemen, "his face drained of color. It became almost grey beneath the white halo of his hair" (*CW* 632). Sheppard loses his halo and is brought to earth when he realizes that by matching wits with Rufus, under the ruse of charity, he has brought about his own destruction.

This young man who claims, "I'm going to hell anyway" illustrates the complexity of O'Connor's prophet figure, serving as a model example (*CW* 626). To begin with, throughout the work, he remains marginalized from mainstream social norms in every sense. Johnson, whose grandfather has disappeared "to the hills" to "bury some Bibles in a cave and take two of different kinds of animals and all ... like Noah," comes from an extremely fundamentalist background (*CW* 607). Analogous to her other prophets, Johnson fits into O'Connor's archetype of "backwoods prophets in the secular city, who carry some overt manifestation of God's 'grace' to the modern world."[27] Moreover, he eats out of trash cans and lives on the street, the type of deviant behavior which disturbs Sheppard. Furthermore, Rufus is further marginalized by his disability, his club-foot, which, along with his high IQ are what attract Sheppard's attention. Although he does

---

[26] Baumgartner, *A Proper Scaring*, 54.
[27] True, "Secular City," 210.

not show the same reluctance for bringing his message as O. E. Parker or Tarwater, Rufus is undoubtedly reluctant to convert to Christianity. Whereas Rufus' message is directed at Sheppard: "Satan has you in his power... not only me. You too," it is young Norton who is convicted, as he begs Johnson to convert, "Repent, Rufus... Repent, hear? You don't want to go to hell" (*CW* 627, 626).

Johnson's message is one of divine judgment and, eventually, annihilation. His background, descending from a prophetic tradition, lends him an inferred credibility as he confidently informs Sheppard "this time it's going to be fire, not flood" (*CW* 607). This fire imagery becomes the central motif of his prophecy. "When I die I'm going to hell... the Bible has give the evidence... and if you die and go there you burn forever" (*CW* 611). True to its biblical antecedent, Johnson's message does not always find fertile ground; Sheppard constantly ridicules Johnson, but the message finds its home not with Sheppard, but with Sheppard's young son, Norton. Johnson prophesizes, "The dead are judged and the wicked are damned. They weep and gnash their teeth while they burn... and it's everlasting darkness" (*CW* 611). By bringing a message of damnation, Johnson quotes the parables of Jesus, where "those who commit lawlessness" will be thrown "into the furnace of fire; in that place there will be weeping and gnashing of teeth" or later where Jesus tells of those who will be thrown "into the darkness, where there will be weeping and gnashing of teeth" (Mt. 13:41–42, 22:13).[28] Rufus' message affects Norton so deeply that he commits suicide to join his mother in Heaven (*CW* 626).

Aside from his own prophecy, Johnson's actions mimic the biblical prophets, on whom his character is modeled. After his belief in the Bible is challenged by Sheppard, Rufus "tore out a page of it and thrust it into his mouth" and taunts Sheppard, "I've eaten it like Ezekiel and it was honey to my mouth" (*CW* 627, 628). Throughout her stories, seldom does O'Connor have a character explicitly elicit biblical allusions— neither the narrator nor O. E. Parker draws readers' attention to the Moses parallels— however, this is exactly what occurs here. This backwoods prophet intentionally alludes to Ezekiel, a situation which, at some level, parallels his own. It may be easier to view Johnson as an antiprophet, like the Misfit, yet he still brings the message of the Lord to both Sheppard and Norton. Ezekiel is told by God, "you shall speak My words to them, whether they listen or not" (Ez. 2:7). Although Sheppard clearly refuses, "what had enraged him [Sheppard] was the Jesus business," Norton hears his message and believes (*CW* 625). Despite the fact that Johnson is not a Christian, he clearly still believes in his own message. Echoing Hazel Motes, Johnson claims, "If I do repent, I'll be a preacher... If you're going to do it, it's no sense in doing it half way" (*CW* 627). By eating the Bible, Johnson acts in parallel with Ezekiel, vision:

> behold, a hand was extended to me; and lo, a scroll was in it... Then He said to me, "Son of man, eat what you find; eat this scroll, and go, speak to the house of Israel." So I opened my mouth, and He fed me this scroll. He said to me, "Son of man, feed

---

[28] This verse appears in several variations through the Bible, especially in Matthew. Notable examples include: Mt. 13:41–42, 13:50, 22:13, 24:51.

your stomach and fill your body with this scroll which I am giving you." Then I ate
it, and it was sweet as honey in my mouth. (Ez. 2:9–3:3)

His identification with Ezekiel illustrates his own associations with a prophetic
tradition, as well as O'Connor's own authorial intent. Rufus is not meant to be an
angelic Christ figure; rather he—much like Mason and Tarwater—is meant as a
contemporary rendering of these peculiar and outlandish prophets in the Bible who
come, not with a message of healing, but of destruction. This would-be prophet,
dragging his clubfoot and eating out of garbage cans, is a flawed vessel for such a
message, yet, ironically, Sheppard—a man oblivious to his own fractured nature—is
intent on trying to fix him, either by purchasing an orthopedic shoe or by trying to
dissuade him of his religious notions as he tells Rufus, "Maybe I can explain your devil
to you" (*CW* 601). Despite Sheppard's feeble attempts, Rufus succeeds, where the inept
Sheppard fails. Rufus' criminal spree indicts Sheppard, as this juvenile delinquent tells
the reporter that he let the police catch him: "To show up that big tin Jesus!" before
telling him, "When I get ready to be saved, Jesus'll save me, not that lying stinking
atheist" (*CW* 630, 631).

Ultimately, Johnson's arrest forces Sheppard to confront his own emptiness, as he
resolves to focus his own energies on Norton, "the image of his salvation" (*CW* 632).
Of course, Sheppard realizes his folly, which is why, much to his chagrin, Norton's
death is such a devastation, not because of a strong paternal bond, but because
Rufus Johnson has succeeded in bringing total destruction to Sheppard's doorstep—
obliterating both his family and his worldview. Sheppard can no longer hide behind
his own charitable deeds. Upon discovering his dead son, Sheppard, as if serving as a
bizarre counterpart of Julian in "Everything that Rises Must Converge," who remains
critical of all those around him until his mother collapses, is forced to realize his
own emotional vacuity and acknowledge the selfishness behind all of his good deeds.
Thus, the story ends with not only Sheppard's discovery of Norton but also Johnson's
reproach: "I lie and steal because I'm good at it! My foot don't have a thing to do with
it! The lame shall enter first! ... When I get ready to be saved, Jesus'll save me, not that
lying stinking atheist" (*CW* 631).

Baptism by the Holy Spirit and fire

O'Connor's *The Violent Bear It Away* presents readers with a novel centered around
her quintessential backwoods prophet young Tarwater, who represents the perfect
amalgamation of her previous attempts. This prophet-in-training combines elements
from both "A Circle in the Fire" and "The Lame Shall Enter First" as well as other
stories. From birth, he has been an outlier; trained as a prophet. Both Tarwater and
his great-uncle, Mason, live in a small, isolated shack in the woods, working an illegal
still. Furthermore, although he "knew that he was called to be a prophet and that the
ways of his prophecy would not be remarkable," Tarwater is extremely reluctant to
follow in his great-uncle's footsteps, which is why he runs away to the city to escape

his destiny (*CW* 388–89). Finally, at the end of the novel, this young prophet brings fire and destruction as well as judgment and obliteration, as he heads into the city to "WARN THE CHILDREN OF GOD OF THE TERRIBLE SPEED OF MERCY" (*CW* 478).

Indicative of her biblical source material, even the novel's title, *The Violent Bear It Away*, alludes to a violent imagery: judgment and destruction. Her use of Matthew 11:12, "from the days of John the Baptist until now the kingdom of heaven suffereth violence, and the violent bear it away," has confused many readers.[29] In fact, Sonnenfeld quotes *The Interpreter's Bible*, which states "We cannot be sure of its meaning."[30] This title is taken from a sermon during which Jesus praises both John the Baptist and Elijah as prophets, acknowledging that the kingdom of Heaven (and Christendom on earth) withstands violence. In Sonnenfeld's exegesis, he points out that "the kingdom of heaven does not suffer *from* violence; it authorizes it—and to the violent belongs the kingdom."[31] By referencing this verse, O'Connor foregrounds her own method of grace through violence, highlighted by these backwoods prophets and their biblical counterparts. It seems only appropriate that O'Connor, the author who viewed herself as a type of prophet, chooses this specific verse, hoping to shock the readers into recognition of the significance of holy violence.

Correspondingly, both of O'Connor's prophets in this novel bring a message of violence and judgment. Mason seems to spend his life courting (or imagining) antagonism and uses any obstacle available as a prophetic trial. Through his conflict with Rayber, O'Connor shows that Mason is unafraid to use violence as a means of making his point. Mason acts "as if Rayber were one of the modern prophets of Baal whom this latter-day Elijah had to vanquish."[32] The combative Mason even scrawled a note to Rayber: "THE PROPHET I RAISE UP OUT OF THIS BOY WILL BURN YOUR EYES CLEAN" (*CW* 422).

Of course, it becomes clear that the prophetic relationship established between Mason and Tarwater mirrors that of Elijah and Elisha, thus, meeting all characteristics of O'Connor's prophetic archetype. Mason, the contemporary embodiment of the biblical Elijah, is an eccentric prophet living on the outskirts who trains his apprentice, Tarwater, to bring a message of judgment to the city.[33] Even the origin of Mason and Tarwater's relationship seems to not only parallel but serve as a bastardization of the lives of their biblical counterparts, Elijah and Elisha.

When Elijah was hiding in a cave in Horeb, God spoke to him and told him, "Elisha the son of Shaphat at Abel-meholah you shall anoint as prophet in your place," so Elijah "departed from there and found Elisha" and "Elijah passed over to him and threw his mantle on him," thus signifying the beginning of their master-apprentice dynamic (1 Kings 19:16, 19). Yet Elisha's inauguration as a prophet comes under fantastic circumstances: as "a chariot of fire and horses of fire" appear and

---

[29] Douay-Rheims Version.
[30] Quoted in Sonnenfeld, "The Catholic Writer as Baptist," 445.
[31] Sonnenfeld, "The Catholic Writer as Baptist," 446 (emphasis added).
[32] Ciuba, *Desire*, 122.
[33] This message and its target (the city) seem to mirror Jonah's calling to Nineveh.

"Elijah went up by a whirlwind to heaven," Elijah's mantle is passed on to Elisha (2 Kings 2:11). In a fantastic parallel, these prophets live together in the woods, and Mason tells Tarwater, "I brought you out here to raise you a Christian, and more than a Christian, a prophet!" (*CW* 338). According to Mason, Tarwater's initiation into prophecy comes under similar circumstances. Mason reveals to Tarwater, "He had been born at the scene of the wreck" and was the lone survivor of the family (*CW* 355). Although there is no chariot of fire, perhaps the closest modern equivalent for O'Connor is a fiery train crash. This extraordinary event is what "set[s] his [Tarwater's] existence apart from the ordinary one and he had understood from it that the plans of God for him were special" (*CW* 355). Mason tells of finding and anointing Tarwater, a scene which evokes Elijah and Elisha allusions. Following his institutionalization, Mason was sent to live with his nephew, Rayber, when he sees Tarwater, his great-nephew. It is then that Mason hears "the voice of the Lord" saying, "HERE IS THE PROPHET TO TAKE YOUR PLACE. BAPTIZE HIM" (*CW* 376). Following his biblical analogue, Tarwater receives a direct revelation about his own successor.

Coincidently, it is Tarwater's birth which introduces the motif of violence in the novel as Mason follows God's instruction and kidnaps his great-nephew, Tarwater. When Tarwater's uncle, Rayber, a schoolteacher, finds out, he travels to Mason's shack in Powderhead to retrieve the young boy. When he arrives, "The old man appeared in the door with his shotgun and shouted that he would shoot any foot that touched his step" and even fired a warning shot, which missed Rayber (*CW* 333). When Rayber refuses to leave, "he had raised the gun slightly higher and shot him again, this time taking a wedge out of his right ear," a shot which will permanently impair Rayber's hearing (*CW* 333). The cycle of violence continues after Mason's death, since Tarwater has been taught "even the mercy of the Lord burns" (*CW* 342).

In a stunning parallel, Mason's life ends with one final Elijah/fire association. Rather than bury Mason, per his great-uncle's wishes, Tarwater "began to set small fires, building one from the other, and working his way out at the front porch, leaving the fire behind him eating greedily at the dry tinder and the floor boards of the house" (*CW* 361). As Tarwater leaves this burning tomb, he felt "the fire behind him. He could hear it moving up through the black night like a whirling chariot" (*CW* 361). Thus, O'Connor begins the novel with this explicit Elijah/Mason allusion.

By Tarwater ignoring his great-uncle's instructions—the old man had insisted that "the hole was deep. He wanted it ten foot, he said, not just eight"—O'Connor establishes that her reluctant prophet is both a conflicted and complex protagonist (*CW* 337). Tarwater had spent his entire life under Mason's thumb, living in a small clearing of woods called Powderhead. The pair embody O'Connor's method of recapitulating the Elijah–Elisha prophetic relationship, a parallel which is consciously evoked when Mason "compared their situation to that of Elijah and Elisha" (*CW* 356). Yet, they resist allegory since they are a more modernized version as the two operate a still in Powderhead. This is an irony not lost on Rayber, who highlights the trope of the ostracized prophet as he notices Mason's own bivocational ministry, "A prophet with a still! He's the only prophet I ever heard of making liquor for a living" (*CW* 358).

It is Tarwater's internal struggle between following his mentor and conforming to his uncle's secular existentialism which keeps him from becoming simply another static character.

Perhaps the strength of O'Connor's modernized portrayal of the Elijah–Elisha relationship is how she captures the eccentricity of the prophets. Besides operating a still and kidnapping young Tarwater, Mason has previously been institutionalized because of his religious zeal: "'Ezekiel was in the pit for forty days, he would say, 'but I was in it for four years'" (*CW* 369). Tarwater's character not only feels as if he walked straight out of the pages of the Old Testament, but he seems to believe he is superior to such prophets. This bravado, coupled with his institutionalization, obviously undermines his already-limited credibility, yet this also makes him a more peculiar and erratic prophet. Mason, "like Jonah[,] had called down God's judgment on an evil city, only to be judged instead," as he was institutionalized for four years.[34] However, although his institutionalization parallels the biblical prophets who were captured or confined, it also makes him an unlikely candidate for prophecy, the perfect exemplar for O'Connor's archetype.

Despite his early exit from the novel, Mason's presence haunts the narrative. He claims that in a vision God had sent him to kidnap and take "the orphan boy to the farthest part of the backwoods and raise him up to justify his Redemption" as he teaches the boy "to expect the Lord's call for himself" (*CW* 332). This prophet raises Tarwater in his stead, and though he has no formal training, Mason educates his grandnephew in matters ranging from "Abel and Enoch[35] and Noah and Job, Abraham and Moses, King David and Solomon, and all the prophets, from Elijah, who escaped death, to John whose severed head struck terror from a dish" (*CW* 340). One of the things that Mason teaches Tarwater is that by raising him as a prophet, he has saved him from a life of secular damnation living with his uncle, Rayber. However, throughout their relationship, Mason emphasizes the importance of baptizing Rayber's own mentally challenged son, Bishop, whom Rayber describes as "a mistake of nature" (*CW* 403). Tarwater, however, does not want to accept Mason's commission. "The boy doubted very much that his first mission would be to baptize a dim-witted child. 'He don't mean for me to finish up your leavings. He has other things in mind for me'" (*CW* 335). Although Tarwater tries to resist, his great-uncle's instructions—Tarwater's commission—continue to dictate his actions through the novel.

After setting the house on fire, Tarwater, ashamed by his actions, sets out for the city to stay with his uncle Rayber. Akin to O. E. Parker, the prophet who is oddly drawn to Sarah Ruth—his polar opposite—despite his hesitancy, Tarwater obsesses over baptizing Bishop, although appearing to be indifferent toward his cousin. When readers first encounter Bishop, it is through Tarwater's eyes. The young developmentally disabled Bishop is eating an apple, which "conjures up symbols of the myth of original

---

[34] Anthony Di Renzo, "And the Violent Bear It Away: O'Connor and the Menace of Apocalyptic Terrorism," in *Flannery O'Connor in the Age of Terrorism*, ed. Avis Hewitt and Robert Donahoo (Knoxville: University of Tennessee Press, 2010), 18.

[35] O'Connor also alludes to the biblical Enoch in her debut novel, *Wise Blood*.

sin and the consequences of Adam and Eve's eating from the tree of the knowledge of good and evil."[36] This act, watching Bishop bite the apple, the ominous symbol of man's own fallen nature, alerts Tarwater to Bishop's need for baptism. When Bishop leaps into a fountain in the park, Tarwater feels compelled to baptize him. However, "the schoolteacher bounded forward and snatched the dimwit out" of the pool just before the young prophet completes his mission (*CW* 432). Tarwater can only respond, "I wasn't going to baptize him … I'd drown him first" (*CW* 432). Yet, despite his obstinacy, he does baptize Bishop, ironically, while drowning him, leading him to fulfill Mason's own prophecy.

For all of his hesitancy, he is no Prince Hamlet. Instead, much like O. E. Parker or Hazel Motes, Tarwater is primarily a man of action. In an effort to reject his prophetic influence, he intends to drown Bishop, both to prove to himself that he is not a prophet—in the same way that Hazel attempts to prove that he does not believe in Christ in *Wise Blood*—and to prove to his uncle, Rayber, that he is a man of action. However, like Motes, Tarwater's resistance is futile. Provoked by Rayber, who leaves both Tarwater and Bishop alone on the lake, Tarwater begins to drown his cousin, yet "He knew with an instinct as sure as the dull mechanical beat of his heart that he had baptized the child even as he drowned him" (*CW* 456).

Tarwater's baptism, and subsequent drowning, of Bishop not only fulfills his great-uncle's prophecy but presents another literalization of a biblical predecessor. In his letter to the Romans, Paul asks, "do you not know that all of us who have been baptized into Christ Jesus have been baptized into His death?" and adds, "we have been buried with Him through baptism into death" (Rom. 6:3-4). Following in the footsteps of her story "Judgment Day," O'Connor's characters recapitulate Paul's metaphor by having Tarwater both baptize and drown young Bishop. This, again, highlights her tendency to literalize biblical stories. As Asals notes, "even the most rabid evangelists recognize the metaphorical sense of Paul's words and tend not to drown their converts while baptizing them."[37] However, as in her earlier story "The River," which relies on the notion of baptism and drowning, through O'Connor's method of biblical recapitulation, "the incarnation of biblical language in fictional action its reverses the relation between literal and metaphorical: as the Bible's metaphors become her literal actions."[38]

Whether he realizes it or not, his actions, drowning Bishop, force Tarwater to accept his own role as a prophet. In much the same way that Johnson serves as a catalyst for Norton's death, Tarwater's murder of Bishop brings annihilation to Rayber and forces this negligent parent to confront the void within himself. Although he is not present, he is somewhat complicit by allowing Tarwater to take Bishop to the lake, alone. Rayber realizes that Tarwater is both baptizing and drowning his son, but he "continued to feel nothing" and "it was not until he realized there would be no pain that he collapsed" (*CW* 456). Similar to Rayber's attempts to make himself "deaf to the

---

[36] Kilcourse, *Flannery O'Connor's Religious Imagination*, 234.
[37] Asals, *The Imagination of Extremity*, 78.
[38] Ibid.

Holy Word" by turning off his own hearing aid, Rayber must accept his own emptiness, the emptiness that his existential worldview creates (*CW* 415).

Unfortunately for Tarwater, even this act of baptism/murder isn't enough to convince him of his call. Following in the footsteps of Jonah, the reluctant prophet who flees from Nineveh, Tarwater leaves the city and returns to Powderhead claiming, "I had to prove I wasn't no prophet and I've proved it...I proved it by drowning him. Even if I did baptize him that was only an accident" (*CW* 458). In this sense, Tarwater is remarkably like several other O'Connor characters—Hazel Motes, O. E. Parker, T. C. Tanner—or even prominent biblical figures—Jonah or Paul—who, despite their doubts are all compelled by some invisible force to deliver God's message, in spite of the consequences. In a resounding reversal, all of these figures do the opposite of what they hoped, instead completing actions that they knew they were destined to fulfill. Tarwater knows he cannot escape his role as *prophet malgré lui*, and his actions and ultimate resignation to accept his own fate reflect that of his biblical models.

As O'Connor and others such as Frederick Asals and Susan Srigley have argued, the crux of this novel lies in the sacrament of Tarwater's baptism of Bishop. The entire action of *The Violent Bear It Away* centers on Tarwater's own internal tug-of-war to baptize Bishop. The novel foregrounds Mason and Tarwater as modern-day Elijah and Elisha; nonetheless, there is very little modern about the pair: they seemed to have walked directly out of the Bible itself. However, ironically, the eccentric Tarwater, obsessed with baptism, also seems to mirror John the Baptist. Sonnenfeld argues that "Francis Marion Tarwater *is* John the Baptist reincarnate."[39] John the Baptist, "an ascetic figure whose dress recalls the ancient prophets,"[40] urged for the "baptism of repentance for the remission of sins" and even, famously, baptized Jesus (Mark 1:4). Yet, Sonnenfeld's argument works, in this context, because John the Baptist, the prophet who emerges from the wilderness eating locusts and drinking honey, embodies the backwoods prophet archetype. He lives on the margins of society and shows up proclaiming, "I baptize you with water for repentance, but He who is coming after me...will baptize you with the Holy Spirit and fire" (Matt 3:11). John the Baptist is even the black sheep amongst internal family strife since his father was a respectable temple prophet, while John the Baptist was an anomalous outlier.

By using John the Baptist, O'Connor is able to connect the Old Testament prophets with the sacrament of baptism since John the Baptist is a throwback to the prophets of old. He is referred to as "a voice crying in the wilderness," and many believed him to be the reincarnation of Elijah, the Old Testament prophet (Mark 1:3). Tarwater, following in the footsteps of both Elijah and John the Baptist, serves as the exemplar of O'Connor's backwoods prophet archetype, fusing the Old and New Testament in this story. He becomes the reincarnation of an Old Testament prophet, who brings John the Baptist's (and possibly Paul's) message of baptism and death to the city.

Much has been written about the novel's end, where Tarwater comes face-to-face with evil in the form of the "pale, lean, old-looking young man" who gives him "an

---

[39] Sonnenfeld, "The Catholic Writer as Baptist," 447 (emphasis added).
[40] Jeffrey, *Biblical Tradition*, 406.

unpleasant sensation" (*CW* 469). Most believe this man, who offers the disgraced prophet tobacco and alcohol in a type of degraded communion scene where Tarwater proclaims, "It's better than the Bread of Life!," to be an archetype of the devil himself (*CW* 471). The man's heinous actions, drugging and raping Tarwater, force him to confront and embrace his own role as a prophet. Echoing the rape of Tamar and the general violence found throughout the Bible, this scene is alarming, but O'Connor reminds reader that Mason "is a prophet. And the boy... prepares to be a prophet himself and to accept what prophets can expect from their earthly lives" (*HB* 350). Following the structure of "A Circle in the Fire," the novels ends, much like it begins, with Tarwater setting the woods on fire. O'Connor leaves readers with the image of "a roaring blaze" and assures that "He knew that his destiny forced him on to a final revelation" (*CW* 472, 473). He realizes that his fate is now to "WARN THE CHILDREN OF GOD OF THE TERRIBLE SPEED OF MERCY" as he intends to return to "the dark city, where the children of God lay sleeping" (*CW* 478, 479).

This final image of fire becomes the essence of regeneration through violence and accentuates the correlation between her backwoods prophets and the regenerative/ destructive power of this fire motif in the novel. The purifying fire appears in Tarwater, as his eyes "looked as if, [they had been] touched with a coal like the lips of the prophet" (*CW* 473). Through this reference, O'Connor likens Tarwater with Isaiah, who cries out, "Woe is me, for I am ruined! Because I am a man of unclean lips, And I live among a people of unclean lips," right before an angel appears "with a burning coal in his hand, which he had taken from the altar" and presses the coals against Isaiah's lips stating, "'Behold, this has touched your lips; and your iniquity is taken away and your sin is forgiven'" (Is. 6:5–7). The coal that touches Isaiah's lips and burns away his sin is "God's glory expressing itself in a form never before anticipated."[41] Tarwater, aligned with Isaiah, who brings a vision of judgment and warning to Judah, is dispatched to bring a message of judgment to Rayber as well as "to wake the sleeping children of God."[42] The repetition of this fire motif emphasizes the connection between O'Connor's prophet figures and their biblical models (Elijah, Elisha, Isaiah, John the Baptist, etc).

While her backwoods prophets lend insight into O'Connor's own religious vision, Tarwater is especially important as the exemplar of this archetype—the backwoods prophet who fits all three categories: outsider, reluctant, and one who brings a message of judgment. The violence surrounding both Mason and Tarwater's vocation as prophets is "consistent with a larger tendency in O'Connor to view her characters as coming to God by way of the most outrageous opposition and antagonism."[43] O'Connor's repetitive use of theological violence in order to bring her readers/characters to this revelation has caused readers to shudder, like the reader who wrote to O'Connor revolted by Tarwater's rape. Yet, in her unpublished response, O'Connor sympathizes with such "repulsion at the episode" yet defends her own actions.[44] She asserts:

---

[41] Gardner, *John*, 121.
[42] Shinn, "Violence of Grace," 58.
[43] Ciuba, *Desire*, 155.
[44] Quoted in Cash, *Flannery O'Connor: A Life*, 332.

It was a very necessary action to the meaning of the book, however, and one which I would not have used if I hadn't been obliged to. I think the reason he doesn't understand it is because he doesn't really understand the ending, doesn't understanding that Tarwater's call is real, that his true vocation is to answer it. Tarwater is not sick or crazy but really called to be a prophet—a vocation which I take seriously, though the modern reader is not liable to. (qtd. in Cash 332)

O'Connor insists that, as strange as it may seem, Tarwater's prophetic call is, indeed, to be understood literally. In another letter O'Connor writes that she believes that Tarwater will return to the city and that "the children of God I daresay will dispatch him pretty quick" (*HB* 342).

Many readers are disturbed by O'Connor's use of holy violence; however, understanding the theological underpinnings and the biblical models, from which these backwoods prophets are based, helps readers recognize O'Connor's own intentions. By recognizing how "O'Connor repeatedly used the analogy of biblical prophecy to characterize the nature of fiction" and used these biblical models as the origin for these characters, the holy violence in her fiction no longer feels like a violation, but rather has a theological—and literary—context.[45]

---

[45] Asals, *The Imagination of Extremity*, 154.

5

So the Last Shall Be First, and the First Last: Biblical Reversals in the Fiction of Flannery O'Connor

The wolf will dwell with the lamb, and the leopard will lie down with the young goat and the calf and the young lion and the fatling together.

Isaiah 11:6

Although she is often remembered for her ability to turn a phrase, it was her penchant for ironic reversals which endeared O'Connor to readers. In classic stories, such as "Good Country People," O'Connor presents readers with characters such as Hulga Hopewell, who tries to disprove her mother's judgment of Manley Pointer as "good" by corrupting him with seduction and sexual initiation, but is outsmarted by the undereducated country boy. Other examples include the would-be iconoclast, Asbury Fox of the "The Enduring Chill," who, in a move of youthful rebellion, deliberately ignores his mother's admonition against drinking unpasteurized milk, yet finds himself more dependent on her than ever after he is diagnosed with undulant fever. Meanwhile, "Everything That Rises Must Converge" features a protagonist, Julian, who tries to teach his mother a lesson about social customs in the "New South," only to see his plans backfire as his mother collapses from shock. This pattern—where the teachers become the students, where children try to outsmart their parents, where tricksters fall prey—is a long-established pattern of reversal found throughout much of O'Connor's work. Although these twists are both humorous and shocking, for seasoned O'Connor readers, they have become expected.

However, readers are right to notice a pattern: her reversals are pervasive, beginning with her early juvenilia[1] through her final works. As many have noticed, O'Connor was the consummate ironist[2] who filled her stories with little ironies such as Ruby's vocal disdain of motherhood, though she is obviously (and obliviously) pregnant in "A Stroke of Good Fortune," and the much more prominent ironies such as the fact that O. T. and E. T. Greenleaf's loose bull kills Mrs. May in "Greenleaf." In fact, it is much more difficult to pick out a story in which there isn't a single ironic reversal. However, this technique should not be oversimplified as a gimmick or one-trick pony, especially since O'Connor herself railed against formulaic prose.

[1] In her early story "The Coat," Rosa's hubris, ironically, gets her husband killed.
[2] O'Connor's "Everything that Rises Must Converge" was reprinted in Wayne Booth's *The Rhetoric of Irony*.

However, as familiar as these turns are to O'Connor's readership, she never intended for these reversals to serve as a literary fingerprint (although they may have become just that); rather she hoped to both shock and teach readers, as Gentry suggests, "the value of the grotesque so often lies in its reversals."[3] In essence, O'Connor tries to introduce readers to the possibility of, and possibly the need for, reversal. It is only after her characters—and readers—have their expectations completely shattered that they can be restored, and it is through this annihilation that they find redemption. Whereas these reversals occur frequently, they have a distinct purpose. As Hazel Motes learned, in the world of O'Connor's fiction, it is only after you are blinded that you receive your sight.

This is precisely why O'Connor gravitated toward this pattern of reversals and why they fit so well into her corpus; however, much like her other literary techniques which made her successful, this method also has its roots in her reading of the Bible—from Genesis to Revelation, the Bible is filled with ironies. Yet, while critics are quick to notice the pattern of reversals, the biblical nucleus of these stories has been neglected. Not only does her fiction follow a biblical model of ironic reversals but, as I will highlight, O'Connor often alludes to these ironies to clue readers into her intentions. O'Connor's stories force readers to the conclusion that God does not play by our rules, whether it is the ever pious Ruby Turpin, who imagines God asking for her help, or Sarah Ruth, who is too holy to even set foot in a church. These characters are shocked out of their own delusions of righteousness.

It has been previously argued that O'Connor viewed herself as a literary prophet, which partially explains her dependency on biblical narratives and her attraction to the rhetorical techniques she found in the Bible. For her, all of these methods were a way of reaching readers: "I have observed that most of the best religious fiction of our time is most shocking precisely to those readers who claim to have an intense interest in finding more 'spiritual purpose'—as they like to put it—in modern novels than they can at present detect in them" (*MM* 165). O'Connor often reverses these characters' positions, expectations, and worldview in order for readers to recognize their own shortcomings. In essence, not only was she writing *about* the self-righteous Ruby Turpin, the spiritually blind Mrs. May, the antagonistically intellectual Hulga Hopewell and Julian, or the restless Tom T. Shiftlet, but she was writing *with* this very same audience in mind.

If the marks and annotations in her Bibles are any indication, O'Connor was attracted to these reversals that she found throughout both the Old and New Testament. She seemed especially interested in the Pauline epistles, which though noted for his logic in constructing arguments, contains several prominent reversals. Perhaps the best examples can be found in 1 Corinthians, a letter consisting of "a series of various forms of parallelism" including "a great number of paradoxes."[4] The letter begins with Paul's contention: "For Christ did not send me to baptize, but to preach the gospel, not in cleverness of speech ... For the word of the cross is foolishness to those who

[3] Gentry, *Religion of the Grotesque*, 94.
[4] F. M. Joop Smit, "'What Is Apollos? What Is Paul?': In Search for the Coherence of First Corinthians 1:10–4:21," *Novuum Testamentum* 44, no. 3 (2002): 236.

are perishing, but to us it is the power of God" (1 Corinthians 1:17–18). Echoing this reversal, "we find the same double move, first dismissal and then appropriation on a higher level"[5] as Paul asks, "Has not God made foolish the wisdom of the world?" (1 Corinthians 1:20). This question mirrors his later claim, which O'Connor marked in her own Bible: "For the wisdom of the world is foolishness before God" (1 Corinthians 3:19). Ironically, Paul's clarification of this reversal sounds like a synopsis of O'Connor's fiction: "God has chosen the weak things of the world to shame the things which are strong and the base things of the world and the despised ... so that no man may boast before God" (1 Corinthians 1:27–29). Paul realizes that the message of Christ seems foolish, something even Jesus acknowledges, yet this is the directive that O'Connor's fiction co-opts.[6]

Of course, Paul's ministry was not the only place where O'Connor found reversals. When Jesus heals the man born blind, he tells the Pharisees, "For judgment I came into this world, so that those who do not see may see, and that those who see may become blind" (John 9:39). Vision, and the reversal of it, is a repeated theme in her work, even though O'Connor realizes that, for her readers, this technique may be hard to notice, yet O'Connor realizes that her Southern readership might recognize the biblical allusions in her work and, more importantly, her intent. She optimistically noted that "in the South the Bible is known by the ignorant as well," and further commented, "Religious enthusiasm is accepted as one of the South's more grotesque features, and it is possible to build upon that acceptance, however little real understanding such acceptance may carry with it" (*MM* 203–204).[7] O'Connor's attitude toward her Southern readership, that the Bible is read and taken seriously by all, whether it is understood or not, explains her use of this technique of reversals. By taking the ironic reversals of the Bible and incorporating them within her own work, she acknowledged:

> I don't wish to defame the word. There is a better sense in which it can be used but seldom is ... This is a sense which implies a recognition of sin; this is a suffering-with, but one which blunts no edges and makes no excuses. (*MM* 165–166)

Flannery O'Connor's own explanation of her intentions seems to parallel a passage in her story "A View of the Woods." Mr. Fortune views his granddaughter as his young double, noting that watching her fight was "like putting a mirror up in front of a rooster and watching him fight his reflection" (*CW* 531). Aside from the veiled reference to Peter,[8] this seems representative of O'Connor's purpose in respect to both her technique of reversals and the genesis of these reversals in the Bible. Her grotesque and ironic reversals hold a mirror up to society, hoping readers would recognize their own traits in her characters. Her work was written with this audience in mind: as

---

5   Michael Goulder, "The Pauline Epistles," in *The Literary Guide to the Bible*, ed. Robert Alter and Frank Kermode (Cambridge: Harvard University Press, 1987), 484.
6   See Luke 10:21.
7   In unpublished manuscripts 281a & 283d, O'Connor elaborates on this idea. See the Flannery O'Connor Collection at the Georgia College and State University Library.
8   The rooster is often symbolic of Peter's three denials of Christ (Luke 22:56–61).

Kinney eloquently points out, "O'Connor's monstrous readers did not always get the point—and *precisely because* they did not always *want* the point, because too they *were* the point."[9] In doing so, she re-creates the axiom of Paul's message, Christ's message, and the gospels' message. By recognizing and celebrating foolishness, readers realize that to celebrate foolishness is to celebrate Christ's wisdom; to celebrate blindness is to celebrate God's ability to make them see.

The point is that O'Connor's biblically based reversals manifest themselves in different ways throughout her stories. In essence, when I use the term "reversal," rather than using the term monolithically, I am talking about many different types of ironic reversals which appear throughout her fiction. Within her many reversals, O'Connor often used a reconciliation of opposites (binary oppositions) or ironic duality,[10] occurring in the form of opposing images or pairs. Following this model, characters are often paired with a doppelganger, such as Hazel Motes, and the "True Prophet," Solace Layfield, in *Wise Blood*, or in "A View of the Woods," where young "Mary Fortune looked like her grandfather" (*CW* 525). However, O'Connor also pairs characters with their exact opposites, for example, "Greenleaf," in which Mrs. May's sons, Wesley and Scofield, are as different "as night and day" (*CW* 504). Often these pairings are so striking that they set the stage for her reversals, as she uses dualities to force her characters to "Believe Jesus or the devil... Testify to one or the other" (*CW* 163). Jill Baumgartner, in her analysis of "The Displaced Person," notes that the conversations between Mrs. McIntyre and the priest rely on both "unusual literalization of a scriptural truth" coupled with "exaggeration and pun, as well as on strange, unsettling juxtapositions."[11] For O'Connor these juxtapositions are intentional; she often sought "one image that will connect or combine or embody two points; one is a point in the concrete, and the other is a point not visible to the naked eye" (*MM* 42). By connecting and contrasting these points, she made duality a means of reversal in her fiction.

Ironic duality is not the only technique that O'Connor uses. In fact, her most stunning reversals are often polarity reversals—reversing the reader's expectations. Much to the delight of audiences, this has become O'Connor's literary staple; yet few, if any, have noticed that it is not only a means of dramatic irony, but rather a rhetorical tool to invite readers into an anagogical reading of her fiction. She hopes readers do more than laugh at Joy-Hulga's misfortune, at Sarah Ruth's reaction to Parker's tattoo, and at the Misfit's final quip "she would have been a good woman... if it had been somebody there to shoot her every minute of her life" (*CW* 153). Instead of solely a means of humor, these reversals enhance the theological dimension of each story. Much like the many ironies of the Bible, O'Connor's stories take the reader's expectations and offer the opposite. It is no wonder that "The Christological passage she most often cited

---

[9]   Kinney, "Fiction of Grace," 95.
[10] This rhetorical technique is used frequently throughout several books of the Bible, the most famous of which is found in Ecclesiastes: "A time to give birth and a time to die; A time to plant and a time to uproot what is planted. A time to kill and a time to heal" (Ecclesiastes 3:2–3), while Ecclesiastes Chapter 7 juxtaposes wisdom and foolishness.
[11] Baumgartner, *A Proper Scaring*, 72.

[Matthew 10:34] gives a precise description of the effect of her double figures: "Think not that I am come to send peace on earth; I came not to send peace, but a sword.'"[12]

By enfolding these reversals in biblical infrastructure, I argue that O'Connor seeks to use this method of ironic reversal to achieve the intended effects the original biblical reversals had on an audience. In "Parker's Back," I intend to show how it is the reader who finds his or her expectations reversed when Parker is shunned by Sarah Ruth (which helps us make sense of these names). In "Revelation," it is Mrs. Turpin herself who undergoes a great reversal based on the prophecy of Mary Grace—in understanding her struggle to understand this message, readers see their own selves reflected within Ruby Turpin. Finally, in "A Temple of the Holy Ghost" everything is reversed, the protagonist's own worldview as well as our ideas of religious leaders. Taking her cue from biblical narratives, within her fictive world, the ordinary is made sacred, a tattoo takes on sacramental importance, the self-righteous are humbled, and the unredeemable are offered grace.

Biblical synthesis in "Parker's Back"

Among all the stories in O'Connor's corpus, "Parker's Back" presents a unique problem. It is one of her most experimental stories and, as Bleikasten noted, one of "O'Connor's most explicitly religious stories" filled with chiasmus and biblically based reversals.[13] Yet, with the exception of the story's final scene, where the pious Sarah Ruth accosts Parker, most do not consider the story as a particularly poignant example of O'Connor's method of reversals. Rather, critically speaking, "Parker's Back" has become a dead issue: a literary problem already solved. Much of the scholarship focuses on the origins of the story, as most critics reference Karl-Heinz Westarp's scholarship, specifically his "Teilhard de Chardin's Impact on Flannery O'Connor: A Reading of 'Parker's Back,'" and concur that Teilhard de Chardin's *The Phenomenon of Man* serves as O'Connor's muse for the story.[14] Others reference *The Augusta Chronicle's* interview with tattooist Ted Don Inman and/or Burchett's *Memoirs of a Tattooist* as O'Connor's source material.

However, long before Parker comes home to unveil his tattoo, O'Connor has meticulously embedded significant biblical allusions throughout "Parker's Back," a foreshadowing for Parker's revelation, which sets up O'Connor's primary reversal. Although some critics acknowledge the theological underpinnings of the story, most give a cursory acknowledgment to the burning tree in "Parker's Back" as the burning bush from Exodus, but disregard the Moses motif, choosing to focus on the Obadiah, Job, or Jonah allusions. Although there is an obvious connection between Parker and Jonah, the locus of the story does not rest on the explicit Jonah allusion, following Parker's banishment, where "a calm descended on the pool hall as nerve

---

[12] Asals, *The Imagination of Extremity*, 121.
[13] André Bleikasten, "Writing on the Flesh: Tattoos and Taboos in 'Parker's Back,'" *The Southern Literary Journal* 14, no. 2 (1982): 9.
[14] See Steven R. Watkins, *Flannery O'Connor and Teilhard de Chardin: A Journey Together Towards Hope and Understanding About Life* (New York: Peter Lang), 2009.

shattering as if the long barn-like room were the ship from which Jonah had been cast" (*CW* 672). These two reluctant prophets, Jonah and Parker, may be analogous, yet by focusing solely on this allusion, the richer tapestry of "Parker's Back" goes largely unnoticed. Rather, few have explored the further biblical allusions embedded within this theologically rich story. By carefully considering Exodus as O'Connor's source material, while noticing the parallels between Parker's and Saul's conversion experiences, I will highlight O'Connor's method of reconciliation of opposites—pairing opposites as a means of subversion and reinterpretation. My central argument is that she not only uses this method of ironic pairing to subvert readers' expectations, but through her conspicuous use of naming, she evokes two seemingly contradictory biblical archetypes seamlessly into the same story—successfully capturing the biblical and integrating it into the modern-day secular world.

Ironically, one of the story's most important reversals occurs before the action begins, embedded within the biblically significant names. Not since *Wise Blood* has O'Connor written a story with such onomastic resonance. Both Obadiah Elihue and Sarah Ruth bear a "double-barreled Old Testament name," an indicator of their significance within the narrative.[15] O'Connor's protagonist, who carries a prophetic moniker—along with his wife—serves as an introduction to her reversal motif, using complementary pairings and juxtapositions as a means of reversal.[16]

There is a central irony regarding O'Connor's use of the names Obadiah and Elihue, especially since this antiprophet had "never revealed the name to any man or woman, only to the files of the navy and the government, and it was on his baptismal record," yet, he decides to disclose it to Sarah Ruth, on the grounds that she swears not to tell anyone (*CW* 662).[17] However, the real irony lies in the initial union of Obadiah and Elihue, a complementary pairing of two paradigmatically different biblical figures—a rhetorical technique that becomes a theme in this story. Not only are their names correlative, but the characters of Parker and Sarah Ruth are, in themselves, a complementary pairing. The name Obadiah itself should make readers recall the minor prophet. Although the name has been interpreted as "servant of Yahweh," Allen suggests that "the term doesn't represent the name of a prophet but is simply symbolic....it is a fairly common name, borne by about a dozen men in the OT."[18] Allen, in fact, argues that there is nothing to indicate that the name is anything more than a marker, indicating a minor or "cult prophet."[19] The use of the name Obadiah serves as the perfect signifier, representative of both prophet (or elect) and extremely commonplace, an apt description of O'Connor's protagonist who was "as ordinary as a loaf of bread" (*CW* 658).

---

[15] James Fowler, "In the Flesh: The Grace of 'Parker's Back,'" *Publications of the Mississippi Philological Association* (2004): 62.

[16] This is especially ironic when noting that O'Connor's use of biblical names is focused in Exodus, which is also known as the Book of Names.

[17] The very fact that Parker's first name is Obadiah, found in the King James Bible, rather than Abdias, found in the Douay-Rheims Bible and Latin Vulgate, alerts readers to the fact that she's using the King James Version of the Bible—which coincides with the story's Protestant version of grace—but whether this is of any real significance within the story is pure conjecture.

[18] Leslie C. Allen, *The Books of Joel, Obadiah, Jonah, and Micah* (Grand Rapids: Eerdmans, 1976), 136.

[19] Allen, *The Books of Joel, Obadiah, Jonah, and Micah*.

However, Elihue is a much more distinctive name attached to a more significant figure in the Book of Job, Elihu, Job's fourth comforter and the only character in the Book of Job with a Hebrew name. Many incorrectly view this name as a pointer to the Book of Job, viewing Obadiah as analogous to Job. However, Obadiah is no Job archetype; instead the name should be read as a direct reminder of Elihu, the youth who comes to comfort Job but who eventually argues that "Job should recognize his own lapses and repent ... instead of demanding the right to be the judge himself."[20] By viewing Parker's names as such, "Obadiah" as Obadiah the Old Testament prophet and "Elihue" as Elihu the final antagonistic voice in Job, O'Connor presents an interesting juxtaposition since Parker's biblical namesakes is represented by two antithetical figures: Obadiah is evocative of a true prophet, while Elihu is far from prophetic status. Obadiah preaches Edom's destruction for actually dealing falsely with Jerusalem, yet the "youthful interloper," Elihu argues, falsely, that "Job is a rebel against his Maker."[21] In thus turning on the righteous Job, Elihu is almost the embodiment of Edom, and for that matter Sarah Ruth, personifying the very deception Obadiah preaches against. Elihu, much like Edom, comes disguised as a friend, a comforter to Job, but instead condemns him in his misfortune. Despite arguing that Job is being punished for his pride, Elihu himself seems inordinately proud, which can be derived from the fact that the youth argues that "they that are aged are not the wise men, neither do the ancients understand judgment" (Job 32:9). Of course, this is why he "decides to speak out ... to refute Job."[22] This instance provides a perfect example of Elihu's disregard for his elders and the Hebrew tradition in the Book of Job.

The combination of these two names, Obadiah and Elihue, is a rhetorical move rich in self-contradiction, combining a condemnation of pride and falsehood (Obadiah) with the incarnation of pride and falsehood (Elihu).[23] The very name of O'Connor's protagonist lays the foundation for her technique, especially considering the two different sides of Parker: the side that is wholly preoccupied with vice and who only works "to pay for more tattoos" and, on the corollary, the side that feels compelled to bring the message of Christ, literally, on his back (*CW* 658).

Sarah Ruth, the very embodiment of O'Connor's method of reversals, like Parker, carries the dual Old Testament namesake. The names suggest the paradigm of virtuous Old Testament women: Sarah and Ruth. Sarah refers to Sarai or Sarah, who is remembered as the wife of the patriarchal Abraham, while Ruth is a reference to Ruth, the Moabite who married Boaz and was heralded throughout the land due to her loyal treatment of her mother-in-law, Naomi. The two ostensibly positive names seem oddly inappropriate for Sarah Ruth's character, suggesting Old Testament archetypes of virtue and loyalty. Of course, it is no accident that O'Connor chose these two figures; as Hebrew scholar Robert Alter notices, Boaz's first words to Ruth in the field[24] parallel

---

[20] Robert Gordis, *The Book of Job: Commentary, New Translation, and Special Studies* (New York, NY: The Jewish Theological Seminary of America, 1978), 555.
[21] Gordis, *The Book of Job*, 550, 551.
[22] Ibid., 554.
[23] The two names have the same bifurcated effect that Enoch has in *Wise Blood*.
[24] See Ruth 2:11.

"God's first imperative words to Abraham that inaugurate the patriarchal tales."[25] This connection which, Alter argues, "sets Ruth up as a founding mother" could certainly be the tie that binds the two names, and yet it makes the names more paradoxical since neither name seems to fit Sarah Ruth's character.[26]

However, readers may recall in Genesis, Sarah banished her husband's son, Ishmael, who almost died, in order to punish him for laughing at her own son, Isaac. This injustice is intensified when considering that it was Sarah who had arranged for Ishmael's conception by suggesting that her husband take Hagar as a concubine, and it was Sarah who later convinced Abraham to exile both Hagar and Ishmael. Furthermore, when God prophesied to Abraham the birth of his son, Isaac, "Sarah laughed to herself saying, 'After I have become old, shall I have pleasure, my lord being old also'" (Gen 18:12). Sarah laughs at God's promise because she did not trust it; thus, she is as wanting in faith as Elihu is in friendship.

On the other hand, Ruth, another biblically significant name, is notable for faith—trusting her mother-in-law, God, and Boaz under trying circumstances. Hence, Sarah Ruth is a perfect archetype suggestive of O'Connor's method of reversals. O'Connor pairs Sarah, the faith-poor wife who casts Parker out in the same way in which Sarah casts out Ishmael, with Ruth, the faithful, compassionate, and trusting woman creating another biblically rich juxtaposition. Thus, O'Connor sets readers up for this reversal when Parker returns home and acknowledges his prophetic calling (embracing the Obadiah part of his name rather than the Elihue); readers will expect Sarah Ruth to embrace her husband's dramatic, yet sacrificial act, but instead she curiously banishes Parker, in turn banishing the image of God—echoing Sarah rather than Ruth. While the holy Sarah Ruth seems bitterly content to crucify Christ and watch Parker, leaning against the pecan tree, in the front yard, "crying like a baby," O'Connor subverts expectations with her complete reversal, undermining readers' expectations of a faithful Old Testament symbolic character (*CW* 675). Yet, for those familiar with the biblical Sarah's betrayal, her literary counterpart's actions should come as no shock.

Furthermore, even their relationship, O'Connor's pairing of both O. E. Parker and Sarah Ruth, presents another complementary pairing. Although Parker may be a man with a numinous awareness, he is, at the same time, a paradigm of "quotidian complacency."[27] Parker carries the noteworthy distinction of a biblical name; however, he prefers to use only his last name, which seems to only affirm his own apathy. Yet, his biblical namesake alone implies that, like many of O'Connor's reluctant prophets, there is more to Parker than meets the eye. Of course, this, in and of itself, seems to be a reversal since upon first encountering Parker, readers are convinced he is an exemplar of self-indulgence whose very means of existence are his tattoos. Oddly enough, Parker, who is obsessed with tattoos, finds a sense of emptiness behind his skin art,

[25] Gen. 12:1; Robert Alter, "Introduction to the Old Testament," in *The Literary Guide to the Bible.* ed. Robert Alter and Frank Kermode (Cambridge: Harvard University Press, 1987), 13–14.

[26] Alter, "Introduction to the Old Testament," 14.

[27] Eben Hewitt, "Diapsalmata and Numinous Recapitulation: The Tropology of 'Parker's Back,'" *Proceedings: Northeast Regional Meeting of the Conference on Christianity and Literature* (Weston, MA: Conference on Christianity, 1996), 62.

realizing that, aesthetically, "the effect was not of one intricate arabesque of colors but of something haphazard and botched" (*CW* 659). Readers realize that there must be something more to this puzzling protagonist.

Sarah Ruth is described as a woman who is "plain, plain," and the complete opposite of the ornamental Parker (*CW* 655). Although he suspects that she secretly "liked everything she said she didn't," she tells Parker that his tattoos—his only distinguishing feature—are "no better than what a fool Indian would do" (*CW* 660). Sarah Ruth, the daughter of "a Straight Gospel preacher" who is "away, spreading it in Florida," refers to Parker's tattoos as "vanity of vanities," an allusion to Ecclesiastes 1:2[28] (*CW* 662). Through her namesake alone, O'Connor gives readers the expectation that the zealous, Bible-quoting, hard-line fundamentalist, who is always "sniffing up sin," will be the moral compass of the story (*CW* 655). However, this initial scene sets the foundation for O'Connor's reversal since Sarah Ruth is by no means the spiritual barometer in the story. The eccentrically pious Sarah Ruth has developed a Pharisaical version of Christianity, in which she forces Parker to get "married in the County Ordinary's office because Sarah Ruth thought churches were idolatrous" (*CW* 663). Needless to say, Parker and Sarah Ruth share a rather unhappy and unaffectionate marriage, serving as just another example of O'Connor's technique of ironic reversals, as Sarah Ruth, in many ways, resembles T. C. Tanner, as the two spend the majority of their time talking about judgment day.

If the names and the initial pairing of these two characters are the most apparent juxtaposition that O'Connor uses to reverse readers' expectations, her depiction of Parker as synthesis of biblical prophets is, perhaps, the most interesting use of this technique. Despite the initial humor, the story, for all intents and purposes, begins the moment Parker slams his tractor into "the tree reaching out to grasp him" and is thrown from the tractor exclaiming, "GOD ABOVE!" (*CW* 665). This scene establishes Parker as the Mosiac prophet, since O. E. Parker, much like Moses, restless, living as a shepherd in Midian, runs from God, living an aimlessly solipsistic existence. When his lewd behavior—besides the tattoos, he "began to drink beer and get in fights"— incited his mother to drag him to church, Parker, in an act of rebellion and spite, joined the Navy to avoid going to church (*CW* 658). Yet, like Moses, God gets Parker's attention in a similar fashion: as "the tractor crashed upside-down into the tree and burst into flame," Parker "saw ... his shoes, quickly being eaten by the fire" (*CW* 665). This passage, much like the barroom scene that proceeds it, has an obvious biblical significance, reiterating the image of God commanding Moses, in front of the burning bush: "remove your sandals from your feet, for the place on which you are standing is holy ground" (Ex. 3:5). At that moment, Parker "knew that there had been a great change in his life," a catastrophic incident indicative of O'Connor's prophetic motif with a jaded Parker as a modern-day Moses (*CW* 666).

Ironically, in her essay "Catholic Novelists and Their Readers," O'Connor comments that "The Lord doesn't speak to the novelist as he did to his servant Moses, mouth to mouth," yet O'Connor has rewritten this scene with Moses in mind (*MM* 181).

---

[28] "Vanity of vanities! All is vanity."

However, the connections extend past the burning bush allusion to include Moses' other direct encounter with God. As Parker scrambles up, "he could feel the hot breath of the burning tree on his face" (*CW* 665). This "hot breath" O'Connor alludes to is more than just the heat from the fire, but the presence of God. In Exodus 34, God summons Moses to the top of Mt. Sinai; as he journeys to the top, "the Lord descended in the cloud and stood there with him as he called upon the name of the Lord. Then the Lord passed by in front of him" (Ex. 34:5–6). Unaware of the result of his direct communion with the Lord, Moses, upon descending from Mount Sinai, "did not know that the skin of his face shone because of his speaking with him" (Ex. 34:29).[29] Thus, the heat that Parker feels on his face is much like the heat of God's presence. Furthermore, even as he leaves the burning tractor, Parker "collapsed on his knees twice," much the way that "Moses made haste to bow low toward the earth and worship" (*CW* 665, Ex. 34:8). This conversion scene, then, alludes not only to Moses in front of the burning bush receiving his call from God but also to his direct communion with God on top of Mount Sinai. By synthesizing both of Moses' encounters into one powerful scene, O'Connor emphasizes the transformation of Parker's life and foreshadows Parker's prophetic destiny.

As is often the case with prophecy, this event serves as the catalyst for the rest of the story. With his numinous awareness, Parker proves to be much more spiritually attuned than the ardently fundamentalistic Sarah Ruth since he "obeyed whatever instinct of this kind" (*CW* 673). Immediately following Parker's encounter with the burning tree, he, instinctively, drives straight for the tattoo parlor, knowing "there had been a great change in his life … It was for all intents accomplished" (*CW* 666). Browsing through a book of possible tattoos, he passes the Byzantine Christ "with all demanding eyes" and a voice immediately tells him to "GO BACK" (*CW* 667). Parker, unwittingly subject to an invisible force, demands to have the tattoo put on his back. Yet, while the tattoo is of Christ's face, even the process by which the face of the Byzantine Christ is etched into Parker's back could be said to, metaphorically, echo the Mosaic motif in the story. Upon choosing the tattoo, Parker demands the artist start immediately. When "the artist said he was ready to quit," Parker is able to get his first look at the tattoo (*CW* 668). Upon examining it, Parker notices that it "was almost completely covered with little red and blue and ivory and saffron squares," which leads Parker to believe he has been duped (*CW* 668). However, the artist uses small squares to form an image; thus, this image of Christ is created from a mosaic. This tattoo, a mosaic on Parker's back, could very well be a punning parallel to the Mosaic motifs circulating throughout the story—the epitome of the Mosaic analogues present throughout Parker's conversion experience.

Furthermore, this tattoo—Christ inscribed on Parker's back—is wholly suggestive of Moses receiving the inscription of the Law. Parker, like Moses, faces and inscribes God's message. Parker goes so far as to have God's eyes boring into his skin, as he

---

[29] NASB edition—According to Propp, there are three rival interpretations: "(a) Moses's face shone; (b) Moses' skin was made horny; (c) Moses' forehead sprouted horns … suffice it to say that Moses comes down the mountain terrifyingly altered" (618).

literally carries God on his back and realizes that "The eyes that were now forever on his back were eyes to be obeyed" (*CW* 672). Much the same way that the Law of Moses becomes the focal point of Exodus, Parker's inscription becomes the focal point of "Parker's Back," since the title alludes to both the anatomical significance as well as the implication of Parker's return, an ominous foreboding that Parker will, indeed, "GO BACK" (*CW* 667).

Yet, the Parker–Moses parallel is reinforced as Parker, immediately after receiving his tattoo, returns to the pool hall he used to frequent. Despite Parker's objections, the men "pulled up his shirt" to reveal his new tattoo, only to be alarmed at the image, at which point, Parker's "shirt fell again like a veil over the face" (*CW* 671). The tattoo takes on a greater significance with this allusion, reminiscent of Exodus 34 as Moses stands before the face of God at Mt. Sinai. When Moses returns, "Aaron and all the sons of Israel saw Moses, behold, the skin of his face shone, and they were afraid" (Ex. 34:30). Therefore, as others were fearful to approach Moses, after he finished "speaking with them, he [Moses] put a veil over his face. But whenever Moses went in before the Lord to speak with Him, he would take off the veil until he came out" (Ex. 34:33–34). This veil imagery is not a coincidence but serves to remind readers of the gravity of the situation. Hence, Parker's shirt acts as a veil for Christ's face tattooed on his back, since displaying the tattoo elicits the same fear that Moses' unveiled face educes for his peers. The veil is a very powerful symbol in Exodus since the veil between God and man, placed in the arc of the covenant represents the distance between the two, as God tells Moses, "And the veils shall be hanged on with rings … and the sanctuary, and the holy of holies shall be divided with it" (Ex. 26:33). In this case, Parker's shirt literally serves as the veil separating the face of God from the men in the pool hall.

O'Connor extends and enriches the Parker–Moses connection as Parker—drunk and confused—decides to, once again, follow his spiritual instinct and "GO BACK" to Sarah Ruth because "She would know what he had to do" (*CW* 672). When Parker returns home, he finds that Sarah Ruth has locked him out of the house and refuses to let him in until he acknowledges his name. As Parker stands locked out of his own home, it is not for a lack of trying that he is refused entry; "it's me, old O. E., I'm back" (*CW* 673). It is only when he finally acknowledges his name that he understands his own transformation:

> Parker bent down and put his mouth near the stuffed keyhole. "Obadiah," he whispered and all at once he felt the light pouring through him, turning his spider web soul into a perfect arabesque of colors, a garden of trees and birds and beasts. (*CW* 673)

Parker feels a change to the "haphazard and botched" "panner-rammer" of his soul that comes with his acknowledgment of his name, an embracing of his prophetic status (*CW* 659, 664). Ironically, as in "The Lame Shall Enter First" or "Good Country People," it is not always the believer who becomes the agent of grace; it is Sarah Ruth's actions which force Parker's acknowledgment of his name and, in turn, his fate.

Yet, readers cannot realize the full impact of Parker's tattoo until he enters the house, removes his shirt, and turns his back to Sarah Ruth, crying, "Look at it!" and asking, "Don't you know who it is?" (*CW* 674). Once again, O'Connor connects both Parker and Moses, as this scene parallels God telling Moses:

> "You cannot see My face, for no man can see Me and live!" Then the LORD said, "Behold, there is a place by Me, and you shall stand there on the rock; and it will come about, while My glory is passing by, that I will put you in the cleft of the rock and cover you with My hand until I have passed by. Then I will take My hand away and you shall see My back, but my face shall not be seen." (Ex. 33:20–23)

God has told Moses that he shall display his back to Moses, as God "passed before" Moses (Ex. 34:6). Of course, it might be hard to understand the connection between God exposing his back to Moses and Parker doing the same for Sarah Ruth. However, Fokkelman notes that "the God of Israel performs a self-revelation which serves believers as a credo."[30] As O'Connor was well aware, God's self-revelation is a way of acknowledging prophetic status. This "self-revelation," as Fokkelman argues, demonstrates Israel's importance as "the chosen people," yet Moses' status as chosen, perhaps even conscripted, certainly mirrors that of O. E. Parker since it is through revelation that both men are imbued with sacralized status.[31]

As God shows Moses his back, while hiding him in a cleft on Mt. Sinai, Parker, in a similar fashion, bares his back to Sarah Ruth. Parker, as well as the reader, believes that a religious-themed tattoo will please her; however, the ultimate irony lies in Sarah Ruth's response as she stands face-to-face with the Byzantine Christ and exclaims, "It ain't anybody I know," dismissing the image as "Idolatry!" (*CW* 674). To complete the parallel, much like the Pharaoh in Exodus, Sarah Ruth's heart hardens and she grabs a broom and proceeds to beat the tattoo until welts form on the face of Christ.

The reformed Parker "felt not quite like himself"; rather he is described as feeling "as if he were himself but a stranger to himself, driving into a new country," a nearly explicit reference to the "stranger in a foreign country" reference found in Exodus (*CW* 672, Ex. 2:22). By the story's end, the Moses allusion comes full circle, as both men, by standing in the presence of God and accepting their, respective, commission, will never be the same. In embracing his own name of Obadiah Elihue, Parker is doing more than accepting his given name; he is accepting his prophetic calling and submitting himself to the will of "the all demanding eyes" of Christ tattooed on his back (*CW* 667).

That Jesus should be imprinted on the back of this modernized Moses, in a way, makes perfect sense. Throughout the New Testament, the teachings of Jesus continually reflect those of Moses. During his famous Sermon on the Mount, Christ reiterates, "Do not think I came to abolish the Law or the Prophets; I did not come to abolish but to fulfill," arguing that his purpose is to serve as the realization of the Law

---

[30] J. P. Fokkelman, "Exodus," *The Literary Guide to the Bible*, ed. Robert Alter and Frank Kermode (Cambridge: Harvard University Press, 1987), 63.

[31] Ibid., 64.

of Moses (Mt. 5:17). Furthermore, throughout his ministry, Christ often quotes from Exodus ("Love the Lord your God with all your heart"; "You shall love your neighbor as yourself"), reiterating the teachings of Moses (Mark 12:30, 31). Moreover, during the transfiguration, "Elijah appeared to them along with Moses; and they were talking with Jesus" (Mark 9:3). Thus, Moses' appearance on the mountain, reminiscent of Mt. Sinai, only strengthens the relationship between the two figures. Throughout the story, Parker's character echoes this chiasmic relationship since he is an archetype of the one to bring the law, yet he is branded with the image of Christ, the fulfillment of this law.

Few have noticed the extent that O'Connor uses the Exodus parallel—the way in which Parker literally brings Christ on his back to Sarah Ruth, who clings to the Law of Moses—as the source material for her story. However, while Parker is an archetype of Moses, there is another biblical allusion that should be noted within this story, an allusion that extends O'Connor's use of complementary pairings as part of the story's system of reversals. Parker is both Mosaic and a bearer of Christ, which is why O'Connor contrasts him with the figure of Paul. Rivaling Hazel Motes in complexity, O'Connor has introduced both Moses and Saul allusions into O. E. Parker's character. Parker's transformation, indirectly, mirrors Saul's conversion on the road to Damascus, an allusion which should be considered to understand the full resonance of the story.

Although Parker's conversion scene is reminiscent of Moses' encounter with the burning bush, there is also a striking similarity to Paul's conversion scene, which A. D. Nock recounts as "the first conversion to Christianity of which we have knowledge."[32] As Parker comes face-to-face with a fire, Saul is encroached upon when "suddenly a light from heaven shined round about him. And falling on the ground, he heard a voice" (Acts 9:3–4). This light from heaven to which Saul is subject corresponds with the analogous flaming tree. Both Saul and Parker are thrown to the ground and are each subject to the same pair of "all demanding eyes" of Christ (*CW* 667). Whereas Parker feels the "hot breath of the burning tree on his face," Saul "saw nothing," being physically blinded by his encounter with God (*CW* 665, Acts 9:8). Undergoing a drastic spiritual transformation, he is commanded to "arise, and go into the city, and there it shall be told thee what thou must do," at which point, Saul, in God's grip, must follow his command (Acts 9:7). Parker, immediately after the tree fire conversion experience, is in a similar state, as he "did not allow himself to think on the way to the city. He only knew that there had been a great change in his life, a leap forward into a worse unknown, and that there was nothing he could do about it" (*CW* 666). Thus, Parker rising up off the ground to head into the city is amazingly like Saul, who is also told to rise up and head toward the city.

The pair not only have similar conversion experiences but also undergo prophetic transformations symbolized by a name change. Following his blinding, Ananias, taking instruction from God, lays his hands on Saul proclaiming:

---

[32] A. D. Nock, *Conversion: The Old and the New in Religion from Alexander the Great to Augustine of Hippo* (London: Oxford at the Clarendon Press, 1933), 191.

"Brother Saul, the Lord Jesus hath sent me, he that appeared to thee in the way as thou camest; that thou mayest receive thy sight, and be filled with the Holy Ghost." And immediately there fell from his eyes as it were scales, and he received his sight; and rising up, he was baptized. And when he had taken meat, he was strengthened. (Acts 9:17–19)

To symbolize his transformation, his name is changed, as "Saul turns to Paul."[33] Evocative of this shift, when Parker arrives home Sarah Ruth forces him to acknowledge his name—his full name: "Obadiah ... Obadiah Elihue! he whispered" (CW 673). The moment he does so, "he felt the light pouring through him, turning his spider web soul into a perfect arabesque of colors, a garden of trees and birds and beasts" (CW 673). This act completes Parker's transformation, allowing him to accept his prophetic sight through the confirmation of his first name, Obadiah, while simultaneously acknowledging the more humbling Elihue.

Both epiphanies lead the men to accept prophetic charges and their name changes reflect the spiritual transformation they each undergo. Parker embraces his full name of Obadiah Elihue, a name he previously disdained since "He had never revealed the name to any man or woman, only the files of the navy, the government, and it was on his baptismal record" (CW 662). Saul, on the other hand, after his conversion becomes known as Paul. With both men, the name change signals the religious paradigm shift that follow.

This use of the Saul/Paul–Moses connection, ultimately, underscores the nature of O'Connor's authorial intent. As Fitzmyer notes, "The Lucan account of Saul's call has often been compared with the call of prophets in the OT," which partially explains O'Connor's use of the two figures.[34] However, Fitzmyer highlights the fundamental difference, arguing that the call stories in the Old Testament "are recounted as a commission for a special mission, but not as a call to change one's way of life, which is the burden of the call of Saul: he is to become the risen Christ's chosen instrument for the evangelization of Gentiles."[35] Readers get the sense that Parker, alienated and ostracized by his friends and family, like Saul, will undergo a major life change. Thus, Parker serves as the conduit bridging Moses from the Old Testament with Paul from the New Testament, while reverberating Paul's message:

For He says to Moses, "I will have mercy on whom I have mercy and I will have compassion on whom I have compassion." So then it *does* not *depend* on the man who wills or the man who runs, but on God who has mercy. (Rom. 9:15–16)

All three figures, Parker, Paul, and Moses embody Paul's own claims that it does not depend on the man who runs, since all three ran away before succumbing to the "all-demanding eyes" (CW 667). As one of O'Connor's last stories published and, obviously, one of her most mature works, "Parker's Back" seems to make the point that what

---

[33] Robert Coles, *Flannery O'Connor's South* (Athens: University of Georgia Press, 1980), 90.
[34] Joseph A. Fitzmyer, *The Acts of the Apostles*, 421.
[35] Ibid.

Moses sees when he encounters the burning bush, what Parker sees in the tree fire, and the force that knocks Saul onto the ground are all one and the same: what these men all encounter in seeing God's glory is really Jesus who said, "He who has seen me has seen the Father" (John 14:9).

Several interesting implications occur when O'Connor combines Parker's story with that of Moses, from the Old Testament, and Saul, from the New Testament. In a sense, this is the key to O'Connor's technique of complementary pairings and the catalyst that allows her to reverse the polarity of both these biblical allusions. When Parker tells Sarah Ruth that the tattoo is actually God, her heart hardens much like the Pharaoh in Exodus, as she screams, "Idolatry! Enflaming yourself with idols under every green tree! I can put up with lies and vanity but I don't want no idolator in this house!" (*CW* 674). Her statement is not only a reference to Isaiah 57:5[36] or Ecclesiastes 1:2[37]; rather O'Connor intended the statement to reference to the second commandment (Ex. 20:4) and Israel's idolatry while Moses is away on Mt. Sinai.[38]

Synthesizing Moses and Paul sets up the fundamental irony of the story: Sarah Ruth uses the Law of Moses and her own version of Old Testament Christianity, in which even "churches were idolatrous" to refuse God's image presented by Parker, a character based on Moses (*CW* 663). Through Sarah Ruth, O'Connor recapitulates the tension, central to Christianity, in seeing Moses and the Law as only a partial revelation of God and Jesus as the full revelation. Essentially, O'Connor has Parker—a version of both Moses and Saul—offering the image of the Byzantine Christ to Sarah Ruth, a religious hypocrite clinging desperately to the Law of Moses, and being rejected the same way that Moses was rejected, Saul was rejected, and, ultimately, Christ was rejected.

Through Parker's action, offering grace through the form of the Byzantine Christ, O'Connor echoes Paul's message that "Jews and Gentiles stand on equal footing before God."[39] Of course, the message is a convergence of both an all-demanding God and a transforming God, which is the significance of the allusion to Saul in the story. Here lies the problem with focusing solely on Job, Jonah, or Obadiah; none of these men experience the same radical conversion, *metanoia*, the immediate reception of grace, which Parker undergoes. Thus, it is necessary, for this story to work, to make the Saul connection, since both men share similar experiences, although there are differences in magnitude. When Parker acknowledges his name and feels "the light pouring through him," this is Saul transformed (*CW* 673). Parker, like Saul, has undergone a reformation, and is now a prophet bearing the message of Jesus. Unfortunately, Sarah Ruth, still clinging to the Law of Moses, cannot accept this message. She considers the mere suggestion of God in human form idolatrous, thus, the irony of her reaction to seeing the face of the Byzantine Christ: "He's a spirit. No man shall see his face" (*CW* 674). As Sarah Ruth rejects and crucifies Christ, in typically O'Connor fashion, it becomes obvious that both Sarah Ruth and Obadiah Elihue are torn between their

---

[36] "Enflaming yourselves with idols under every green tree (from KJV)".
[37] "Vanity of vanities; all is vanity".
[38] Exodus 32:8.
[39] E. P. Sanders, *Paul and Palestinian Judaism: A Comparison of Patterns of Religion* (Philadelphia: Fortress Press, 1977), 516.

contrasting Old Testament namesakes. Sarah Ruth can either embrace Parker, as Ruth would, or reject him as Sarah would. This is more than just an ironic detail; it is a fundamental example of the reversals found throughout O'Connor's corpus.

The central reversal in "Parker's Back" derives from the fact that she is retelling the story of Moses through O. E. Parker, an AWOL discharged Navy vet, who only finds pleasure in drinking, debauchery, and tattooing. Parker, much like Moses, is a wanderer-turned-prophet who receives a miraculous calling from God, encounters God face-to-face, is inscribed, veiled, and told to "GO BACK" becoming "a stranger to himself...into a new country" (*CW* 667, 672). Although there are significant differences, Parker is a modernized Moses, a man who brings the image of Christ to the people. If the image of a modern-day Moses as a tattooed sailor is not enough, O'Connor further complicates the story by juxtaposing Parker's conversion with Saul's conversion. O'Connor synthesizes Moses, the man who receives the Law directly from God, with Paul, the New Testament preacher who preaches "the role of divine grace" as freedom from the Law.[40] Both Moses and Paul are influential biblical figures, yet they stand for different theological paradigms in the Old and New Testament. The blending and reconciling of the two archetypes is something that no theologian, or fiction writer for that matter, would normally attempt to do; however, O'Connor successfully merges elements from both Moses and Paul into her protagonist.

Although a peculiar pairing, the Moses and Paul connection is crucial to the success of "Parker's Back." The Moses connection is important for the setting and development of O'Connor's intended theme. Parker, like Moses, stands barefoot in front of the burning tree before the glory of God. The Old Testament elements running through the story desensitize the reader to O'Connor's intentions. Most readers, like Parker, believe that Sarah Ruth will love the tattoo since "she can't hep herself...She can't say she don't like the looks of God," and are surprised when she rejects Christ (*CW* 670). Yet O'Connor's use of ironic juxtapositions prepares us for Sarah Ruth's reaction. The Moses connection is the rhetorical device allowing O'Connor to reverse the reader's expectations; however, the Saul–Paul connection helps us make sense of this rejection. When Parker returns to show Sarah Ruth the face of God, whom she crucifies, O'Connor illustrates—through Parker's acknowledgment of his name and his own prophetic transformation—that he brings the same message Paul brings: grace. The New Testament allusions in "Parker's Back" incorporate "Pauline theology, justification by faith...as an explanation of forgiveness of sins," a concept that Sarah Ruth seems to miss entirely.[41] O'Connor's authorial intentions can be found in the final striking juxtaposition, which features Sarah Ruth—reminiscent of the New Testament Pharisees—refusing prophecy, the image of God that Parker bears, which is a "testimony to the terrible price of grace" with the hope that she might catch the reader's attention and wake him or her up to his own potential rejection of God's image.[42]

[40] Fitzmyer, *The Acts of the Apostles*, 520.
[41] Ibid., 508.
[42] A. R Coulthard, "From Sermon to Parable: Four Conversion Stories by Flannery O'Connor," *American Literature* 55, no. 1 (1983): 70.

Biblical reversals in "Revelation"

With the notable exception of, perhaps, "Good Country People," few stories match the ironic final scene of "Parker's Back." The sanctimonious Sarah Ruth seems so pious that it is difficult to make sense of her rejection. Yet, no ending is more striking and no reversal more drastic than Ruby Turpin's vision in "Revelation." Although the reversal of "Parker's Back" lies mainly with the readers, in "Revelation," it is the character who is paradigmatically "reversed." Published in the spring of 1964, the last story printed during her lifetime, "Revelation" stands as a testament use of reversals. In many ways, "Revelation" offers the quintessential elements of an O'Connor story, including her literary hallmark, the ironic ending. Yet, the story is also one of O'Connor's most complex, theologically, due to the multiple biblical analogues ranging from Job to the gospels (Luke 18:9–14) to the Book of Revelation (Rev. 21:27). Thus, the biblical reversals to which she was drawn in developing her story—specifically Matthew 20:16 ("So the last shall be first, and the first last")—not only fit into her anagogical framework, but help create one of the most drastic reversals in her corpus.

In his study of the "Parables of Reversal," Crossan notes that "Jesus' parables of reversal are not single reversals and not even double or parallel reversals. They are what might be best termed polar reversals."[43] It is this rhetorical structure, the parables of reversal, in which "Revelation" is modeled. Although the names Ruby and Mary Grace offer a "Parker's Back"-like juxtaposition, since neither name seems suitable for the character—the reversal is not a reversal of expectations as much as a polarity reversal or great upheaval of almost everything that Ruby Turpin thinks she knows.

This story—set in a doctor's waiting room, a clever ploy to force interactions between cross sections of societies, it features characters described solely by appearance ("well-dressed," the "old," "the trashy woman," etc.) who would otherwise remain segregated—seems more progressive and socially conscious than many of her previous works. This technique, the waiting room, serves as the device to incorporate both biblical analogues and reversals. Although, the doctor's office serves as the great social equalizer, Ruby Turpin remains entirely unaware of this fact. Rather, she spends her time "naming the classes of people," although, for her, this task is more difficult than it seems:

> On the bottom of the heap were most colored people ... then next to them—not above, just away from—were the white-trash; then above them were the home-owners, and above them the home-and-land owners, to which she and Claude belonged. Above she and Claud were people with a lot of money and much bigger houses and much more land. (*CW* 636)

At this point, "the complexity of it would begin to bear in on her, for some of the people with a lot of money were common and ought to be below she and Claud" (*CW* 636).

---

[43] John Dominic Crossan, *In Parables: The Challenge of the Historical Jesus* (New York: Harper and Row, 1973), 55.

As was the case with a growing middle class and the South's shift from a bourgeois aristocratic system to a meritocracy, Mrs. Turpin slowly realizes that social standing cannot be determined solely based on socioeconomics. Of course, she finds this upsetting since she is a woman "most comfortable with clear definitions, with distinct, unambiguous categories."[44] However, when Mrs. Turpin's amateur sociology project gets too difficult, she continues her self-righteous dialogue with God, imagining:

> If Jesus had said to her before he made her, "There's only two places available for you. You can either be a nigger or white-trash," what would she have said? "Please, Jesus, please," she would have said, "just let me wait until there's another place available," and he would have said, "No, you have to go right now and I have only those two places so make up your mind." She would have wiggled and squirmed and begged and pleaded but it would have been no use and finally she would have said, "All right, make me a nigger then—but that don't mean a trashy one." And he would have made her a neat clean respectable Negro woman, herself but black. (*CW* 636)

O'Connor's omniscient narrator allows readers to penetrate Mrs. Turpin's private conversations with God. It is this internal monologue which O'Connor uses as parallel to its biblical counterpart, the story "The Pharisee and the Publican" (Luke 18: 9–14).[45]

The parable begins as Jesus tells the crowd, "Two men went into the temple to pray one a Pharisee and the other a tax collector [Publican]" (Luke 18:10). Yet, by moving it out of the church, O'Connor still garners the same effect, a place where social classes interact. Jesus continued:

> The Pharisee stood and was praying this to himself: 'God, I thank You that I am not like other people: swindlers, unjust, adulterers, or even like this tax collector. I fast twice a week; I pay tithes of all that I get.' But the tax collector, standing some distance away, was even unwilling to lift up his eyes to heaven, but was beating his breast saying, 'God, be merciful to me, the sinner!'
> I tell you, this man [the Publican] went to his house justified rather than the other; for everyone who exalts himself will be humbled, but he who humbles himself will be exalted. (Luke 18: 10–14)

O'Connor sets "Revelation" in the secular world of a doctor's office, but it is not far removed from the setting of the parable, the temple. The temple in Israel was more than a place of worship; it was a social and community pillar. Friedrichsen argues that "neither the Pharisee nor the tax collector would have been praying in the temple building itself"; rather they would have been in the temple area, since the term "temple implies the corporate, public nature of worship."[46] Thus, the fact that

---

[44] Baumgartner, *A Proper Scaring*, 114.
[45] The story of the Pharisee and Publican precedes the story of the "Rich Young Ruler" (Luke 18:18–30), which O'Connor references in other stories such as "A Good Man Is Hard to Find."
[46] Timothy A. Friedrichsen, "The Temple, A Pharisee, A Tax Collector, and the Kingdom of God: Rereading A Jesus Parable (Luke 18:10–14A)," *Journal of Biblical Literature* 124, no. 1 (2005): 105.

O'Connor moves her story into the religious sphere makes it an apt parallel to the spirit of the original parable.

When the Pharisee enters the temple, he is sure to distance himself from the tax collector since "Pharisees were known for their concern about ritual purity; to stand apart from others is one way for the Pharisee of this parable to ensure that he does not come into contact with anything or anyone who is unclean."[47] Throughout "Revelation," Ruby Turpin tries to distance herself from the unclean masses in the doctor's office. However, as the trashy-lady points out, it is Ruby, herself, who is unclean since she raises pigs: "One thang I don't want … Hogs. Nasty stinking things, a-gruntin and a-rootin all over the place" (*CW* 638).

As Mrs. Turpin brags that she has "a little of everything," her biblical counterpart, the Pharisee, is also fairly wealthy since "both the Pharisee's fasting and his tithing reflect a man of some financial means"[48] (*CW* 642). Ironically, the Pharisee thanks God for his upper-class status, just as Ruby Turpin is thankful: "He had not made her a nigger or white-trash or ugly! He had made her herself" (*CW* 642).

This prayer, however, is the strongest connection between the two. The Pharisee's prayer is a repudiation of God; instead of a prayer, he offers self-justification as to why he doesn't need God—to paraphrase the Misfit, the Pharisee tells God, "I'm doing all right by myself." Essentially, the Pharisee has arrived at the temple to proclaim that he doesn't need to be there, in the same way, Mrs. Turpin arrives at the doctor's office to support Claud—she also makes it clear that she does not belong here, either. In fact, she revels in the idea of her own generosity: "to help anybody out that needed it was her philosophy of life. She never spared herself when she found somebody in need" (*CW* 642).

The Pharisee, who publically announces his holiness, prays aloud, "God, I thank You that I am not like other people" (Luke 18:11). Echoing this prayer, almost verbatim, Mrs. Turpin's dialogue mirrors the Pharisee: " 'Jesus, thank you!' she said. 'Thank you thank you thank you!' " (*CW* 642). As if to re-emphasize the connection, O'Connor has Mrs. Turpin continue audibly praying, "If it's one thing I am … it's grateful. When I think who all I could have been besides myself and what I got, a little of everything … I just feel like shouting, 'Thank you, Jesus, for making everything the way it is! It could have been different!' " (*CW* 644). Ironically, it is directly after this middle-class defender of the status-quo cries aloud, "Oh thank you, Jesus, Jesus, thank you!" that the *Human Development* book "struck her directly over her left eye" (*CW* 644). This act changes her outlook as "Mrs. Turpin's vision suddenly reversed itself and she saw everything large instead of small" (*CW* 645). It is Mary Grace, whom Ruby criticizes for her poor disposition, patronizingly telling her, "It never hurt anyone to smile," who delivers a message to Ruby Turpin (*CW* 644). Mary Grace's attack serves as the catalyst for Ruby's paradigm shift in the story, in turn, reversing everything for Mrs. Turpin.

This biblical allusion also provides an excellent example of O'Connor's method of reversals, which follows in the tradition of "the Lukan theme of reversal" of the original

---

[47] Friedrichsen, "The Temple, a Pharisee, a Tax Collector, and the Kingdom of God," 97.
[48] Ibid., 111.

parable.[49] In fact, Christ's concluding comment, "for everyone who exalts himself will be humbled, but he who humbles himself will be exalted" might as well be the mantra for O'Connor's reversal stories—the arrogant (Julian in "Everything that Rises Must Converge," Asbury Fox in "The Enduring Chill," Mrs. Turpin, etc.) are humbled (Luke 18: 14). By reading this story as an analogue to Christ's parable, it seems clear that O'Connor does not want us to sympathize with Ruby Turpin. Rather, the reversal—akin to its biblical correlative—surfaces after the story's climax, as readers realize that it is those surrounding Ruby Turpin, whom she judges (the white-trash lady, etc.), who are marching toward redemption—a complete reversal of expectations from the story's beginning, which focuses on Mrs. Turpin's own righteousness. While the Lukan account "announces eschatological judgment by God," O'Connor's story does much the same thing.[50]

This story of the Pharisee and Publican is more than "another parable of Jesus about prayer"; instead, this story was one of the great reversals of the Bible, which reversed the polarity of listeners' expectations.[51] By now, O'Connor's attraction to such a parable should become clear. The biblical underpinnings of this story serves as the framework for which her reversals often operate. Her *modus operandi* is to immerse these ironic twists within a biblical grounding. The initial audience of Christ's parable expected the righteous Pharisee to be justified, not the publican, who was looked upon as a traitor to the Israelites. Yet this is Christ's point. Jesus' critiques of the Pharisees—the context of several of his reversals, including this one—are meant to condemn absolute doctrinal correctness. Had the Pharisee been genuine in his faith, then he would be the hero of the story; however, he "did not really go to pray to God. He prayed *with himself*."[52] While he "stands afar off, casts his eyes down, strikes his breast, and begs God for mercy, as a 'sinner,'" the Pharisee, much like Ruby Turpin, was not praying, but "giving himself a testimonial before God."[53] He strives for repentance "by the avoidance of thievery, adultery, and evildoing," much like Ruby Turpin's own admitted self-righteousness, yet his "conduct and attitude turn out to be fundamentally misguided."[54] Like the Pharisee, Mrs. Turpin's prayer, whether she realizes it or not, is a public testimonial of her own goodness. In this sense, her prayer seems to reflect not only the story of the Pharisee and the Publican but also Jesus' own teaching on prayer, as he warns:

> Beware of practicing your righteousness before men to be noticed by them; otherwise you have no reward with your Father who is in heaven … When you pray, you are not to be like the hypocrites; for they love to stand and pray in the synagogues and on the street corners so that they may be seen by men … they have their reward in full. (Mt. 6:1, 5)

---

[49] Friedrichsen, "The Temple, a Pharisee, a Tax Collector, and the Kingdom of God," 102.

[50] Crossan, *In Parables*, 68.

[51] Fitzmyer, *The Gospel According to Luke X–XXIV* (1183).

[52] William Barclay, *Introduction to the First Three Gospels* (Philadelphia: The Westminster Press, 1966), 232.

[53] Fitzmyer, *The Gospel According to Luke X–XXIV*, 1184; Barclay, *Introduction to the First Three Gospels*, 232.

[54] Fitzmyer, *The Gospel According to Luke X–XXIV*, 1184.

Mrs. Turpin's own prayer, ironically, stands in stark contrast to Jesus' instructions on prayer. Hence, these parallels serve as a complexity to O'Connor's own anagogical vision. Her point is interwoven within the intent of the original stories; she means to condemn absolute doctrinal inflexibility, the absolute certainty that prioritizes self over God.

Although "Revelation" may feel allegorical, it is not a complete retelling of any specific biblical account. If anything, one could consider her interaction with the Pharisee and the Publican as a monologic retelling of the biblical account, since it offers no corollary, no humble Publican in the waiting room and since neither the white-trash nor the stylish lady fits this mold. Rather, Brinkmeyer argues—effectively—that the entire story of "Revelation" is itself a dialogic; however, I would also add that much like the Pharisee's self-righteous prayer in the temple, Mrs. Turpin's own conversation with God "is itself un-dialogical."[55] This is exactly why O'Connor includes this allusion to the story of the Pharisee and Publican; she intends to align Mrs. Turpin with this tradition of arrogance and self-righteousness.

Moreover, the reference to the Pharisee and the Publican is neither the only biblical allusion nor is it the only example of reversals in the story. True to O'Connor's style, "Revelation" is a complex and multilayered short story. Mrs. Turpin's own self-righteous standards, when used against her, clearly demonstrate her own faults—it is as if Mrs. Turpin is a prototype of Hazel Motes claiming that no one with a good car needs to be justified, only to realize that she does not have a good car. One of these self-revelations comes through her inane waiting-room conversations. Though she is freely critical of those she believes to be below her—a trait highlighted through her critique of footwear (the "well-dressed lady had on red and grey suede shoes" and the "white-trashy mother had on what appeared to be bedroom slippers")—Mrs. Turpin is completely unaware of her own flaws (*CW* 635). Throughout the first half of the story, Mrs. Turpin is unapologetically judgmental. As the trashy woman claims, "You can get you one with green stamps... Save you up enough you can get you most anything. I got me some joo'ry," Mrs. Turpin's implicit response was "Ought to have got you a wash rag and some soap" (*CW* 637). Yet, Mrs. Turpin's criticism of the trashy lady's hygiene becomes ironic when Mrs. Turpin reveals her profession: "We got a couple acres of cotton and a few hogs and chickens" (*CW* 638). This comment, meant to enhance Mrs. Turpin's social status, becomes the trashy woman's central critique of Mrs. Turpin. Although Mrs. Turpin is sure that God would put "the white-trash" at the bottom of his hierarchy, far below, "home-and-land owners, to which she and Claud belonged," the white-trash lady offers a new hierarchy: "One thang I don't want... Hogs. Nasty stinking things, a-grunting and a-rootin all over the place" (*CW* 636, 638). Yet, to Mrs. Turpin's dismay, her own retort, "Our hogs are not dirty and they don't stink... They're cleaner than some children I've seen," referring to the woman's child, falls on deaf ears, unable to dissuade the trashy woman who repeats, "I know I wouldn't scoot down no hog with no hose" (*CW* 638). Unexpectedly for readers, the trashy woman presents readers another reversal since she rejects the social hierarchy.

---

[55] Sykes, *Aesthetic*, 79.

In examining their exchange, it should be noted that Mrs. Turpin's response to the woman's criticism provides another potent biblical symbol: O'Connor's use of swine as a spiritual marker. Mrs. Turpin's insistence that "Our hogs are not dirty and they don't stink... Their feet never touch the ground. We have a pig-parlor—that's where you raise them on concrete" seems to suggest she has literally laid her pearls before her own swine (*CW* 638). With its repeated pig imagery, echoing *Wise Blood*, Mrs. Turpin's pigs function as a potent symbol, representing an animal that is "both unclean and sacred."[56] This imagery resonates of God's command to Israel: "And the pig, though it has a split hoof completely divided, does not chew the cud; it is unclean for you" (Lev 11:7). Although Mrs. Turpin considers herself virtuous, the trashy woman's condemnation highlights the fact that no matter how many times she scoots them down, her pigs will always be unclean. It is not until Mrs. Turpin receives her revelation that she realizes, through her association with these animals which "appeared to pant with a secret life," that she too is unclean and in need of redemption (*CW* 653).

Throughout their conversations on race, parenting, and farming, Mrs. Turpin and the pleasant lady establish an implicit agreement: "they both understood that you had to *have* certain things before you could *know* certain things" (*CW* 639). Both the pleasant lady and Ruby Turpin look down upon the white-trashy lady, as Mrs. Turpin, stereotyping, thinks "if you gave them everything, in two weeks it would all be broken or filthy or they would have chopped it up for lightwood" (*CW* 642). Yet, directly after Mary Grace strikes Mrs. Turpin in the eye with a book, the pleasant lady's daughter is restrained: the "only sounds in the room were the tremulous moans of the girl's mother," the implication being that she will be institutionalized (*CW* 646). Ironically, it is the white-trash woman who gets the final say: "That there girl is going to be a lunatic, ain't she?" she asks the nurse aloud, only to receive no answer; she reiterates, "Yes, she's going to be a lunatic... Po' critter" (*CW* 647). In a stunning reversal, the white-trash woman becomes the doppelganger to Mrs. Ruby Turpin: "'I thank Gawd,' the white-trash woman said fervently, 'I ain't a lunatic'" (*CW* 647). Upending Ruby's moral pyramid completely, the incident ends with the white-trash lady pitying the stylish lady and looking down upon Mrs. Turpin.

Mrs. Turpin has worked hard to construct a "divinely-inspired" order to the world in which she has created God in her own image, but this hierarchy is problematized by Mrs. Turpin, herself, and the very members of the hierarchy who do not willingly accept her judgments. Ironically, it is the trashy lady who believes herself to be better than both Mrs. Turpin and the pleasant lady. Furthermore, Mary Grace's attack on Mrs. Turpin certainly affects her judgment of the pleasant lady—a woman Mrs. Turpin eagerly allied with and tried to please in the waiting room—since no other children, including the naturally mean son of the white-trash lady, attacked her in the waiting room. Thus, Mrs. Turpin's apparent frustration when she realizes the limits of her personal taxonomy as "all the classes of people were moiling and roiling around in her head" (*CW* 636). For Mrs. Turpin, the true revelation becomes clear: judge not lest ye be judged.

---

[56] Sir James George Frazer, *The Golden Bough* (New York: MacMillan, 1963), 546.

The most prominent of the many reversals in the story is clearly foreshadowed by the story's title. O'Connor's limited-omniscient narrator allows readers access to Mrs. Turpin's private, albeit superfluous, conversation with God; yet after Mary Grace heaves a book at her head, Ruby confronts her by saying, "What you got to say to me," staring at the girl, "waiting as for a revelation" (*CW* 646). Ruby Turpin is the type of woman who not only believes in divine revelation but also anticipates it. In her hubris, she spends her time imagining various scenarios where Jesus consults her about her possible social status, imagining she has a say in God's dominion. Until this point, her prayers and conversations with God have been monologic, yet she finally receives an answer in the form of her revelation, God's response to Mrs. Turpin's prayers—completing the dialogic as anticipated.

After she is accosted by Mary Grace, Mrs. Turpin, distancing herself from Claud, no longer has the outgoing, sanctimonious, self-gratified personality from the waiting room; rather she is downcast and moans, "'I am not...a wart hog. From hell'" (*CW* 647). This message cuts to her very core and, much like "David's interpretation of Shimei's curses, Mrs. Turpin's response to Mary Grace's insults is to consider them to be a message from God."[57] Yet, O'Connor is sure to draw another biblical connection as her protagonist, Ruby Turpin, sits at home: "she raised her fist and made a small stabbing motion over her chest as if she was defending her innocence to invisible guests who were like the comforters of Job, reasonable-seeming but wrong" (*CW* 648). O'Connor explicitly alludes to the comforters of Job, as she does as well in "Parker's Back," but does so in order to reinforce another motif which develops, chiefly, at the end of the story.[58] However, it should come as no surprise to readers that Mrs. Turpin, a lady who imagines herself an advisor to God, begins to equate herself with Job. The righteous Job is tested with simultaneous disasters as "the fire of God fell from heaven and burned up the sheep and the servants," yet returning home, the self-righteous Mrs. Turpin "would not have been startled to see a burnt wound between two blackened chimneys" (Job 1:16, *CW* 647). So strong is her belief that, like Job, her virtue is being tested by God "that she expects God's rage to have been visited even upon her own farm house."[59]

O'Connor's fiction is so steeped in biblical intertextuality that her characters begin to mirror biblical figures: Hazel Motes is a comic Saul, O. E. Parker mimics a modern-day Moses, and Mrs. Turpin becomes a contemporary version of Job arguing with his comforters. Like Job, Mrs. Turpin seeks comfort from those around her by recounting the story of her attack to her farmhands, yet her retelling shows readers that she is still judgmental of others. "There was this girl there. A big fat girl with her face all broke out...and all of a sudden WHAM! She throws this big book she was reading at me" (*CW* 649). It is obvious, however, that Mrs. Turpin receives no solace in their attempts to comfort her: "She [Mary Grace] belong in the sylum" (*CW* 650). Instead, their final

---

[57] Brian Britt, "Divine Curses in O'Connor's 'Revelation' and 2 Samuel 16," *Flannery O'Connor Review* 1 (2001–2002): 53.

[58] Not only do both stories, written during the same time frame, contain explicit allusions to the Book of Job, but both stories reference Job's comforters.

[59] Wood, *The Comedy of Redemption*, 129.

words are haunting: "Jesus satisfied with her!" (*CW* 650). This response torments her, as she knows there is a literal truth that Jesus is satisfied with Mary Grace, which seems to add authenticity to the young girl's prophets. Infuriated by their solace, Mrs. Turpin walks away, dismissing the farmhands as "Idiots!"(*CW* 650). Yet, even Mrs. Turpin's condemnation of her comforters is reminiscent of Job: "Fools... And now I have become their taunt, I have even become a byword to them" (Job 30:5–6). Despite who tries to assuage her woes (Claud, the doctor, the farmhands), Mrs. Turpin feels mortified by other people's pity. In the same way "Job feels humiliated because his suffering allows those who should be below him to assume a superiority," Mrs. Turpin realizes that her own hierarchy is now complicated even further.[60]

This motif culminates with Mrs. Turpin's Job-like questioning of God. Dejected, Job vocalizes his frustration, crying out to God, "Will You never turn Your gaze away from me... Have I sinned? What have I done to You, O watcher of men?" (Job 7:19–20). Mrs. Turpin, following his lead, finally asks God, "What do you send me a message like that for? ... How am I a hog and me both? How am I saved and from hell too?" (*CW* 652). In a final act of provocation, "Job-like ... she raises her fist in self-defense against her accuser."[61] Her confusion seems strangely emblematic of "the pig's double nature—polluted but close to divinity."[62] Yet, it is through her complex interplay of both the theological dimensions and the religious imagery that O'Connor's anagogical vision emerges—through the dual nature of Mrs. Turpin's question—as she wonders: how is she simultaneously a Pharisee (self-righteous) and Job (righteous)? Her question is one that "articulates the duality" of O'Connor's use of reversals.[63] Within many of her stories, as I have pointed out, is a tendency toward duality, which is often manifest through juxtaposing the secular and sacred, the body and the spiritual, "a touching of the human with the grotesque luminosity of the divine."[64]

Ruby Turpin's question is a theologically poignant inquiry: "Both the question and the reply [Ruby's vision] are central to the Christian faith: How can one be the reborn child of God while remaining a miserable offender."[65] Yet, ironically, the answer to this question comes in the form of God's dialogical reply, which seems to suggest "grace" is brought to her courtesy of Mary Grace.

At first, the absence of an answer bothers her: "Why me? ... It's no trash around here, black or white, that I haven't given to. And break my back to the bone every day working. And do for the church" (*CW* 652). She continues to question God, asserting her own righteousness, "I could quit working and take it easy and be filthy ... It's too late for me to be a nigger ... but I could act like one. Lay down in the middle of the road and stop traffic. Roll on the ground" (*CW* 652–653). Mrs. Turpin's reaction demonstrates

---

[60] Michael L. Schroeder, "Ruby Turpin, Job, and Mystery: Flannery O'Connor on the Question of Knowing," *The Flannery O'Connor Bulletin* 21 (1992): 78.
[61] Kilcourse, *Flannery O'Connor's Religious Imagination*, 285.
[62] Dennis P. Slattery, "In a Pig's Eye: Retrieving the Animal Imagination in Ruby Turpin's 'Revelation,'" *The Flannery O'Connor Bulletin* 25 (1996): 141.
[63] Asals, *The Imagination of Extremity*, 68.
[64] Ibid., 67.
[65] Wood, *South*, 263.

that she is still as judgmental and biased as she was before her encounter with Mary Grace. She is not only cavalier enough to expect an answer from God; she is deluded enough to demand one. However, this confrontation seems to parallel Job's response to God as Job asserts his own righteousness: "If I have walked with falsehood and my foot has hastened after deceit, Let him weigh me with accurate scales, And let God know my integrity" (Job 31:5–6). Schroeder asserts that Job "is proud of his goodness, which had previously won him respect as well as wealth," yet the same could be said for Mrs. Turpin, who is extremely proud of her own perceived beneficence.[66] She relentlessly defends her own assertions: "Call me a wart hog from hell. Put that bottom rail on top. There'll still be a top and bottom!" (*CW* 653). She believes that social standing is based on economic status "rather than moral qualifications," so she "assumes that social status has religious overtones" (Schroeder 79). With one last "surge of fury," Mrs. Turpin demands, "Who do you think you are?" (*CW* 653).

When "the Lord answered Job out of the whirlwind," God asks him, "Who is this that darkens counsel By words without knowledge" (Job 38:1–2). Yet in O'Connor's parallel, God responds to Ruby Turpin with a vision. She sees the "purple streak in the sky, cutting through a field of crimson"; this combination of crimson and purple gives the sky a ruby tint as:

> [A] visionary light settled in her eyes. She saw the streak as a vast swinging bridge extending upward from the earth through a field of living fire. Upon it a vast horde of souls were rumbling toward heaven. There were whole companies of white-trash, clean for the first time in their lives, and bands of black niggers in white robes, and battalions of freaks and lunatics shouting and clapping and leaping like frogs. And bringin up the end of the procession was a tribe of people whom she recognized at once as those who, like herself and like herself and Claud... They were marching behind the others with great dignity... They alone were on key. Yet she could see by their shocked and altered faces that even their virtues were being burned away. (*CW* 654)

This final image of her vision suggests that her own perceived virtues are meaningless; thus, reversing her perceived hierarchy. Upon seeing this, "She lowered her hands and gripped the rail of the hog pen" (*CW* 654). For the first time, readers are not told if it is the top or bottom rail, suggesting that Mrs. Turpin's vision will lead to a less hierarchical order.

Responding to early drafts, Catharine Carver believed "Revelation" to be one of O'Connor's blackest stories, as she "Found Ruby evil" and assumed that the end vision was meant to confirm this (*HB* 554). In fact, Carver thought that the end vision made Ruby seem too evil and "suggested I [O'Connor] leave it out" (*HB* 554). Of course, O'Connor responded, "I am not going to leave it out. I am going to deepen it so that there'll be no mistaking Ruby is not just an evil Glad Annie" (*HB* 554). By weaving various biblical narratives into the final allusion, O'Connor strengthens the vision to

---

[66] Schroeder, "Question of Knowing," 78.

make its redemptive possibilities clear to readers. O'Connor has Mrs. Turpin clearly follow in Job's image. Both figures challenge "God's authority" and are "put into ... place by His answer" transformed by their, respective, vision.[67] Job answers God, "I know that You can do all things. And that no purpose of Yours can be thwarted," just as Mrs. Turpin is humbled by the vision she receives as she walks home and "the invisible cricket choruses had struck up, but what she heard were the voices of the souls climbing upward into the starry field and shouting hallelujah" (Job 42:2, CW 654). Although the story is not allegorical (one could hardly compare the honorable Job to the busybody Mrs. Turpin), their responses to God's divine message are the same.

Some have compared Mrs. Turpin's vision of the "vast swinging bridge extending upward from the earth" to Jacob's own dream where "a ladder was set on the earth with its top reaching to heaven," in which "the angels of God were ascending and descending on it" (Gen. 28:12). However, the most remarkable biblical allusions are apparent in this ending. The story seems to have a biblical resonance from its namesake, Revelation, the final book of the New Testament. The author envisions heaven as a place where "The nations will walk by its light" as the "glory and honor of the nations will be brought into it" and "Nothing impure will ever enter it" (Rev. 21: 24, 26–27). This image resonates throughout Mrs. Turpin's own revelation, where she sees "whole companies of white-trash, clean for the first time in their lives" with "bands of black niggers in white robes" (CW 654). It seems perfectly reasonable to assume that O'Connor would turn to this source, the Revelation of John, while writing Ruby Turpin's own revelatory vision. Through certain aspects of Ruby Turpin's prophetic experience, O'Connor seems to re-create this biblical account. Throughout Revelation, the author emphasizes the many different nations represented within his vision, yet O'Connor includes a variety of social classes—all of which are included previously in Ruby Turpin's own social hierarchy.[68] Furthermore, the author's emphasis on purity, "Nothing impure will ever enter it," seems to be signified in Ruby's vision, which includes those who were "clean for the first time" as others wear "white robes" and everyone's "virtues were being burned away" (Rev. 21:27, CW 654).

The final biblical allusion circulating throughout the text not only is one of the most explicit theological references but also provides perhaps the strongest examples of O'Connor's method of polarity reversals. Ruby Turpin's vision, the parade into heaven, literally embodies the most famous reversal in the Bible: "Nevertheless, many who are first will be last, and the last first" (Mt. 19:30). This becomes obvious since the order of the procession is of great consequence to Mrs. Turpin—surprisingly, it is the people and their position in the queue, rather than their destination, serving as the focal point of the vision as she notices that the "white-trash" and the "bands of black niggers" are leading the march into heaven. Yet, this is a great divergence from her own belief that "On the bottom of the heap were most colored people" and "next to them—not above, just away from—were the white trash" (CW 636). Through her vision, Ruby Turpin realizes that her own social hierarchy has been toppled, but she also now understands that "God

---

[67] Schroeder, "Question of Knowing," 75–76.
[68] The author identifies himself as John and is traditionally believed to be John the apostle, although some believe the author is John the Presbyter, who was also writing during this time.

has not shown himself to be the Protector of white middle-class virtues that she had thought him to be."[69] Hence, it is ironic that "bringing up the end of the procession was a tribe of people whom she recognized at once as those who, like herself and Claud[,] had always had a little of everything," inverting her own caste system and personifying Jesus' statements in Matthew: "Nevertheless, many who are first will be last, and the last first" and later, "So the last shall be first, and the first last" (*CW* 654, Mt. 19:30, 20:16). Albright and Mann assert that this passage is "equally a warning against any assumption on the part of the disciples that privilege and reward in the Kingdom belong in higher degree to those first called," or in Mrs. Turpin's case, those with the most goods.[70] Additionally, these reversals are "repeated in reverse order" forming "a chiasm, a device often employed by Matthew."[71] Following in the biblical tradition of Matthew, O'Connor mirrors this rhetorical technique, employing chiasm throughout "Revelation."

Through her revelation, Mrs. Turpin is "turned upside down in her final eschatological vision, for she is made to see things as God sees them."[72] Readers can assume that Mrs. Turpin has undergone a great change and now understands the meaning of her prophetic message—a great social upheaval which reverses everything Ruby Turpin knows about race, class, and holiness since the theological hegemony which she once assumed has been completely eviscerated. Her final vision, this great reversal, seems to echo God's response to Mrs. Turpin's question—the same response Jesus gives to the chief priests and members of the Sanhedrin as he tells them, "the tax collectors and prostitutes will get into the kingdom of God before you" (Mt. 21:31). Throughout the gospels, "Jesus did not need to spend time in denouncing the obvious sins of the publicans and harlots"; rather his effectiveness lies in the fact that "His major effect was to awaken so-called good people to discover the shortcoming which they did not know they had."[73] Following this model, through this revelation, Mrs. Turpin is awakened, quite forcefully, to her own shortcomings. Through O'Connor's ultimate attentiveness to these biblically nuanced and explicit allusions peppered throughout the text, she establishes the foundation for her ironic reversals. Not only does this augment her rich attraction to biblical source material but it also further illustrates the complexity of her technique of biblically based reversals.

All things sacred: Redemptive reversal in "A Temple of the Holy Ghost"

When listing the most controversial stories in O'Connor's corpus, most would consider "A Good Man Is Hard to Find," "The Artificial Nigger," and *The Violent Bear It Away*, yet "A Temple of the Holy Ghost," a story in which no one is harmed or killed, supersedes

[69] Wood, *The Comedy of Redemption*, 130.
[70] W. F. Albright and C. S. Mann, *Matthew: Introduction, Translation, and Notes.* (Garden City: Doubleday, 1971), 238.
[71] Ibid., 234.
[72] Wood, *South*, 264.
[73] Sockman, *The Paradoxes of Jesus*, 61.

all others in terms of precarious rhetorical strategies. This work, featuring a character possessing a rare sexual anomaly and is transformed into a redemptive figure—an agent of God's own transforming grace—represents perhaps the most bizarre, yet successful reversal in her corpus. However, although "Good Country People," "Parker's Back," and "Revelation" are among O'Connor's most beloved stories, "A Temple of the Holy Ghost" is among the most critically conspicuous. Askin argues that the story "can be a stumbling block even for experienced O'Connor readers because it has neither her paradigmatic plot nor her signature ironic ending."[74]

A theological experiment for O'Connor, "A Temple of the Holy Ghost" does not follow the same precedents set by her other fictions; rather the locus rests on a mild brand of Catholicism while maintaining an anagogical framework consistent with her work. This divergence from her signature ironic ending to a more nuanced use of reversals augments her authorial intent within the story—to transform the grotesque into the sacred—signaling the importance of "A Temple of the Holy Ghost" within her corpus. It is a story which seemingly does not fit into the prescriptive form, yet still falls into her framework of reversals, through the dual function of the hermaphrodite as both carnival freak and incarnation of a Christ-like priestly figure, embracing his own sacrificial suffering.

While it lacks the stark contrasts found in her other works, "A Temple of the Holy Ghost," a bildungsroman tale about the young protagonist's own initiation into sexual maturation, may be one of her most dualistic stories. Following the pattern established in *Wise Blood*, "A Temple of the Holy Ghost" is filled with doubles, beginning with the unnamed protagonist, a stand-in for the author, herself.

Most who have written about the story have noticed the similarities between O'Connor's precocious narrator and the author who commented that she wanted to stay arrested at the age of 12 because "There was something about 'teen' attached to anything that was repulsive to me" (*HB* 136–137). Much like O'Connor living in Andalusia, the story's 12-year-old unnamed protagonist, the author's doppelganger, is quite intelligent, yet surrounded by the remarkably banal. The girl's two cousins are shallow teenagers and Miss Kirby, a schoolteacher who boards with the family, is obliviously tedious. The characters in her household provide the witty protagonist with plenty of fodder for satire. Biographer Jean Cash recounts Loretta Feuger Hoynes' firsthand account of O'Connor's fiery temper. When a young boy "invited Loretta to go to the movies with him," the couple "sat on the porch to swing and smoked."[75] After the date, "Mary Flannery became so angry that she put Loretta out of the house with her suitcase, declaring her a 'wayward woman,'" an experience which "later found its way into 'A Temple of the Holy Ghost.'"[76] O'Connor's incorporation of her childhood experiences supports Westling's theory that O'Connor's fiction often presented "doubles of herself."[77]

---

[74] Denise T. Askin, "Carnival in the 'Temple': Flannery O'Connor's Dialogic Parable of Artistic Vocation," *Christianity and Literature* 56, no. 4 (2007): 557.

[75] Cash, *Flannery O'Connor: A Life*, 18.

[76] Ibid.

[77] Louise Westling, *Sacred Groves and Ravaged Gardens: The Fiction of Eudora Welty, Carson McCullers, and Flannery O'Connor* (Athens: University of Georgia Press, 1985), 180.

The young girl's cousins, Joanne and Susan, offer a more visible version of this motif. Readers are first introduced to these two cousins, the embodiment O'Connor's doppelganger motif, who come to visit their aunt. Instead of a juxtaposition of opposites, readers are immediately introduced to two indistinguishable characters who jokingly referred to themselves as "Temple One and Temple Two" in reference to Sister Perpetua's advice on dating, as she informs the girls that if a gentleman should "behave in an ungentlemanly manner with them in the back of the automobile," they are to exclaim, "Stop sir! I am a Temple of the Holy Ghost!" (*CW* 199). Although Sister Perpetua's advice is an example of her own sexual naivety, through her ill-informed counsel she provides readers with an explicit example of biblical recapitulation, a reference to Paul's own advice: "What? Know yet not that your body is a temple of the Holy Ghost which is in you, and ye are not your own?" (1 Cor. 6:19).[78] This motif from which O'Connor derives the title of the story becomes the most important within the work.

As the cousins mock Sister Perpetua, the young protagonist "didn't see anything so funny" as Miss Kirby repeats to herself "I am a Temple of the Holy Ghost" (*CW* 199). It is the aunt who speaks for readers as she tells her immature nieces, "I think you girls are pretty silly ... After all, that's what you are—Temples of the Holy Ghost" (*CW* 199). Yet, through their mockery, both Joanne and Susan, unknowingly, "literalize the trope of the 'Temple.'"[79] This literalization provides another example of both O'Connor's method of biblical rewriting and her fondness for dualities. Furthermore, the two cousins' own nicknames support Eggenschwiler's assertion that "the central theme of the story is Paul's teaching that man is a temple of the living God."[80]

Unsure of how to relate to her immature nieces, the aunt decides to find dates to entertain her two new houseguests. It seems telling that the young protagonist recommends twins Wendell and Cory Wilkins, yet not because they are twins, but because "They are sixteen and they got a car" adding "they were both going to be Church of God preachers because you don't have to know nothing to be one" (*CW* 200). The boys' own doubleness and indeterminacy offer both a perfect corollary for the girls since the pair of doppelgangers could not be more dissimilar, offering a subtle example of O'Connor's technique of reconciling opposites as a means of reversal. Of course, O'Connor is neither concerned with the cousins, who laughed until "they were positively ugly," nor their dates, who "sat like monkeys, their knees on a level with their shoulders and their arms hanging down between" (*CW* 197, 201). Rather, the focus is on the curious protagonist observing this dating ritual firsthand for presumably the first time.[81]

Through the narrator's description, readers are privy to this bizarre courting as Wendell and Corey serenade the girls with gospel hymns such as "I've Found a Friend

---

[78] Quoted from the Douay-Rheims edition. The NASB edition reads: "Or do you not know that your body is a temple of the Holy Spirit?" (1 Cor. 6: 19).

[79] Askin, "Carnival in the 'Temple,'" 561.

[80] David Eggenschwiler, *The Christian Humanism of Flannery O'Connor* (Detroit: Wayne State University Press, 1972), 20.

[81] The only other romantic relationship she has observed is Mr. Cheatam's awkward courtship of Miss Kirby.

in Jesus" and "The Old Rugged Cross" (*CW* 201). The girls, who "held their lips stiff so as not to giggle but Susan let out one anyway," respond with a song of their own, *Tantum Ergo* (*CW* 201).[82] When the Protestant Wilkinses do not understand the song (Wendell xenophobically comments "That must be Jew singing"), instead of being offended, the girls respond with their familiar giggles (*CW* 202). Rather it is the young protagonist who is outraged that these boys miss the sacralized nature of the song, stamping her foot and yelling, "You big dumb ox!...You big dumb Church of God ox!" (*CW* 202).[83] This guarded St. Thomas allusion offers another example connection between the young protagonist and the author herself. O'Connor, obviously aware of this Ox–St. Thomas connection, famously claimed to be "a hillbilly Thomist," who read Aquinas's *Summa Theologica* "for twenty minutes every night before I go to bed"(*HB* 81, 93).

However, the story's central reversal concerns the most poignant juxtaposition in the story, and possibly within her entire corpus, which is literalized through the holy hermaphrodite who holds court at the local fairgrounds. When Joanna and Susan return from the carnival, the young girl persuades them to tell her about a particular "freak" that they saw at the fair. The hermaphrodite, described by the cousins as abhorrent, presents a popular trope within O'Connor's fiction. As May writes, "There is scarcely a story of O'Connor's, especially among her truly great short stories," which does not contain this offer of grace, foregrounding "the grotesque figures, con artists, and demonic characters who are paradoxically sources of grace."[84] However, although this sideshow act typifies her use of ironic reversals, offering readers the very embodiment of O'Connor's rhetorical technique, the decision to make this sideshow "freak" a priestly figure reverses the readers, expectations as well.

Although the cousins are, initially, hesitant to discuss the hermaphrodite, they describe a tent "divided into two parts by a black curtain" (*CW* 206). As in "Parker's Back," O'Connor uses the same veil imagery from Exodus, since the veil was meant to serve "as a partition between the holy place and the holy of holies"—a divider between God and man (Ex. 26:33). Fittingly, the "freak" uses this same curtain to partition the sexes from his own duality as both person and "temple of the holy ghost" (*CW* 207). Yet, the hermaphrodite's promises seem strangely indicative of the Old Testament curses, as he claims "God made me thisaway and if you laugh He may strike you the same way. This is the way He wanted me to be and I ain't disputing His way" (*CW* 206).

The young girl is quite affected by this image, yet the two cousins seem completely apathetic to the hermaphrodite's suffering. She, alone, recognizes the sacred nature

[82] As Kilcourse notes, *Tantum Ergo* is a Latin hymn which would be "familiar to them from the ritual of Benediction at the convent school" (147).

[83] The young girl's reaction, of course, provides a telling allusion since *Tantum Ergo* was written by St. Thomas Aquinas. When she calls Wendell a big dumb ox, she is unintentionally alluding to Aquinas, who was called "the Dumb Ox of Sicily...a huge heavy bull of a man, fat and slow and quiet" (Chesterton 2, 3).

[84] John R. May, "Flannery O'Connor and the Discernment of Catholic Fiction," in *Inside the Church of Flannery O'Connor: Sacrament, Sacramental, and the Sacred in Her Fiction*, ed. Joanne Halleran McMullen and Jon Parrish Peede (Macon: Mercer University Press, 2007), 211.

of the hermaphrodite, while "Joanna and Susan, the convent cousins, are gigglers who trivialize the idea that God might dwell in each person. It would be particularly unthinkable to them that God inheres in the hermaphrodite."[85] Unbeknownst to Joanna and Susan, their younger cousin sympathizes with the hermaphrodite; through the young girl's vision, the hermaphrodite's suffering becomes redemptive. She imagines the figure saying to the crowd, "God done this to me and I praise Him ... He could strike you thisaway," as she reinterprets her cousins' taunts, "Raise yourself up ... You are God's temple, don't you know?" (*CW* 207).

Through his sermon, the story's central message is clear: "everyone is a temple of the Holy Ghost, though less obviously so than the hermaphrodite," who is able to embody a trinity being a man, woman, and temple of the Holy Ghost.[86] In a literal juxtaposition paralleling Ruby Turpin's question for God (How am I saved and from hell?), the hermaphrodite's two genders become one, actualizing, as Giannone suggests, "the mystery of two natures, divine and human."[87] While the story includes O'Connor's method of ironic juxtaposition, it strays from this framework as, atypical of other reversals, the young girl does not have a divine epiphany, but rather through her vision, as Sykes notes, she "identifies sexual struggle with the suffering of Jesus" and equates his "pain as a gift to God" since "Divine and human can only unite through voluntary suffering."[88] In essence, her dream allows her to reconcile this binary opposition. Through her internalization of the hermaphrodite's message, he, ultimately, becomes the embodiment of Paul's claim: "There is neither Jew nor Greek, there is neither slave nor free, there is neither male nor female, for you are all one in Christ Jesus" (Gal. 3:28).

This turn, the lack of a sudden ironic reversal at the story's end, complicates the story's placement. Although Sarah Gordon argues that O'Connor uses "A Temple of the Holy Ghost" as a method of rewriting Christ's parable of the foolish virgins (Matthew 25: 1–3), the story does seem to fit the qualifications for O'Connor's method of biblical recapitulation, but not as the parable of the foolish virgins as much as a literalization of Paul's claims of the holiness of the physical body—the same way O'Connor literalizes Paul's views of the resurrection in "Judgment Day." However, it seems that there is something more than just biblical retelling at work in this story. Throughout "A Temple of the Holy Ghost," O'Connor's tone seems more subdued; the story lacks the bombastic characters such as Hulga Hopewell, the grandmother, or Mrs. Turpin, yet she still makes use of her literary staple of polarity reversals centered around a central, self-righteous protagonist. In fact, the reason that I argue that this story fits into the reversal framework is that, in many ways, though the 12-year-old protagonist shares similarities with Sarah Ruth (and the author, herself), this female spitfire, our young protagonist, is actually an early version of Ruby Turpin.

---

[85] Giannone, *Hermit*, 100.
[86] James W. Horton, "Flannery O'Connor's Hermaphrodite: Notes Towards a Theology of Sex," in *The Flannery O'Connor Bulletin* 23 (1994–1995): 37.
[87] Giannone, *Hermit*, 101.
[88] John Sykes, "Two Natures: Chalcedon and Coming-of-Age in O'Connor's 'Temple of the Holy Ghost,'" *Flannery O'Connor Review* 5 (2007): 89, 96.

Following Mrs. Turpin, this young girl is filled with judgment for others, from her cousins, whom she calls morons, to the Wilkinses who were "going to be Church of God preachers because you don't have to know nothing to be one," to the Baptist preacher she mimics: she "would pull down her mouth and hold her forehead... and groan, 'Fawther, we thank Thee,' exactly the way he did" (*CW* 200, 204). Without hesitation, O'Connor's protagonist is unapologetically judgmental and, as Sykes notices, "Her own point of pride is that she is smarter than everyone else."[89] Her outright criticisms lead the cook to warn her: "God could strike you deaf dumb and blind... and then you wouldn't be as smart as you is"; her response demonstrates her own hubris: "I would still be smarter than some" (*CW* 203).

Furthermore, in a striking parallel to Mrs. Turpin, the young narrator occupies herself with self-righteous fantasies, imagining she "would have to be a saint because that was the occupation that included everything you could know" (*CW* 204). This young idealist's "Catholic conscience reminds her, however, that she is unworthy to be a saint,"[90] so she settles for the next best thing, "she thought she could be a martyr if they killed her quick" (*CW* 204). Borrowing from the Book of Daniel, this charismatic young protagonist imagines being thrown in a pit of lions, only to emerge unscathed: "The first lion charged forward and fell at her feet, converted. A whole series of lions did the same" (*CW* 204).[91] Next, this exercise continues as she imagines that the Romans "were obliged to burn her, but to their astonishment she would not burn" (*CW* 204, Dan 3:15).[92] Finally, her mind shifts to the New Testament, as she imagines that "they finally cut off her head very quickly" (*CW* 204).[93]

Although she thinks of herself in terms of these quintessential biblical figures—and has the audacity to consider saint and martyr as possible occupations—she practices a very hypocritical version of Christianity. Ironically, the unnamed girl's prayers function as an exemplar of her own Pharisaical nature; echoing Mrs. Turpin, who imagines herself as an advisor to the Almighty, this young girl has an exaggerated sense of self. As the young protagonist begins to pray, starting with the Apostle's creed, readers are told that "Her prayers, when she remembered to say them, were usually perfunctory"; another O'Connor character who reflects the negative example of prayer that Jesus offers: "And when you are praying, do not use meaningless repetition" (*CW* 205, Mt. 6:7).

To add insult to injury, as she continues, her prayer becomes a predecessor of Ruby Turpin's waiting-room prayer, as the young girl "almost weeping with delight" says, "Lord, Lord, thank You that I'm not in the Church of God, thank You Lord, thank You!" (*CW* 205). Through the young girl's prayer, O'Connor alludes to Jesus' Parable of

[89] Sykes, "Two Natures", 94.
[90] Ralph Wood, "Why 'The Dixie Limited' Is Indeed *Limited*: Moral Transformation in Faulkner and O'Connor" (Paper presented at The Stories of Flannery and Faulkner: A Conference and Celebration, Milledgeville, GA., April, 2008) 11.
[91] A reference to Daniel, who was "cast into the lions' den" because he would not denounce his God in favor of King Darius, yet Daniel told the king, "My God sent His angel and shut the lions' mouths and they have not harmed me" (Dan. 6:16, 22).
[92] A reference to Shadrach, Meshach, and Abednego, who refuse to submit to Nebuchadnezzar and are "cast into the midst of a furnace of blazing fire" yet emerge from the fire unscathed (Dan 3:15).
[93] An allusion to John the Baptist, since King Herod "had John beheaded in the prison" (Mt. 14:10).

the Pharisee and the Publican. Her delight, "thank You that I'm not in the Church of God," offers an analogue to the Pharisee as well as serving for a model for "Revelation" (*CW* 205). Although O'Connor's protagonist is intelligent for her age and has a respect for the sacred, demonstrated by her outrage at Wendell's misunderstanding of *Tantum Ergo*, she is also extremely self-righteous. Like her biblical model (and future doppelganger), this young girl is "eaten up also with the sin of Pride," and, as Wood notes, "seeks her own power and glory" (*CW* 204).[94]

Here, however, lies the key to the differences of "A Temple of the Holy Ghost" from other stories in O'Connor's corpus, including "Revelation." Almost all of O'Connor's stories have a Protestant view of grace, often incorporated within an ironic ending, but neither the readers nor the characters will find such "Instant Enlightenment" within this story (*MM* 108). Rather, O'Connor presents a much more Catholic view of grace, a grace that comes gradually over time, as evidenced through the young girl's recasting of the hermaphrodite from the carnival, the story's very emblem of redemption.

After hearing her cousins' description of the hermaphrodite, the curious protagonist becomes obsessed with the figure: "She lay in bed trying to picture the tent with the freak walking from side to side" and "could hear the freak saying 'God made me thisaway and I don't dispute hit'" (*CW* 207). The child's vision imbues a much richer religious connotation than Joanna and Susan's original recounting of the event. Presumably most in the audience, such as Joanna and Susan, are obsessed with the grotesque aspects of "the freak" who is "a man and woman both," which is why "Some of the preachers from town gone out and inspected it and got the police to shut it down" (*CW* 206, 209). However, their actions must be seen as the stunning irony; this carnival "which local preachers will force to close is, ironically, fraught with God's presence," as the young girl's own sacramental vision demonstrates.[95] The spiritual nexus of the story lies in the fact that the young protagonist sees the holiness of the message, where the religious leaders see only the controversy associated with the carnival. Paralleling the reception to the message of the Pharisee and the Publican, readers expect the preachers to have the town's spiritual health in mind, but it is the girl—rather than the legalists—who views the hermaphrodite's message as Pauline theology—embodying Sister Perpetua's theological dictum that everyone is a temple of the holy ghost.

Therein is the heart of the story's core reversal: within her recasting of the event, the young girl imagines the hermaphrodite not as a freak on display at a carnival, but as a clergyman leading a congregational service:

"God done this to me and I praise Him."
"Amen. Amen."
"He could strike you thisaway."
"Amen. Amen."
"But he has not."
"Amen."

---

[94] Wood, "The Dixie Limited," 11.
[95] Baumgartner, *A Proper Scaring*, 78.

"Raise yourself up. A temple of the Holy Ghost. You! You are God's temple, don't you know? Don't you know? God's Spirit has a dwelling in you, don't you know?" (*CW* 207)

The girl imagines the hermaphrodite not only in the role of a preacher, but has him say, "Know you not that your bodies are the members of Christ? ... know you not, that your members are the temple of the Holy Ghost, who is in you, whom you have from God?" (1 Cor. 6:16, 19).[96] It is important to note that the girl imagines the hermaphrodite quoting Paul, the Pharisee-turned-Christian prophet, indicative of her own role in the story as the pharisaical judge of those around her. Yet, she alone identifies the hermaphrodite's embrace of God's will for him. In a sense, this girl reverses the hermaphrodite's function, placing him squarely in the central role as a clerical figure, turning this carnival, associated with sin and vice, into a sacramental form of worship. Ironically, it also serves as an important part of the girl's own spiritual development.

O'Connor's placement of the hermaphrodite as a minister who claims "A temple of God is a holy thing" is incongruous because it presents such a distorted image of a religious leader (*CW* 207). Clearly, she is not concerned with the sexual ramifications of placing a hermaphrodite in this role as much as she is with the spiritual connotations. It is through this hermaphrodite that "the Body of Christ is made vividly present as the agent of the child's moral and spiritual formation."[97]

Herein lies one of the story's major reversals: the girl imagines the hermaphrodite leading a call-and-response style congregational sermon, a literal tent revival, akin to the Church of God members or the Baptist preacher whom she mocks. Although the hermaphrodite's sermon is Protestant, the girl does not imagine such discourse in jest, but rather there is a reverence as the hermaphrodite ends his sermon reminding everyone, "I am a temple of the Holy Ghost," as the crowd responds, in kind, "Amen" (*CW* 207). Through her dream, she transforms the hermaphrodite from a freak on display at a public carnival, available for petty consumption, into a sacred object, a religious figure leading a religious service. Her imagination distorts the audience's relationship with the freak as well. He is no longer a product, but a producer, offering his own redemptive message: "The liturgical exchange between preacher and audience concerns not only acceptance but transformation as well."[98]

There are a few ways in which I view this as a reversal, the most obvious being the fact that transforming a carnival freak into a venerated religious figure functions as a subversion of expectations. Many writers have a tendency to instill religious leaders with eccentric characteristics—O'Connor herself is not known for traditional representations—most depictions of religious leaders in Western literature are somewhat monolithic. While religious personas are often endeared with quirks, there is a fairly narrow spectrum of delineation. They tend to be pious—often naively and comically so, such as Father Finn in "The Enduring Chill" or the unnamed Baptist

---

[96] Douay-Rheims edition.
[97] Wood, "The Dixie Limited," 10.
[98] Ibid., 12.

preacher whom the young protagonist mocks in "A Temple of the Holy Ghost." Other common depictions include the fainthearted and/or conflicted such as Rev. Hightower in Faulkner's *Light in August* or Rev. Dimmesdale of Hawthorne's *The Scarlet Letter*, the fraudulent and/or power-hungry found in title characters of *Elmer Gantry* and *The Damnation of Theron Ware*, or even the comic and/or bumbling such as Mr. Collins in Jane Austen's *Pride and Prejudice* or Graham Greene's Whiskey Priest in *The Power and the Glory*.[99] However, O'Connor's hermaphrodite departs from all pre-existing paradigms. Her portrayal of a clergy member as a marginalized outsider, a gender-neutral freak, who praises God for his own affliction, is simultaneously risky, yet innovative. This representation could be seen as offensive, but this does not seem to be O'Connor's intent, as the hermaphrodite's message is redemptive. Through her recasting of the hermaphrodite as both preacher and Christ-like, she gives readers an innovative representation as complex as any in her corpus. The hermaphrodite's depiction, therefore, perfectly epitomizes O'Connor's own artistic and religious vision in her fictive world where anyone—thieves, murders, conmen, and even carnival freaks—can be an agent of the sacred.

O'Connor uses both ironic juxtaposition and a complete role reversal; the second reason I believe this story should be read as an example of her use of biblical-based reversals is the way in which the young protagonist undergoes a Ruby Turpin–like role reversal at the story's end. Of course, structurally, the story deviates from O'Connor's typical narrative fare since most of her works offer an immediate (and often ironic) ending after the introduction of grace—whether it is through banishment in "Parker's Back" and *The Violent Bear It Away*; abandonment in "Good Country People" and "A Circle in the Fire"; a spiritual vision/divine revelation in "The Artificial Nigger," "The Enduring Chill," and "Revelation"; or even death in "Greenleaf," "The Displaced Person," "A Good Man Is Hard to Find," *Wise Blood*, and, presumably, "Everything that Rises Must Converge," the common thread between these stories is that they offer the reader little in terms of resolution. However, "A Temple of the Holy Ghost," one of the shorter works within her corpus, does not end immediately after the young girl's dream. Instead, the story offers a subtle dénouement, providing readers not only with a paradigm-shifting reversal but also with a finite sense of closure (or as close to an ending as possible in an O'Connor short story).

As the young girl and her family arrive at St. Scholastica to drop off Joanna and Susan, "A big moon-faced nun came bustling to the door" to embrace the party en masse, an embrace that the protagonist narrowly escapes, laconically commenting, "You put your foot in their door and they got you praying" (*CW* 208). However, the young girl's transformation, her religious polarity shift and "acceptance of God's will," which "comes not from abstract angelism, but from its shocking opposite—from the discourse of the freak," is evidenced by her newfound reverence for the Eucharist.[100]

As the "priest was kneeling in front of the monstrance" and the congregation was "well into the '*Tantum Ergo*'" the girl's "ugly thoughts stopped and she began to realize

---

[99] Greene's "Whiskey Priest" is portrayed in a comically reverent fashion.
[100] Askin, "Carnival in the 'Temple,'" 568.

that she was in the presence of God" (*CW* 208). Her prayer begins similarly to her previously monotonous attempts at prayer, reflecting the "meaningless repetition" that Jesus has previously warned against. "Hep me not to be so mean, she began mechanically," yet she begins to have another epiphany as "Her mind began to get quiet and then empty" (*CW* 208).[101] As the priest raised the Host, emblematic of Christ, she begins "thinking of the tent at the fair that had the freak in it," as he proclaimed, "I don't dispute hit. This is the way He wanted me to be" (*CW* 209). The little girl is able to embrace her own shortcomings, like the hermaphrodite, but in comparing the host with the freak, she equates the hermaphrodite's own redemptive suffering with that of Christ. It is this very means of reconciliation that typifies Paul's claim: "But the one who joins himself to the Lord is one spirit with him" (1. Cor. 6: 17). Through O'Connor's use of a hermaphrodite—two genders—she literalizes the message of how "two shall become one" (1 Cor. 6: 16). For the girl, watching the Eucharist and understanding the division of Christ's own humanity and divinity, she realizes that "the hermaphrodite's embrace of his sexual suffering is a sacramental instance of the crucified Christ's embrace of the ultimate suffering."[102]

As the young girl leaves the convent with her mother, "the big nun swooped down on her mischievously and nearly smothered her" in an embrace (*CW* 209). Although this precocious prophet-in-training had strategically avoided the nun, the confrontation is unavoidable. Instead, as the unnamed nun hugs the young girl, the nun is, unintentionally, "mashing the side of her [the young girl] face into the crucifix hitched onto her belt" (*CW* 209). O'Connor herself has claimed that this act, much like the grandmother's gesture to the Misfit, is central to understanding the story:

> Remember that when the nun hugged the child, the crucifix on her belt was mashed into the side of the child's face, so that one accepted embrace was marked with the ultimate all-inclusive symbol of love. (*HB* 124)

The crucifix leaves a physical indentation and, more likely, a lasting impression on this young girl, who, at this moment, recognizes that "The sun was a huge red ball like an elevated Host drenched in blood" (*CW* 209). This ending imprints the Catholic imagery—"the spiritually pregnant allusion to the bloody Eucharist"—upon the readers in the same manner that the nun imprints the cross on the child's head.[103]

The nun's action signals this, implicit reversal, as O'Connor transforms both the girl and the hermaphrodite from Pharisee and "freak" to the humble and holy. O'Connor's portrayal of the freak as both a preacher and a part of Christ represents the theological nexus of the story and perhaps her most meaningful reversal. By recasting the hermaphrodite "as a preacher proclaiming the Good News of Affliction," he not only

---

[101] This prayer, ironically, parallels the prayer/confession Solace Layfield gives during his death in *Wise Blood* (CW 115).

[102] Wood, "Dixie Limited," 14.

[103] Stephen C. Behrendt, "Partaking of the Sacraments with Blake and O'Connor: A Reading," in *Inside the Church of Flannery O'Connor: Sacrament, Sacramental, and the Sacred in Her Fiction.* ed. Joanne Halleran McMullen and Jon Parrish Peede (Macon: Mercer University Press, 2007), 136.

becomes a bizarre and grotesque representation of the clergy, with the carnival itself serving as a "vulgarization of the church," but also the girl equates him with Christ himself, as the hermaphrodite paces back and forth and describes his own suffering: "This is the way He wanted me to be and I ain't disputing His way" (*CW* 206).[104] Instead of attempting to be healed of this condition, in the tradition of Bevel Summers, the hermaphrodite embraces his own suffering; hence, "he lives not as a bitter freak of nature but one who has consented to be afflicted by God."[105]

Giannone correctly argues that "it would be entirely in keeping with O'Connor's sensibility to say that the story levels charges against a Christianity, modern or ancient, that has been complacent, smug, sentimental and antithetical to Logos," all characteristics the young girl possesses.[106] Yet, O'Connor seems less interested in condemnation than she does in redemption in this story. By the story's end, the little girl realizes during the Eucharistic mass that "she was in the presence of God"; however, while the priest continues the mass, her mind shifts to a vision of the hermaphrodite (*CW* 208). Through this vision, the young child "powerfully connects like and unlike, equating the Eucharist—the body of Christ—with the body of the hermaphrodite, emphasizing the silencing mystery of both."[107]

Ironically, the young girl's ultimate realization, which provides "a textual definition ... of the Real Presence" of the Eucharist, is juxtaposed with the "comic eccentricity, adolescent jokes and carnival distortion toward this sacred presence."[108] Yet, it is the girl's recognition of the sacred that illustrates O'Connor's method of reconciliation of opposites, transforming the bizarre grotesqueries found in the carnival into the sacrosanct. Not only does she imbue these objects with a religious resonance, but, by turning the risqué into the sacred, she presents readers with a key inversion or reversal and reinvents the hermaphrodite into a spiritually pregnant figure, a hermaphrodite who is connected in redemptive suffering to the body of Christ.

Strangely, by enjoining the hermaphrodite with the figure of Christ, she is—in essence—solidifying and exemplifying the message of Hebrews 5. The author asserts that the role of the priest in Christianity is "to offer sacrifices for sins, as for the people, so also for himself" (Hebrews 5:3). Yet, the author adds that Jesus himself "became a high priest" through this physical incarnation, and "Although He was a Son, He learned obedience from the things which He suffered" (Hebrews 5:5,8). For both the hermaphrodite and Christ, suffering becomes an agent of submission, in which both seem to implicitly say, "I don't dispute hit. This is the way He wanted me to be"—a message that the lupus-stricken O'Connor simultaneously wishes to convey to her readership (*CW* 209).

---

[104] Ralph Wood, "'God May Strike You Thisaway.': Flannery O'Connor and Simone Weil on Affliction and Joy," in *Renascence: Essays on Values in Literature* 59, no. 3 (2007): 192; Horton, "Theology of Sex," 36.
[105] Wood, "Thisaway," 192.
[106] Giannone, *Hermit*, 100.
[107] Lake, *The Incarnational Art*, 137.
[108] W. A. Sessions, "Real Presence: Flannery O'Connor and the Saints," in *Inside the Church of Flannery O'Connor: Sacrament, Sacramental, and the Sacred in Her Fiction*, ed. Joanne Halleran McMullen and Jon Parrish Peede (Macon: Mercer University Press, 2007), 20.

Bibliography

Albright, W. F. and C. S. Mann. *Matthew: Introduction, Translation, and Notes*. Garden City: Doubleday, 1971.

Allen, Leslie C. *The Books of Joel, Obadiah, Jonah, and Micah*. Grand Rapids: Eerdmans, 1976.

Alter, Robert. "Introduction to the Old Testament." in *The Literary Guide to the Bible*. Edited by Robert Alter and Frank Kermode, 11–35. Cambridge: Harvard University Press, 1987.

Aquinas, St Thomas. *Summa Theologica*. Vol. 4 (Part 3). New York: Cosimo Classics, 2007.

Asals, Frederick. *Flannery O'Connor: The Imagination of Extremity*. Athens: University of Georgia Press, 1982.

Askin, Denise T. "Carnival in the 'Temple': Flannery O'Connor's Dialogic Parable of Artistic Vocation." *Christianity and Literature* 56, no.4 (2007): 555–572.

Barclay, William. *Introduction to the First Three Gospels*. Philadelphia: The Westminster Press, 1966.

Baumgaertner, Jill P. *Flannery O'Connor: A Proper Scaring*. Wheaton: Harold Shaw Publishers, 1988.

Behrendt, Stephen C. "Partaking of the Sacraments with Blake and O'Connor: A Reading." in *Inside the Church of Flannery O'Connor: Sacrament, Sacramental, and the Sacred in Her Fiction*. Edited by Joanne Halleran McMullen and Jon Parrish Peede, 117–137. Macon: Mercer University Press, 2007.

Bellamy, Michael O. "Everything Off Balance: Protestant Election in Flannery O'Connor's 'A Good Man Is Hard to Find.'" *Flannery O'Connor Bulletin* 8 (1979): 116–124.

Bleikasten, André. "Writing on the Flesh: Tattoos and Taboos in 'Parker's Back.'" *The Southern Literary Journal* 14, no.2 (1982): 8–19.

Bloom, Harold. "Introduction." in *On the Bible: Eighteen Studies*. By Martin Buber. Edited by Nahum N.Glatzer, ix–xxxii. New York: Schocken Books, 1982.

Brinkmeyer, Robert. *The Art and Vision of Flannery O'Connor*. Baton Rouge: Louisiana State University Press, 1989.

———. "'Jesus, Stab Me in the Heart!': *Wise Blood*, Wounding, and Sacramental Aesthetics." in *New Essays on "Wise Blood"*. Edited by Michael Kreyling, 71–90. New York: Cambridge University Press, 1995.

Britt, Brian. "Divine Curses in O'Connor's 'Revelation' and 2 Samuel 16." *The Flannery O'Connor Review* 1 (2001–2002): 49–55.

Brueggemann, Walter. *The Prophetic Imagination*. Minneapolis: Fortress Press, 2001.

Bryant, Hallman B. "Reading the Map in Flannery O'Connor's 'A Good Man Is Hard to Find.'" *Studies in Short Fiction* 18, no.3 (1981): 301–307.

Byars, John. "Prophecy and Apocalyptic in the Fiction of Flannery O'Connor." *Flannery O'Connor Bulletin* 16 (1987): 34–42.

Cash, Jean. *Flannery O'Connor: A Life*. Knoxville: University of Tennessee Press, 2002.

Cash, W. J. *The Mind of the South*. New York: Vintage Books, 1960.

Chesterton, G. K. *St. Thomas Aquinas*. New York: Sheed & Ward, 1933.

Ciuba, Gary M. *Desire, Violence & Divinity in Modern Southern Fiction: Katherine Anne Porter, Flannery O'Connor, Cormac McCarthy, Walker Percy.* Baton Rouge: Louisiana State University Press, 2007.

Coles, Robert. *Flannery O'Connor's South.* Athens: University of Georgia Press, 1980.

Coulthard, A. R. "From Sermon to Parable: Four Conversion Stories by Flannery O'Connor." *American Literature* 55, no.1 (1983): 55–71.

Covington, Dennis. *Salvation on Sand Mountain: Snake-Handling and Redemption in Southern Appalachia.* New York: Penguin, 1996.

Crossan, John Dominic. *In Parables: The Challenge of the Historical Jesus.* New York: Harper and Row, 1973.

"Damnation of Man." *Savannah Morning News* (May 25, 1952).

Daujat, Jean. *The Theology of Grace.* New York: Hawthorn Books, 1959.

Detweiler, Robert and David Jasper, eds. *Religion and Literature: A Reader.* Louisville: Westminster John Knox Press, 2000.

DiRenzo, Anthony. "And the Violent Bear It Away: O'Connor and the Menace of Apocalyptic Terrorism." in *Flannery O'Connor in the Age of Terrorism.* Edited by Avis Hewitt and Robert Donahoo, 3–24. Knoxville: University of Tennessee Press, 2010.

Driskell, Leon V. and Joan T. Brittain. *The Eternal Crossroads: The Art of Flannery O'Connor.* Lexington: The University Press of Kentucky, 1971.

Edmondson III, Henry T. *Return to Good and Evil: Flannery O'Connor's Response to Nihilism.* Lanham: Lexington Books, 2002.

Eggenschwiler, David. *The Christian Humanism of Flannery O'Connor.* Detroit: Wayne State University Press, 1972.

Fee, Gordon D. *The First Epistle to the Corinthians.* Grand Rapids: Eerdmans, 1987.

Feeley, Kathleen. *The Voice of the Peacock.* New York: Fordham University Press, 1982.

Ferguson, Paul. "Onomastic Revisions in Flannery O'Connor's." *Wise Blood. Literary Onomastics Studies* 13 (1986): 97–110.

Fike, Matthew. "The Timothy Allusion in 'A Good Man Is Hard to Find.'" *Renascene: Essays on Values in Literature* 52, no.4 (2000): 311–322.

Fitzmyer, Joseph A. *The Gospel According to Luke: Introduction, Translation, and Notes. Vol. 2 of the Anchor Bible.* New York: Doubleday, 1981.

———. *The Gospel According to Luke X–XXIV: A New Translation with Introduction and Commentary. Vol. 28A of the Anchor Bible.* New York: Doubleday, 1985.

———. *The Acts of the Apostles: A New Translation with Introduction and Commentary. Vol. 31 of the Anchor Bible.* New York: Doubleday, 1998.

Fokkelman, J. P. "Exodus." in *The Literary Guide to the Bible.* Edited by Robert Alter and Frank Kermode, 56–65. Cambridge: Harvard University Press, 1987.

Fowler, James. "In the Flesh: The Grace of 'Parker's Back.'" *Publications of the Mississippi Philological Association* (2004): 60–66.

Frazer, Sir James George. *The Golden Bough.* New York: MacMillan, 1963.

Friedman, Melvin J. "Flannery O'Connor: Another Legend in Southern Fiction." *The English Journal* 51, no.4 (1962): 233–243.

Friedrichsen, Timothy A. "The Temple, A Pharisee, A Tax Collector, and the Kingdom of God: Rereading A Jesus Parable (Luke 18:10–14A)." *Journal of Biblical Literature* 124, no.1 (2005): 89–119.

Frye, Northrope. *The Great Code: The Bible and Literature.* New York: Harcourt Brace, 1982.

Furnish, Victor Paul. *New Testament Theology: The Theology of the First Letter to the Corinthians.* New York: Cambridge University Press, 1999.

Gafford, Charlotte Kelly. "Fiction of Flannery O'Connor Mission of Gratuitous Grace" (Part III). *The Catholic Week* (October 16, 1964).

Gardner, Thomas. *John in the Company of Poets: The Gospel in Literary Imagination.* Waco, TX: Baylor University Press, 2011.

Gentry, Marshall Bruce. *Flannery O'Connor's Religion of the Grotesque.* Jackson: University Press of Mississippi, 1986.

Giannone, Richard. "Paul, Francis, and Hazel Motes: Conversion at Taulkingham." *Thought* 59 (1983): 483–503.

———. *Flannery O'Connor, Hermit Novelist.* Urbana: University of Illinois Press, 2000.

Giroux, Robert. "Introduction" in *The Complete Stories.* Edited by Flannery O'Connor. New York: Farrar, Straus, and Giroux, 1971.

Gomes, Peter. *The Scandalous Gospel of Jesus: What's So Good About the Good News?* New York: Harper, 2007.

Gordis, Robert. *The Book of Job: Commentary, New Translation, and Special Studies.* New York, NY: The Jewish Theological Seminary of America, 1978.

Gordon, Sarah. *Flannery O'Connor: The Obedient Imagination.* Athens: University of Georgia Press, 2000.

Goulder, Michael. "The Pauline Epistles." in *The Literary Guide to the Bible.* Edited by Robert Alter and Frank Kermode, 479–502. Cambridge: Harvard University Press, 1987.

Greenberg, Martin. "Books in Short." *American Mercury* 75 (1952): 111–113.

Hannon, Jane. "The Wide World Here Parish: O'Connor's All-Embracing Vision of the Church." *Flannery O'Connor Bulletin* 24 (1995): 1–21.

Hawkins, Peter. *The Language of Grace: Flannery O'Connor, Walker Percy, and Iris Murdoch.* New York: Seabury Classics, 2004.

Hewitt, Eben. "Diapsalmata and Numinous Recapitulation: The Tropology of 'Parker's Back.'" *Proceedings: Northeast Regional Meeting of the Conference on Christianity and Literature,* October 10–12, 1996. Weston, MA: Conference on Christianity (1996): 61–64.

Horton, James W. "Flannery O'Connor's Hermaphrodite: Notes Towards a Theology of Sex." *The Flannery O'Connor Bulletin* 23 (1994–1995): 30–41.

Howarth, William. "Land and Word: American Pastoral." in *The Changing America Countryside: Rural People and Places.* Edited by Emery Castle, 13–38. Lawrence: University of Kansas Press, 2005.

Jameson, Fredric. *The Political Unconscious: Narrative as a Socially Symbolic Act.* New York: Routledge, 1983.

Jasper, David. *The Study of Religion and Literature: An Introduction.* Minneapolis: Fortress Press, 1989.

Jeffrey, David Lyle. ed. *A Dictionary of Biblical Tradition in English Literature.* Grand Rapids: William B. Eerdmans, 1992.

Kermode, Frank. "Matthew." in *The Literary Guide to the Bible.* Edited by Robert Alter and Frank Kermode. Cambridge: Harvard University Press, 1987.

Kierkegaard, Søren. *Fear and Trembling.* Translated by Alastair Hannay. New York: Penguin Books, 2003.

Kilcourse, George A. *Flannery O'Connor's Religious Imagination: A World with Everything Off Balance.* Mahwah: Paulist Press, 2001.

Kinney, Arthur F. "Flannery O'Connor and the Fiction of Grace." *Massachusetts Review* 27, no.1 (1986): 71–96.

Kreyling, Michael. *Inventing Southern Literature*. Jackson: University Press of Mississippi, 1998.

Lake, Christiana Bieber. *The Incarnational Art of Flannery O'Connor*. Macon: Mercer University Press, 2005.

Lewis, R. W. B. "Eccentrics Pilgrimage." Review of *Wise Blood* by Flannery O'Connor. *The Hudson Review* 6, no.1 (1953): 144–150.

Liguori, Saint Alphonsus. *The Glories of Mary*. Liguori: Liguori, 2000.

Lytle, Andrew Nelson. "The Hind Tit." in *I'll Take My Stand: The South and the Agrarian Tradition*. Edited by Louis Rubin, 201–245. New York: Harper, 1930.

Maritain, Jacques. *The Living Thoughts of Saint Paul*. Edited by Alfred O. Mendel. Philadelphia: David McKay Company, 1941.

Martin, W. R. "A Note on Ruby and Revelation." *The Flannery O'Connor Bulletin* 16 (1987): 23–25.

May, John R. "Flannery O'Connor and the Discernment of Catholic Fiction." in *Inside the Church of Flannery O'Connor: Sacrament, Sacramental, and the Sacred in Her Fiction*. Edited by Joanne Halleran McMullen and Jon Parrish Peede, 205–220. Macon: Mercer University Press, 2007.

McMullen, Joanne. *Writing Against God: Language as Message in the Literature of Flannery O'Connor*. Macon: Mercer University Press, 1996.

Montgomery, Marion. "Flannery O'Connor: Realist of Distances." in *Realist of Distances: Flannery O'Connor Revisited*. Edited by Karl-Heinz Westarp and JanNorby Gretlund, 227–235. Aarhus: Aarhus University Press, 1987.

Musurillo, Herbert. "History and Symbol: A Study of Form in Early Christian Literature." *Theological Studies* 18 (1957): 357–386.

Nabokov, Vladimir. *Lectures on Russian Literature*. Edited by Fredson Bowers. New York: Harcourt Brace, 1981.

Nissinen, Martti and Peter Machinist. *Prophets and Prophecy in the Ancient Near East*. Atlanta: Society of Biblical Literature, 2003.

Nock, A. D. *Conversion: The Old and the New in Religion from Alexander the Great to Augustine of Hippo*. London: Oxford at the Clarendon Press, 1933.

O'Connor, Flannery. "My Dear God: A Young Writer's Prayers." *The New Yorker* (16 September 2013):26–30

O'Connor, Flannery. *Mystery and Manners: Occasional Prose*. Edited by Sally and Robert Fitzgerald. New York, NY: Farrar, Straus, and Giroux, 1970.

———. *The Complete Stories*. New York, NY: Farrar, Straus, and Giroux, 1971.

———. *The Habit of Being*. Edited by Sally Fitzgerald. New York, NY: Farrar, Straus, and Giroux, 1979.

———. *O'Connor: Collected Works*. New York, NY: Library of America, 1988.

———. *Peculiar Crossroads: Flannery O'Connor, Walker Percy, and Catholic Vision in Postwar Southern Fiction*. Baton Rouge: Louisiana State University Press, 2004.

———. *The Presence of Grace*. Edited by Leo Zuber (Compiler) and Carter Martin. Athens: University of Georgia Press, 2008.

———. "My Dear God: A Young Writer's Prayers." *The New Yorker* (16 September 2013): 26–30.

Patte, Daniel. *The Gospel According to Matthew: A Structural Commentary on Matthew's Faith*. Philadelphia: Fortress Press, 1987.

Percy, Walker. *How to Be An American Novelist In Spite of Being Southern and Catholic*. Lafayette: University of Southwestern Louisiana, 1982.

Phipps, William E. *Assertive Biblical Women*. Westport: Greenwood Press, 1992.

Propp, William H. C. *Exodus 19–40: A New Translation with Introduction and Commentary. Vol. 2A of the Anchor Bible*. New York: Doubleday, 2006.

Ragen, Brian. *A Wreck on the Road to Damascus: Innocence, Guilt & Conversion in Flannery O'Connor*. Chicago: Loyola University Press, 1989.

Ramsey, Michaels, J. "Eating the Bread of Life: Muted Violence in *The Violent Bear It Away*." in *Flannery O'Connor in the Age of Terrorism: Essays on Violence and Grace*. Edited by Avis Hewitt and Robert Donahoo, 59–70. Knoxville: University of Tennessee Press, 2010.

Rath, Sura. "Ruby Turpin's Redemption: Thomistic Resolution in Flannery O'Connor's 'Revelation.'" *The Flannery O'Connor Bulletin* 19 (1990): 1–8.

Robinson, Marilynne. *Home*. New York: Farrar, Straus and Giroux, 2008.

Sanders, E. P. *Paul and Palestinian Judaism: A Comparison of Patterns of Religion*. Philadelphia: Fortress Press, 1977.

———. *The Historical Figure of Jesus*. New York: Penguin Books, 1993.

Satterfield, Ben. "*Wise Blood*, Artistic Anemia and the Hemorrhaging of O'Connor Criticism." *Studies in American Fiction* 17, no.1 (1989): 33–50.

Schleifer, Ronald. "Rural Gothic: The Stories of Flannery O'Connor" in *Critical Essays on Flannery O'Connor*. Edited by Melvin J. Friedman and Beverly Lyon Clark, 158–168. Boston: Hall, 1985.

Schoeps, H. J. *Paul: The Theology of the Apostle in the Light of Jewish Religious History*. Philadelphia: Westminster Press, 1962.

Schroeder, Michael L. "Ruby Turpin, Job, and Mystery: Flannery O'Connor on the Question of Knowing." *The Flannery O'Connor Bulletin* 21 (1992): 75–83.

Sessions, W. A. "Real Presence: Flannery O'Connor and the Saints." in *Inside the Church of Flannery O'Connor: Sacrament, Sacramental, and the Sacred in Her Fiction*. Edited by Joanne Halleran McMullen and Jon Parrish Peede, 15–40. Macon: Mercer University Press, 2007.

Shinn, Thelma J. "Flannery O'Connor and the Violence of Grace." *Contemporary Literature* 9, no.1 (1968): 58–73.

Singer, Isidore. Ed. *The Jewish Encyclopedia*. Vol.6. New York: Funk and Wagnalls Co., 1912.

Slattery, Dennis P. "In a Pig's Eye: Retrieving the Animal Imagination in Ruby Turpin's 'Revelation.'" *The Flannery O'Connor Bulletin* 25 (1996): 138–150.

Slotkin, Richard. *Regeneration Through Violence: The Mythology of the American Frontier, 1600–1860*. Norman: University of Oklahoma Press, 1973.

Smit, Joop F. M. "'What Is Apollos? What Is Paul?': In Search for the Coherence of First Corinthians 1:10–4:21." *Novuum Testamentum* 44, no. 3 (2002): 231–251.

Smith, Martha. "Georgian Pens 'Wise Blood,' A First Novel." *The Atlanta Constitution* (May 1952).

Sockman, Ralph. *The Paradoxes of Jesus*. Nashville: Abingdon Press, 1964.

Sonnenfeld, Albert. "Flannery O'Connor: The Catholic Writer as Baptist." *Contemporary Literature* 13 (1972): 445–457.

Sparrow, Stephen. "Wisdom: Simple or Idiotic Religious Vision and Free Will in Flannery O'Connor's Novel *Wise Blood*." *The Comforts of Home*. Last modified January 22, 2002. http://mediaspecialist.org/sswisdom.html

Srigley, Susan. "Review of Richard Giannone's 'Flannery O'Connor, Hermit Novelist.'" *Religion & Literature* 35, no.1 (2003): 129–131.

———. *Flannery O'Connor's Sacramental Art*. Notre Dame: University of Notre Dame Press, 2004.

Stephens, Martha. *The Question of Flannery O'Connor*. Baton Rouge: LSU Press, 1973.

Sykes, John. *Flannery O'Connor, Walker Percy, and the Aesthetic of Revelation*. Columbia: University of Missouri Press, 2007.

———. "Two Natures: Chalcedon and Coming-of-Age in O'Connor's 'Temple of the Holy Ghost.'" *Flannery O'Connor Review* 5 (2007): 89–98.

Terrien, Samuel. *Till the Heart Sings*. Philadelphia: Fortress Press, 1985.

True, Michael D. "Flannery O'Connor: Backwoods Prophets in the Secular City." *Papers on Language and Literature* 5 (1969): 209–223.

Walker, Alice. "Beyond the Peacock: The Reconstruction of Flannery O'Connor." *Ms* (December 1975): 77–79, 102, 104–106.

Westarp, Karl-Heinz. "Flannery O'Connor's Development: An Analysis of the Judgment-Day Material." in *Realist of Distances: Flannery O'Connor Revisited*. Edited by Karl-Heinz Westarp and Jan Nordby Gretlund, 46–54. Aarhus: Aarhus University Press, 1987.

Westling, Louise. *Sacred Groves and Ravaged Gardens: The Fiction of Eudora Welty, Carson McCullers, and Flannery O'Connor*. Athens: University of Georgia Press, 1985.

Whitt, Margaret. *Understanding Flannery O'Connor*. Columbia: University of South Carolina Press, 1995.

———. "Letters to Corinth; Echoes from Greece to Georgia in O'Connor's 'Judgment Day.'" in *Flannery O'Connor and the Christian Mystery*. Edited by J. P. Murphy, Linda Hunter Adams, Richard H. Cracroft, and Susan Elizabeth Howe, 61–74. Provo: Brigham Young University Center for the Study of Christian Values in Literature, 1997.

Wilson, Charles Regan. *Baptized in Blood: The Religion of the Lost Cause (1865–1920)*. Athens: University of Georgia, 1983.

Wood, Ralph. *The Comedy of Redemption: Christian Faith and Comic Vision in Four American Novelists*. Notre Dame: University of Notre Dame Press, 1988.

———. "Obedience to the Unenforceable: Mystery, Manners, and Masks in 'Judgment Day.'" *The Flannery O'Connor Bulletin* 25 (1996–1997): 153–174.

———. *Flannery O'Connor and the Christ-Haunted South*. Grand Rapids: Eerdmans Publishing Company, 2004.

———. "'God May Strike You This Away.': Flannery O'Connor and Simone Weil on Affliction and Joy," *Renascence: Essays on Values in Literature* 59, no.3 (2007): 181–195.

———. "Why 'The Dixie Limited' Is Indeed *Limited*: Moral Transformation in Faulkner and O'Connor." Paper Presented at The Stories of Flannery and Faulkner: A Conference and Celebration, Milledgeville, GA, April, 2008.

Wright, N. T. *What Saint Paul Really Said*. Grand Rapids: William B. Eerdman's Publishing, 1997.

Index

Note: The locators followed by 'n' refer to note numbers.

Index of Biblical References

CPSIA information can be obtained at www.ICGtesting.com
Printed in the USA
LVOW07s1711161115

462812LV00008B/201/P